The Northern Lights

The Northern Lights

LUCY JAGO

Alfred A. Knopf  New York   2001

THIS IS A BORZOI BOOK
PUBLISHED BY ALFRED A. KNOPF

Originally published in Great Britain by Hamish Hamilton, an
imprint of Penguin Books Ltd., London.

Library of Congress Cataloging-in-Publication Data
Jago, Lucy.
The northern lights / Lucy Jago.—1st ed.
p. cm.
Includes bibliographical references.
ISBN 0-375-40980-7 (alk. paper)
1. Birkeland, Kr. (Kristian), 1867–1917. 2. Auroras.
3. Geophysicists—Norway—Biography. I. Title.

QC805 .B57 J34 2001
538'. 7'092—dc21
[B]   2001029895

Manufactured in the United States of America
First American Edition

For Lily

Contents

Contents

Illustrations

Author's Note

THE EXTRAORDINARY EVENTS in this story actually occurred and the characters involved existed, although in an attempt to prevent the book becoming an academic text or a standard biography, I have kept references to a minimum and there are no footnotes. Exhaustive research has been done into all available archives and resources concerning Birkeland, his contemporaries, and his environment in Norway, Britain, Egypt, Greece, and Japan. Most details that appear in the book, from the wallpaper used in the Haldde observatory to the number of servants Birkeland employed while working in Sudan, have come from written sources (mentioned in the Select Bibliography). Portraits of characters and descriptions of Christiania (Oslo), Cairo, Tokyo, and other towns come from photographs or written accounts contemporary with Birkeland. Very occasionally I have telescoped events in order to avoid making the story too long or have made assumptions that are not documented but are reasonable. I have visited most of the locations mentioned, several of which are little changed. Place names used in the book are those current in Birkeland's time, and his scientific discoveries have been written from a perspective contemporary with him; the epilogue contains an assessment of Birkeland's contribution to the field of auroral science in the light of the latest scientific research.

Acknowledgments

THE GENEROSITY of many individuals in helping with the research for this book has been extraordinary. First and foremost, my thanks go to Truls Lynne Hansen at the Auroral Observatory in Tromsø, Northern Norway, who, as he put it, has been my "Norwegian eyes and ears," helping me find and translate documents from all the major archives in Norway and many minor ones as well. He was a constant reference point when I was trying to understand some of the more complicated scientific elements in Birkeland's work and has enabled me to enjoy many memorable sightings of the aurora. Concerning the science, I would also like to thank Stanley Cowley, professor of solar-planetary physics and head of the Radio and Space Plasma Group at the Department of Physics and Astronomy, University of Leicester, and Dr. Robert H. Eather, author of *Majestic Lights: The Aurora in Science, History, and the Arts* (1980), both of whom are eminent experts in the field of auroral physics and have kindly given their time and knowledge in offering suggestions for this book.

Many other people have also helped my research and I am grateful to them all. In Norway, in no particular order, they are Åse Lauritzen of Oslo University, who has written her thesis on Birkeland's technology and has been very helpful in providing me with information about the Norsk Hydro period and in general research; Ketil Gjølme Andersen, who has written extensively on Norsk Hydro during Birkeland's time; Professor Asgeir Brekke, with whom I shared a memorable skimobile journey up Haldde Mountain and who was generous in lending me books; Terje Brundtland, formerly of the Auroral Observatory and now at Oxford University and a leading expert in Birkeland's terrella experiments; Solveig Berg, librarian at the Institute of Theoretical Astrophysics, University of Oslo; Professor Alv Egeland, formerly of the physics department of Oslo

Acknowledgments

University; Professor Egil Leer of the Institute of Theoretical Astrophysics, University of Oslo, for an inspirational discussion; Robert Marc Friedman, Institute of History, Oslo University, for his essay on Birkeland as a space pioneer; Mr. Søren Sem, formerly a director of Norsk Hydro, who very kindly allowed me access to Hydro's archives and gave me a guided tour of the hydroelectric plants, factories, and museum at Notodden; Ragnar Moen who helped with research in the Notodden archives; Hans Thorleif Lundeby, grandnephew of Ida Birkeland, and his wife, Bjørg Lundeby, in Raade, who lent me photographs and provided important biographical detail; and Destinasjon Alta Tourism Group, which arranged for me to visit Birkeland's observatory in midwinter. I would also like to thank the helpful staff at the Riksarkivet, Oslo (National Archives), Statsarkivet i Oslo (State Archives, Oslo), Statsarkivet i Tromsø (State Archives, Tromsø), Nasjonalbiblioteket i Oslo Håndskriftsamlingen (National Library of Norway Manuscript Department), the Astrophysics Institute Library, Norsk Teknisk Museum (Norwegian Technical Museum), the University Library of Tromsø, Bredriftshistorisksamling, Norsk Hydro, Notodden (Industry Museum), the Tromsø Auroral Observatory Library, and the departments of physics at the Universities of Tromsø and Oslo.

In England, Richard Dale, science executive producer at the BBC, offered me tremendous help and encouragement; the distinguished and lovely Professor Dungey; Dr. Peter Hingley from the Royal Astronomical Society in London, who helped in my search for information about Helwan Observatory in Egypt; Richard Wellm gave me extremely useful translations; staff at the Royal Society, the Institute of Electrical Engineers, the Rutherford-Appleton Laboratory, the Royal Society of Chemistry, the Royal Institution, and the British Library provided valuable assistance.

In Egypt, eminent botanist Loutfy Boulos kindly arranged a trip into the desert to search for the Zodiacal Light; Professor Galal, formerly of the Helwan Observatory, and Professor Essa Ali, its current director, helped me find Birkeland's house in Helwan and provided access to the observatory; thank you also to Iman Sayed of the Old Cataract Hotel in Aswan for her kindness and help with finding archives; Peter Knox-Shaw, son of Harold Knox-Shaw, for his great generosity and trust in lending me precious photographic plates of his father, the observatory, and Helwan in Birkeland's time. My uncle and aunt, Peter and Hoda Jago, kindly

Acknowledgments

arranged for me to be looked after in Egypt; Nehad Abd Elsalam was my cheerful guide; Mr. Samir Hares and El Said M. Hassanin were extremely generous with their hospitality during my research. The members of the Greek community in Alexandria could not have been more helpful in searching through numerous archives and libraries for biographical details of Hella Spandonides.

In America, thanks go to Professor Alex Dessler of the Lunar and Planetary Laboratory, University of Arizona, for interesting articles and debates about the suppression of Birkeland's work by Chapman; and Professor Anthony Perratt at Los Alamos National Laboratory, New Mexico.

In Japan, Professor Fukushima drew attention to Terada's account of Birkeland's final weeks and, in conjunction with Professor Brekke in Norway, provided a translation from Japanese. Professor Ryochi Fuiji of Nagoya gave helpful information about Japanese archives.

The Pasteur Institute in France gave historical advice.

In Greece, Angelos Vryonis found valuable information about Hella Spandonides.

Stephanie Cabot, "agent extraordinaire" at William Morris UK, and Owen Laster in New York have done great deals, ably supported by Eugenie Furniss and Rhiannon Williams.

My editor and publisher, Simon Prosser, has steered me through the process of writing my first book with tremendous tact and encouragement, shaping *The Northern Lights* into something I am proud of. It has been a great pleasure to work with the team at Penguin—Charlie Greig, Joanna Prior, Carol Baker, John Bond, John Gray, Michele Hutchinson, Juliette Mitchell, the account managers, and the reps. Bela Cunha, the copy editor, corrected the manuscript with great skill. Robin Desser, editor for the American edition, has been hugely supportive and her assistant, Bonnie Schiff-Glenn, has made transatlantic communication enjoyable.

Lastly, but sincerely, thank you to my family and friends, who have been constant in their support and encouragement.

Lucy Jago
London, December 2000

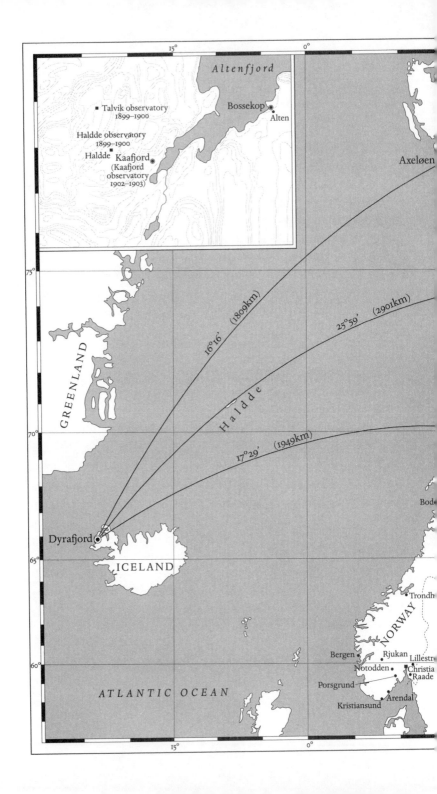

Altenfjord

Talvik observatory
1899–1900

Halldde observatory
1899–1900

Haldde Kaafjord
(Kaafjord
observatory
1902–1903)

Bossekop
Alten

Axeløen

15°

0°

75°

GREENLAND

16°16′ (1809km)

25°59′ (2901km)

H a l d d e

70°

17°29′ (1949km)

Bodø

Dyrafjord

ICELAND

65°

Trondh

NORWAY

Bergen

Rjukan Lillestr

Notodden

Christia

Raade

60°

Porsgrund

Kristiansund

Arendal

ATLANTIC OCEAN

15°

0°

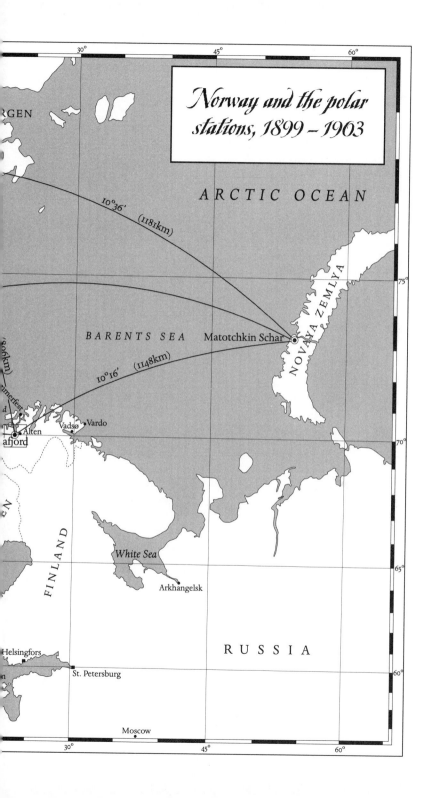

30°　　　　　　　45°　　　　　　　60°

RGEN

Norway and the polar stations, 1899 – 1963

ARCTIC OCEAN

10°36′ (1181km)

75°

NOVAYA ZEMLYA

BARENTS SEA　Matotchkin Schar

906km)

10°16′ (1148km)

mmerfest

Alten　Vadsø　Vardo
afjord

70°

FINLAND

White Sea

65°

Arkhangelsk

RUSSIA

Helsingfors

St. Petersburg

60°

Moscow

30°　　　　　　　45°　　　　　　　60°

PART I

Aurora Borealis

Kristian Birkeland with his three assistants—Riddervold, Koren, and Schaaning—and Samoyed guide at Litovsky's Studio, Archangelsk, Russia, 1902. Copyright by the Norwegian Technical Museum, Oslo

I

Odin's Messengers

14 October 1899

Finnmark, Northern Norway, within the Arctic Circle

It is true of the northern lights, as of many other things of which we
have no sure knowledge, that thoughtful men will form opinions and
conjectures about it and will make such guesses as seem reasonable. But
these northern lights have this peculiar nature, that the darker the night
is, the brighter they seem, and they always appear at night but never by
day, and rarely by moonlight. They resemble a vast flame of fire viewed
from a great distance. It also looks as if sharp points were shot from this
flame up into the sky, they are of uneven height and in constant motion,
now one, now another darting highest; and the light appears to
blaze like a living flame . . .

KONGESPEILET (The King's Mirror), c. 1220–30, Norse epic

*I*T WAS TEN in the morning and −25° Celsius when the
group left the small mining town of Kaafjord for the summit of Haldde Mountain, Haldde being a Lappish word for
"guardian spirit." The cold should have scattered the clouds but
halfway to the top the wind engulfed the men in blinding eddies of
snow and ice. Their guide, Clement Isaakson Hætta, was a Lapp
who had abandoned the traditional activity of herding reindeer to
become the local postman serving the few Norwegians, Swedes,
and immigrant workers from Finland, the Kvens, living in this
northerly outpost. Short, with bandy legs, he bent his body at the

hips into a right angle and pushed on through the storm like a sway-ing battering ram. Firmly wrapped around his wrist were the leather reins of the leading reindeer that was struggling to pull a sled piled high with a bizarre cargo of instrument boxes, trunks, and tripods. Seven reindeer, similarly yoked, were lashed behind the leader, and roped to them were five huddled figures.

Directly behind Hætta was the instigator of the expedition, Kris-tian Olaf Birkeland. He yelled to the guide above the screeching wind, wanting to know whether it was safe to continue. He could not hear the response, as the storm scrambled Hætta's words and Birkeland was partly deaf from conducting noisy radio-wave experi-ments as a student. Festooned with reindeer skins, he appeared shorter than his five feet five inches. Only thirty-one years old, he was already balding across the dome of his fine-boned scalp. The snow stuck to his round spectacles but he had long given up scrap-ing ice off the lenses and instead squinted between the rims and his fur hood. This unlikely adventurer had been made a professor of Norway's only university one year previously. He was the youngest of his colleagues in the Faculty of Science and Mathematics, his prophetic genius as a scientist emerging in his twenties when he solved problems that had defeated some of the brightest minds in Europe. Despite his youth, Birkeland was not a fit man; he loathed physical hardship and was more accustomed to long hours in the laboratory, hunched over diagrams and experiments. It was a com-ment on his devotion to scientific discovery that he was stranded on a mountain in eighty-kilometer-an-hour winds that howled continuously.

The storm was worsening; the men had been walking for six hours and had covered a distance that would take only two in good conditions. The guide shuffled onward, chewing on black tobacco, damp wads of which he spat into the wind. To reach the summit of the mountain, and the hut that would provide them with shelter, it was necessary to leave the narrow plateau they were traversing and climb the exposed mountainside. The peak they were heading toward was engulfed in a mass of swirling snow and ice as dense as black smoke.

Roped behind a breathless Birkeland came Bjørn Helland-Hansen, a gifted student in the medical department of Christiania University who was training to be a surgeon. Talented in science as well as medicine, he had attended Birkeland's lecture course and been inspired to join him on this adventure. He had just celebrated his twenty-second birthday. Tied to him was Elisar Boye, a Latin scholar who had been the first to volunteer for the expedition, presenting himself just a few hours after Birkeland posted a notice on the boards in the main hall of the university, requesting strong and able science students for a unique expedition to the Arctic Circle. At first Birkeland had thought that a Latin graduate would be of little use to him on a scientific mission, but Boye explained that he had achieved the best mark possible in mathematics, and eventually Birkeland relented in the face of the young man's enthusiasm. Boye looked much younger than his twenty-two years, with a smooth, pale complexion and clear blue eyes, on this day hidden inside his reindeer hood. He had stopped trying to see where he was going through the lashing snow and simply followed the direction of the tugging rope. Behind Boye came Kristoffer Knudsen, a twenty-three-year-old telegraphic engineer who had been working for the Norwegian railway until Birkeland lured him away with promises of adventure and pioneering science. He did not know the other members of the group and was the quietest when they began the ascent. As the storm intensified, he retreated ever further into his jacket and squinted at the ground immediately before his feet through the hairs of his hood. The tallest in the party, Sem Sæland, brought up the rear. Just turned twenty-five, Sæland had studied mathematics, astronomy, physics, and chemistry at the university, then traveled to Iceland, where he spent a year teaching before returning to Christiania University for further studies. There he met Birkeland, and was so interested in the professor's ideas that he had volunteered to join him on his expedition. Sæland repeatedly checked the knot in the rope linking him to the others as the driving snow was so thick he could see no more than a few centimeters beyond his nose.

By four o'clock the light was fading. Hætta decided that they should turn round and head back down the mountain, but then immediately changed his mind, suggesting they continue to the hut as it could not be more than two kilometers away and it would be more difficult to go down than up. He cajoled and harried the reindeer, which would not face the wind and nervously shook their heads at the sharp points of ice pricking their eyes and noses. It was impossible to sit in the sleds as they lay so close to the ground that the men were pelted with ice and small stones. Soon some of the reindeer lay down flat and refused to move. Hætta, a large part of his face white with frostbite, followed their lead and threw himself onto his sled, declaring he could go no further and could not find the way forward. He told Birkeland to continue without him, keeping the wind in his face, but the professor knew that abandoning their guide would be a fatal mistake and told the group to make camp as best they could. Hætta crawled under his sled while the others dragged the remaining sleds and baggage to form a barricade, behind which they erected a low tent. They struggled into their reindeer sleeping bags with all possible haste while Helland-Hansen weighed down the guy ropes with boxes and trunks. By the time he entered the tent less than five minutes later, the tips of his fingers had turned white with frostbite.

For twenty hours the five men lay in the cramped tent. They rubbed Helland-Hansen's fingers every quarter of an hour in an attempt to bring them back to life, and almost as regularly one of the five men had to push snow from the roof of the tent to prevent the suffocation of all those inside. Wherever there was a little shelter the snow heaped into thick, compact drifts that would trap them in a freezing vise if allowed to settle. They had nothing to drink or warm themselves with, having been assured by Hætta that the ascent was a matter of six hours' gentle climbing with a short, steep section at the summit. Birkeland had half a loaf of bread in his jacket that he tossed to Hansen in the darkness, hoping some food might distract him from the pain in his hands, but the noise of the wind was so great that he did not hear Birkeland yelling to him to eat the bread, and it froze to the consistency of rock within a few minutes. Gradually the little light that glowed through the snow-filled air was extinguished by the black night that fell by five o'clock. Inside the tent Birkeland was painfully aware that only a thin strip of canvas trembled between them and the lethal storm outside; one fierce gust and it could be ripped off. Without the tent they would be unlikely to survive.

The men lay shivering in their sleeping bags, dozing fitfully through the night but being frequently awoken by particularly violent blasts of wind and ice or by hunger and thirst. They had put a bucket of snow inside the tent in the hope that it would melt with their body heat and they would have water to drink, but it remained frozen. Birkeland felt responsible for the safety of his talented charges who had followed him on this hazardous expedition. Aware that this area sometimes experienced week-long tempests of unbroken ferocity, he worried throughout the night about how they could survive if the storm continued the next day. Lying awake listening to the air howling through the mountain pass and over their tent, he waited for the slightest sign that the gale-force winds were easing.

At ten the following morning Birkeland untied one of the leather strings holding down the tent flap but could see no more than a meter ahead. Not until midday did the wind abate sufficiently to risk venturing out. Birkeland banged on Hætta's sled to make sure the postman was still alive. Hætta shouted in reply that he was too cold to move but Birkeland insisted that they take advantage of the lull. Camp was struck, the sleds reloaded, and a reluctant Hætta once again led the group onward. They had only a few hours of daylight left to make the ascent, and without food and water it was imperative they find the shelter.

As the six men trudged on, the snow finally stopped and only tiny ice crystals spun in the eddies of wind left behind by the fierce zephyrs now en route to central Finnmark, Kautokeino, and the Lapp reindeer camps of the plains. The clouds dispersed as quickly as they had arrived, and in the gathering twilight the Pole Star appeared, reassuring and constant. Without the cloud cover the cold intensified rapidly, and moisture frosted on their lips, while their breath trailed behind them in crystal plumes. The drifting snow made walking in boots impossible, so the men strapped small skis to their feet. The undersurface of the skis was covered in reindeer skin in such a way that gliding forward was easy but the hairs sticking in the snow prevented them from slipping backwards. Nearly two hours later they reached a gently sloping plateau at the foot of the summit. Hætta pointed to the top of the peak. In the deepening twilight the group could faintly discern the shape of a small building. The sky was almost dark and the final slope was littered with sharp, icy rocks and narrow crevices. The reindeer coughed and snorted with the effort of pulling the heavy sleds up the incline and the group stopped frequently to allow them to rest. At the steepest sections, the men put their weight behind the sleds and pushed with all their failing strength as the delicate-limbed reindeer slipped and scrabbled on the icy rocks and patchy snow. After twenty minutes of backbreaking struggle the exhausted group arrived at a small area of smooth snow, a ledge of flat ground at the base of the final peak. Above them stood their sanctuary, a black shape against an inky sky.

In the dark the men could discern a small stone building with wooden steps leading up to the doorway in a low tower. After struggling to crack away the ice that had sealed the door to the jamb, Birkeland managed to get inside. It was nearly seven o'clock by the time the stove was lit and a bucket of snow brought in to thaw. Hansen immersed his hands in it in the hope that the frostbite could still be reversed. The others unpacked the sleds and staggered up the slope with the boxes and bags.

As the last of the packages were carried in and Hætta tethered the reindeer, a crack appeared in the night. On the eastern horizon

the darkness was splitting to reveal a gentle, tremulous luminescence—just a sliver, a streak. One by one the men stood still on the
summit and stared at the vision appearing before them. The
streamer of light began to move toward them in a huge arc across
the heavens, pulsating and writhing as it advanced. The streak
became a pennant with points of light coursing down in parallel
lines like the strings of a harp, attached at one end to heaven and at
the other to the sinuous curve of light as it crept from horizon to
horizon. Then another bolt of the green-white light stretched out
beside the first and both arced together. Even more wildly the
strings were plucked and the shapes changed to the music—now
curling, now forming great circles, then breaking again to roll away
to join another arc of green-white light. No one spoke. The hairs on
the backs of their necks stood up, as if awoken by static electricity.
Birkeland understood for the first time why the Lights had defied
neat explanation: they appeared not to belong to Earth but to space.
Seemingly beyond human comprehension, they reached straight
into the souls of those who witnessed them as an appearance of the
angelic host or the Holy Spirit might do. The glowing banners in
the sky were so entrancing that the group forgot the cold and
remained outside, entering the hut occasionally to eat or drink but
re-emerging to watch the breathtaking display dancing over their
heads. Only Hætta did not look. He took the reins and bells off his
animals and went into the hut without an upward glance.

For the Lapps, the Northern Lights were a fierce and powerful
presence. They were the messengers of God, to be respected and
feared. Hætta had removed the harnesses from the reindeer to avoid
attracting their attention, for Lapps believed that whistling, waving
handkerchiefs, or the sound of tinkling bells would provoke the
Lights into attacking the offender. Stories abounded of Lapps who
ignored this warning being struck down, their charred reindeer
jackets remaining as a warning to others. The Lapps would chant a
special rhyme repeatedly if they feared that they had angered the
Lights:

The northern light, the northern light
Flickering, flickering,
Hammer in its leg
Birch bark in its hand.

The hammer signified the vengeance of the angels if God was not respected and the birch bark created the flames with which they could burn transgressors to a cinder.

The ethereal phenomenon of the Northern Lights had inspired centuries of myth and terror. In Norway they were sometimes called Blood Lights to recall the belief that they were the souls of dead warriors fighting, a portent of war and death. The Vikings thought that the magical apparitions were Valkyries, female messengers of the god Odin, riding from Valhalla to mark out those who would be killed in battle. The streaks of luminescence were their fiery spears, the flashing sparks the reflections from their shields, and the great arcs the mythical bridge, Bifrost, across which the souls of the dead passed to the next world.

Sem Sæland had noticed Hætta's fear of the Lights; he had seen similar reactions the year before in Iceland. There, the people believed the Lights to be the spirits of those unhappy to be dead, trying to signal to their living relatives. The spirits could be vengeful, and the villagers would bring their children inside for fear that the Lights would sweep down and cut off their heads to use for ball games. An Eskimo word for aurora, *arssarneq,* meant "ball player." Icelanders would never cut their hair when the Lights shone or venture outside without a cap in case their hair was singed off.

The perception of the Lights as wrathful and violent spread throughout Europe in the Middle Ages. Every fifty to a hundred years a display dramatic enough to light up the skies above Paris, Vienna, and Rome occurred, blood-red in color. The frightening sight of the sky ablaze with pulsating flames led commentators to believe they predicted war, plague, and conflagration.

When Birkeland set out on his expedition, the earliest known record of the Lights was more than 2,000 years old, written in China in 208 B.C.:

> During the night luminous clouds were seen, gold and white, with long streamers, which lit up the hills. Some think it is Heaven's Sword, but others think that it is a deep hole, with a large blazing fire in the sky.

The earliest written attempt to provide an explanation for the aurora in Scandinavia was in the epic Norse poem *The King's Mirror:* "It seems to me not unlikely that the frost and the glaciers have become so powerful there that they are able to radiate forth these flames." As generations passed, other folkloric explanations gained ground—that the Lights were reflections from the silvery shoals of herring swimming close to the water's surface, or that they were the light bouncing off icebergs rocking in the polar sea; that they were created by sunlight reflecting off the wings of migrating geese, or off swans trapped in the polar ice flapping desperately to free themselves.

The aurora was one of the last unsolved mysteries of the natural world, puzzled over, feared, or worshipped. In an audacious plan, Birkeland intended to spend a whole winter on the mountaintop to study the Lights, which were known to appear in this region more frequently than elsewhere in the country. It was not only their beauty that compelled him and his fellow scientists to make this dangerous trip, but their challenge. He had a theory that, if he could prove it, would solve the riddle of the Lights and overturn conventional wisdom about the solar system and the Earth's place within it. For him, the Lights marked the threshold between the visible and invisible worlds; they were the link between the planet and the vast, uncontrollable, and unseen forces that shaped the universe.

After nearly an hour of celestial entertainment, weariness over-took the explorers and they went into the hut and shut the door against the cold night. The tiny building stood proud on the summit of Europe as the Earth turned its diurnal course around the sun. As the night wore on the beautiful Lights wound their path across the heavens, retreating from the dawn. Inside, the six men lay sleeping around the dying embers of the fire.

2

Land of the Lapps

October 1899
Auroral observatory, Haldde Mountain

> *A Valkyrie rests*
> *On the rock in steep,*
> *Flickering fire*
> *Flames about her:*
> *With the seep-thorn Ygg*
> *Her erst did prick:*
> *Other heroes she felled*
> *Than he had willed.*

The Prophecy of the
Seeress, *Older Edda,*
A.D. 1000–1100

*T*HE FOLLOWING morning Hætta woke first and brewed the very strong black coffee of which Lapps were extremely fond. After sharing it with the others, he went outside to slaughter four of the reindeer—they were to be the main item on the observatory's menu for the next six months. He kept two alive for the men remaining behind and harnessed two to take himself and Helland-Hansen down the mountain. Helland-Hansen's fingertips were still white and needed to be examined by a doctor. If lifeless, they would be amputated to avoid the risk of gangrene infection and he would have to abandon his hopes of becoming a surgeon. If they could be saved, Hansen would return to the observatory.

Hætta was anxious to leave. Already one of the group was injured and the Lapp saw this as an omen that the expedition was ill-fated. He tried to tell Birkeland of his disquiet, but the professor disliked superstition and dismissed his warning. The postman untied the reindeer and they skidded and lurched down the steep slope until they reached the shallow basin at the foot of the summit. In the deep snow that had gathered in the hollow the animals leapt in great bounds toward the head of the trail that would lead them to Kaafjord. From there, Hansen would catch the steamer to Hammerfest, the nearest town with a hospital—a journey that might take two days if they had to wait for the steamer. Hansen's departure was a stark reminder for the others of their isolation and vulnerability. Hansen had been the only one with any medical training and they were now reliant on the tiny printed instructions in their first aid box.

After a quick breakfast, the four remaining men inspected the observatory in the deep gloom of early morning. Birkeland was immensely proud of the sturdy little observatory, which was capable of withstanding some of the most extreme weather conditions to be found anywhere on Earth. Commissioned in the spring by Birkeland and built during the mild months of summer by men and horses, dragging over forty tons of building material from the valley to the peak, it should have been finished by September. A freak snowstorm in August had caused delays, forcing the observers to climb to the peak three weeks later than planned, when the weather was worse and the task of equipping and preparing the observatory more difficult. The four men had to pick their way carefully around the base of the walls as the building was perched on the rocky mountain tip, with sheer cliffs plummeting several hundred meters on two sides and steep, rocky inclines on the others. The stone and concrete walls were nearly thirty centimeters thick. The roof was of sturdy Norwegian design, layers of timbers covered in gravel, bark, earth, and more wood, with steel guy ropes added to keep it fixed to the house during the gales that ripped through the mountains. The house itself was probably solid enough, although the ground was too hard for foundations to be dug. On the south wall was a short, flat-roofed observing tower with the entrance set into it, a meter off the ground, reached by climbing ten wooden steps. Birkeland had insisted on raising the level of the doorway to prevent large snow-drifts blocking the entrance and trapping the men inside the hut, or worse, outside. In these parts the wind was so strong that even hard compacted drifts could be blasted away and reformed in minutes.

Inside the observatory were four rooms, all lined with pine and wallpapered in the workroom and kitchen. The ground floor of the tower provided a buffer between the outside world and the kitchen and contained the wood, coke, coal, and paraffin that had been delivered in the late summer. Once the men had unpacked, it would also house their outdoor clothes, boots, spades, skis, and snow-shoes. A wooden ladder led to a trapdoor that gave on to the roof. The kitchen was the warmest room in the building, containing the only stove and, at one end, bunks and a small window. A door led to the workroom—depository of the forty trunks and boxes hurriedly stacked there the previous night—and beyond that was the window-less instrument room.

A sheet was strung across the kitchen to separate the bunks from the cooking area. The kitchen table was placed near the fire and domestic utensils hung on nails in the walls. A wooden parti-tion was built to divide the workroom into two sections, the smaller of which became a darkroom for developing their photographs of the Lights. A larder for the dead reindeer was fashioned out of pack-ing cases filled with ice and roped to the exterior of the building along the south wall. The far side of a rocky outcrop was designated as the latrine; when it was too windy, a chamber pot in the vestibule would have to suffice.

2 reindeer-skin hats	3 mattresses
2 reindeer skins	kitchen utensils, casseroles,
Skis and snowshoes	kettles
5 reindeer jackets	stove for cooking
4 pairs snowshoes	5 pairs skin mittens
2 pairs Sami shoes	tools
medicine chest	copper nails
flag	2 sleds
2 mirrors	3 sets reindeer reins
alarm clock	cups, wine and beer glasses
2 buckets	scissors, etc.
3 lamps	2 tents
5 pillows	6 simple chairs
4 sleeping bags	2 office chairs
10 blankets	2 chaises longues (not elegant)

Inventory of items bought for the Haldde observatory, not including fuel, food, drink, and live animals.

As the weather that morning was good, Birkeland decided to start with the instruments designed to be fixed onto the roof of the observatory tower. He checked the boxes, trunks, cases, and bags of instruments he had brought with him from Christiania University. Most of them had been shipped from overseas—Germany, France, Russia, Britain—their postmarks testimony to the breadth of his knowledge of the latest scientific advances occurring throughout Europe. Birkeland had chosen the very best he could afford, and no previous expedition to study the Northern Lights had been as well equipped. Here, on top of a mountain in Northern Norway, the fruits of centuries of scientific research and experimentation were being harnessed to study the Lights.

First he picked out a strong anemometer, built to survive hurricane-strength winds up to seventy-five knots or one hundred forty kilometers an hour. By recording wind speeds he could determine whether the appearance of the auroras was linked to any particular weather conditions. For this purpose he also chose a sturdy electrometer for the roof, to record the electric condition of the atmosphere, which was known to vary during thunderstorms but had not been studied in connection with the aurora. An alcohol thermometer that could withstand temperatures as low as $-117°$ Celsius was unpacked to verify numerous anecdotal reports that auroras looked brighter the colder the temperature. The lowest recorded temperature in Finnmark was $-51.4°C$ on 1 January 1886, a temperature at which it would be impossible to be outside observing the aurora for more than a few minutes. In the vestibule Birkeland also fixed a mercury thermometer that would work down to $-38°$ Celsius. Norway was, in fact, the best place on Earth to study the Northern Lights because the Gulf Stream that ran along its western coast mitigated the worst of the Arctic cold. Although the storms across Finnmark could be fierce, the temperature tended to be a few degrees higher than in other Arctic regions where the Lights appeared. A barometer would tell whether air pressure changed during auroral displays, and a hygrometer measured air humidity. The photographic equipment was stored in the darkroom until needed, and wind kites, to record wind velocities up to 2,000 meters above the ground, were left in the vestibule until official recordings began on 1 November.

These instruments, Birkeland hoped, would give him the evidence he needed for his theory of how the auroras were formed, and the observations would provide answers to some contentious minor questions, such as were auroras accompanied by a crackling noise? Could they make hair stand on end, burn flesh, or cause headaches in the way thunderstorms could? Did they touch the ground? Did they occur during "daytime"? By the end of the winter

Birkeland hoped to have definitive answers to all these questions, ending centuries of speculation.

There were also numerous ledgers into which records and descriptions of the auroras would be entered, including their shapes, longevity, brightness, position in the sky, movement, and related weather phenomena. Auroras were generally divided into four basic forms—bands, arcs, crowns, and rays—but during a display, the luminous threads of light rarely remained in a single shape but swayed from one form to the next, frequently defying categorization. Trying to describe and explain the Northern Lights had taxed the world's greatest minds, their beauty and inconsistency snubbing even the most poetic and daring attempts. Around 450 B.C., the Greek Anaxagoras put forward the idea that auroras were caused by fiery vapors that poured down from the sky and accumulated in the clouds until they burst into flames. These explosions gave rise to the auroras, comets, and lightning, a vaguely heretical idea that challenged the presumed perfection of the heavens but might have been overlooked had Anaxagoras not also asserted that the sun was a large ball of fire. For this outrageous impiety he was exiled in disgrace. A century later, Aristotle contradicted Anaxagoras's heresy and denied that there could be any interaction between the heavens and the Earth because the heavens were perfect and unchanging—an erroneous belief that persisted to Birkeland's day. In a letter to Alexander the Great in 349 B.C., Aristotle described a rare occurrence of the auroras as blood-red, some remaining stationary while others shot out at great speed, some flickering up and dying out while others lingered. He categorized them as "torches," "small rays," "round vessels," "chasms," and, in his more scholarly work *Meteorologica*, as "jumping goats."

Aristotle grouped the Lights under the general heading "Comets," and they were not clearly separated from other "heavenly bodies" until the early 1600s when Galileo Galilei described them as the *boreale aurora* or "the northern dawn." In 1621 the designation was modified slightly to *aurora borealis* by the eminent

French astronomer Pierre Gassendi, who, like Galileo and Aristotle, had witnessed a display tinged with pink. Auroras seen in lower latitudes often had a rosy hue, reminiscent of dawn. Birkeland himself preferred the Latin term *lumine boreali,* "the northern light," or *aurora polaris,* "polar light," as in the far north the auroras were usually white or yellowish green and bore no resemblance to dawn.

Once Birkeland was satisfied that he had chosen all the instruments he needed for outdoors, they were hauled up the wooden ladder in the tower and through the trapdoor. The observatory roof was the highest point on the mountain and free from all obstructions. The weather was clear and cold and the panorama stretched for hundreds of kilometers in every direction. In the west, the sharp blue peaks of the Kvænangen Mountains jutted out of the Earth's crust; to the east the horizon was interrupted by the softer outlines of the Porsanger Mountains. The precipitous cliffs of Lang fjord and Stjernø Island could be glimpsed fifty kilometers to the north, while the northernmost glaciers of Norway glittered on the neighboring island of Seiland. The mountain plateau of the south stretched inland in undulating lines as far as the eye could see, toward the winter home of the mountain Lapps, and far below lay the fjord, a dark channel with numerous branches that continued into the Alten valley.

Haldde Mountain was a little known and desolate place when Birkeland came to Finnmark, the largest and most northerly of Norway's provinces, in search of the ideal location for an aurora observatory. He had first seen it in the summer when the midnight sun illuminated the peaks with a soft radiance and the grass and moss on the slopes housed clouds of mosquitoes that made the climb to the top unpleasant. Birkeland was warned by the villagers living along the fjord that the mountain changed character after the end of autumn, when the summit could be shrouded in snow for days on end, the route to the top blocked by drifts up to nine meters high. Then the mountain was a harsh and capricious place, no one attempted to ascend it and certainly no one had spent a whole winter there. Even the Lapps abandoned the Haldde area at the first sign of snow and guided their reindeer herds to the winter grazing plateau of Kautokeino.

For a scientist, however, Haldde Peak was the perfect site from which to study the aurora. By choosing this vantage point, nearly 1,000 meters above sea level, Birkeland would be as close to the Lights as possible with a view unhindered by trees, buildings, or the electric lights and factory smoke that were beginning to pollute the skies over the capital and other cities. Several earlier reports about the Lights had suggested that they reached so close to the Earth as to touch the mountaintops. Others who witnessed them thought that the Lights were emitted from the peaks themselves, like smoke from a volcano. By siting the observatory on such a high peak Birkeland would be able to test these hypotheses and maybe stand among the Lights themselves. No one knew where the Lights originated, and no one had yet proved where in the sky they appeared. In order to reveal how near to the ground they came and how high into space they stretched, Birkeland had had another small hut built on a neighboring peak, Talvik. By sending one man there, they could measure the Lights against the stars from the two locations, nearly four kilometers apart, and determine their height with simple geometry.

From the tower the men could look toward the north, beyond Stjernø and Seiland Islands to the long, bluish silhouette of Sørø Island, the last barrier of land against the Arctic seas and the unconquered North Pole, nearly 2,000 kilometers away. Before Birkeland left Christiania, news had broken that an Italian team was trying to reach it, but nothing was yet known of their progress. It was just the latest in a string of attempts starting twenty years earlier with George de Long's tragic expedition, during which twenty of the thirty-three crew members perished, including de Long himself. An American explorer, Adolphus Greeley, had tried the following year and only six of his team of twenty-five were alive when rescue eventually came. Birkeland's countryman Fridtjof Nansen, who spent three years drifting in the polar ice in the ship *Fram,* had come the closest, missing the pole by only 400 kilometers in 1896. Other attempts, including a foolhardy scheme to fly over the pole in a hot-air balloon, had ended in failure and death. Birkeland himself had thought of becoming an explorer when he was young, although not of the Arctic but of Africa. While Birkeland was studying for his degree in physics he had been captivated by the professor of Egyptology Jens Lieblein, a mesmerizing speaker in his seventies, who recounted his journeys along the Nile and the discoveries he and his fellow archaeologists had made about the country's pharaonic past. Egypt still held a fascination for Birkeland but otherwise Africa seemed to have been overrun by unpleasant European prospectors, the motivation of discovery having been displaced by that of greed and exploitation. He had turned his sights instead to the glittering, uncharted mysteries of the polar regions and the skies above them.

Once all the instruments were securely fastened to the roof, the little group gathered around the flagpole that Birkeland had requested be built into the supporting wall. He opened the parcel that he had carried with him from Christiania and pulled out a large flag. It was the Norwegian standard, a thin dark blue cross on a broader white cross on a red background, free of the Swedish colors that the government had decreed must appear in the upper corner nearest the flagpole. Birkeland improvised a short speech, invoking the history of their small country whose people had been great explorers since the days of the Vikings. As the old century drew to a close, Norway was enjoying a renaissance, with figures of the stature of Ibsen, Grieg, Nansen, and Munch retrieving its politics, culture, and status from the doldrums of foreign domination. The expedition to the mountain summit was to further this process and to uncover new territory—not in places where flags could be planted but in space, and in the world of ideas. Birkeland dedicated his team's pioneering research to Norway, that it might one day be released from the shackles of Swedish supremacy to ride to independence with dignity and pride.

The others applauded the nationalism of Birkeland's speech. Norway had lost its independence 400 years earlier and was then the frustrated partner in a union with Sweden, formed in 1814 after Carl Johan, heir apparent of Sweden, defeated the forces of Denmark and Norway. By the time Birkeland was born in 1867, a rapidly developing Norway was chafing under Swedish hegemony, and increasingly vociferous demands for autonomy were made during the last two decades of the century, focusing primarily on the inequality of the partnership: the prime minister of Norway and three principal ministers were required to reside in Sweden, the Swedish king had power of veto, and the Norwegian national flag was supposed to carry the Swedish colors—"scrambled egg" as it was known—a symbol of Norway's inferior role that was widely resented. In matters of foreign affairs the situation was yet more galling. Norway was not allowed its own foreign office, minister, consuls, or even merchant marine flag: Sweden sought control over Norway's shipping contacts abroad, even though Norway had become a more important sea-trading nation than Sweden. Relations between the two countries became so strained by 1895 that both sides began rearmament in preparation for possible war and Sweden ended the Scandinavian Common Market, a move that hit sections of Norway's economy very hard.

Birkeland had always been vociferous in his view that his country should be autonomous and defended Norway's honor at every opportunity. While studying in Leipzig a few years earlier, he had been forcibly ejected from a performance of *Little Eyolf,* by the great Norwegian playwright Henrik Ibsen, for objecting loudly that a Swedish, rather than a Norwegian, flag had been raised in the second act of the play. He had gone straight to the local paper to submit a furious letter. The next day the flag was changed. Birkeland's sentiments were shared by all standing on the observatory roof with him, particularly by Sæland, who had narrowly missed a jail sentence for hissing at the Swedish king, Oscar, and Crown Prince Gustav when they visited the capital. He had been forced to resign from the Students' Society and a number of professors argued that he should be prevented from taking his final examinations. Sæland had opted to take a sabbatical and travel to Iceland while the debate about his future died down, and he had eventually been allowed to return to continue his studies in the mathematics and science department. Birkeland was glad to have Sæland with him. He was a capable organizer, a talented scientist, and blessed with a good sense of humor. He also possessed great musical abilities and would often start a round of singing after meals.

Once the outdoor instruments had been properly sited, Birkeland began setting up the most important machines, the magnetometers. These were designed to measure changes in the strength and direction of the Earth's magnetic field and were housed in the interior instrument room, on pillars built into the floor. He spent many days adjusting the exquisitely made instruments with their perfectly turned brass fittings, quartz threads, and steel needles, having first removed door hinges, nails, pipes, and any other object made of iron and replaced them with brass hinges, copper nails, and ceramic pipes—materials that would not affect the magnetic readings.

It had been known for nearly 150 years that the Northern Lights disrupted compass readings and were a threat to navigation. With this in mind, a young man called Olaf Peter Hiorter, brother-in-law of the famous Swedish scientist Anders Celsius who invented the temperature scale, had spent an entire year, from 19 January 1741 until 19 January 1742, watching a compass needle, recording its position every hour. He took 6,638 readings (out of a possible 8,760), stopping only for a short trip home in August and a ten-day Christmas holiday. In his treatise he gave evidence to show that a compass needle would move, left and right of the magnetic north, when the auroras appeared. He did not know why this strange phenomenon occurred but implored travelers to be careful when using a compass in the regions where the auroras could appear. Birkeland was convinced that the relationship between the compass needle and the

Lights was crucial. His sophisticated magnetometers would do the job of Hiorter's compass, recording movements of the needle photographically, without Birkeland having to watch them night and day.

Birkeland was well read in previous explanations of the Lights, his favorite being an experiment performed in the 1740s by a Swedish man of letters, Samuel von Triewald, who shone a beam of light through a prism, over a glass of cognac and onto a screen. Von Triewald was hoping to prove that the Lights were caused by sunlight striking clouds of "vapors" in the atmosphere. The fumes from the cognac created swirling patterns in the light, and the experimenter wrote:

> One was surprised to see a naturally occurring northern light on the screen that nothing could more resemble . . . Never be a man tired regardless how long he looks at this experiment, for in addition it is far the most beautiful one can produce in a dark room.

During the nineteenth century a rash of theories for the aurora had been posited. Birkeland was aware of at least two dozen competing ideas, and there were probably more. The most sophisticated concentrated either on magnetic, electric, or cosmic forces as the main causal element in the appearance of the Lights. Unlike his predecessors, Birkeland considered that all these elements were involved in the complicated processes the aurora revealed. Although Newton had written, "It is the perfection of all God's works that they are done with the greatest simplicity," the aurora seemed to defy that belief.

Once the magnetometers were working correctly, Sem Sæland organized a recording timetable, to come into effect on 1 November. The timetable listed all the instruments in the observatory, the intervals at which they needed to be read and which member of the team was to do so. Readings needed to be taken, indoors and out, throughout each twenty-four-hour period, although the busiest time was between six in the evening and one in the morning when the Northern Lights most frequently appeared. During auroral displays the skies would be monitored constantly and readings for the outdoor instruments entered in a ledger every few minutes and, on occasions, every thirty seconds.

As the days of preparation passed, the sun sank lower on the horizon and the hours of daylight dwindled rapidly. The Arctic winter was just over the horizon and within a few weeks there would be no daylight at all. Even now they saw the sun for only four or five hours when the clouds permitted, but this did not depress the group. A sense of urgency and excitement permeated their every action: they would be the first men to spend a whole winter in this harsh environment. As the instruments began to click and tick, whirr and swing, the hope that nature would surrender her secrets to them became palpable. No one grumbled about the cold or the long dark afternoons but all looked instead for the first glimpses of the aurora.

Sæland had accepted the unenviable task of manning the second auroral station on the neighboring peak, originally with Hansen, but no word had arrived from the injured scientist. Sæland was perhaps the best suited of the group for the task—calm, experienced with the instruments, and trusted by Birkeland to be rigorous in rising to the scientific challenges of the months ahead. He visited the Talvik building as soon as Birkeland was able to release him. It was a single tower with a sloping lean-to against one wall, hurriedly built of rock and concrete, drafty and cheerless, with one window and a thin roof. The tower would be equipped with the same instruments as the other observatory but without magnetometers. The lean-to was Sæland's living and working area. The two observatories would be connected by telephone, but there was a tacit recognition that contact would be frequently broken during storms or large auroral displays, when huge currents in the ground often disrupted telegraph and telephone links. It would be Knudsen's job to repair the telephone cable to maintain communication between the two buildings.

During the last two weeks of October, Knudsen and Boye frequently traveled between the two peaks, inspecting the cable that had been installed during the summer. After much deliberation, Knudsen had decided that it was better to suspend the cable from wooden poles where it was vulnerable to wind and ice but out of reach of snowdrifts and nibbling reindeer. As he moved beneath the cable, checking for faults and weak points, Boye would practice his reindeer driving skills or, as was more frequently the case, reveal his lack of them. Fortunately, after the first few trips from peak to peak, the reindeer had learned the route and trotted off without instruction. This worked well when the men were already sitting in their sleds, less well when they were inside finishing their coffee. Boye spent many frustrating hours chasing the echoes of their bells and soon realized that tethering them loosely to poles did not work as they could chew through them or undo the tether by sucking at it with their strong lips. They were masters of escape and Boye had to learn quickly in order not to lose the group's fastest means of transport. It would be hard to replace the reindeer at this time of year as the Lapps had moved from the fjord into the hinterland of Finnmark, where they roamed over the immense high plateau with their animals, guarding them day and night from wolves. In the summer, when Birkeland had come looking for a good position for the observatory, the shores of the Alten fjord were bristling with thousands of reindeer, large herds grazing on the slopes or swimming with their magnificent spreading horns towering above the sea, appearing from a distance like a floating forest. The herders came to the coast only in summer, when they met with the Lapps who had abandoned the herding life to be fishermen. During the first week in the observatory, the scientists could see the last herders, retreating to the plateau beyond the mountains.

Birkeland and his team were not ignorant of the ways and customs of the indigenous people of Finnmark, for Norwegians had lived as neighbors with the Lapps for centuries and marriages between them were common. The Lapps belonged to a wider group called the Sabme, Sami, or Sabmeladsjak who inhabited nearly the whole of Europe north of the sixty-sixth degree of latitude, the parts of Russia, Finland, Sweden, and Norway that jutted into the Arctic Ocean—250,000 square kilometers, populated by around 30,000 Sami. During the winter they moved camp every three days or so, looking for the moss on which the reindeer fed, and avoiding wolves. Although they would hunt and fish, the nomads lived mainly on reindeer, occasionally eating their meat but mostly subsisting on frozen reindeer milk mixed with berries, reindeer milk cheese, and rye-meal cakes baked over the fire. Birkeland and his team followed their lead in terms of diet, eating mainly reindeer but supplementing the strong meat with delicacies they had brought from the city, such as biscuits, chocolate, honey, and dried fish.

By the end of October, after less than a month in the observatory, the instruments were calibrated and ready and Birkeland had time to invent contraptions designed to make their lives more comfortable. The first was a pump and a series of pipes connected to the stove that would heat their bunks through the freezing nights. On the trial night, the pump somehow slipped and instead blew freezing air into their beds, resulting in Birkeland catching a cold and the others waking with stiff necks. More successful was an alarm system that would alert the group when readings were due. Birkeland powered the alarm with a battery, wondering whether one had been used so far north before. Volta, an Italian chemist, had first made a battery in 1800, but no one, including the inventor, understood why it worked, just that it did. So Birkeland was curious to find out if the battery would perform in low temperatures, but after a few days' trial run, it died, and the alarm, up to that point accurate and useful, had to be abandoned. Birkeland's great triumph, however, was a mechanical cable car that could carry supplies up the final, steep section of the summit. He sent his drawings to Meyer, the engineer who had built the observatories, explaining that the cable should be 200 meters long and the car large enough to carry 100 kilos of goods, or snow for water. Five weighty, misshapen boxes arrived in Kaafjord two weeks later and Hætta struggled up the mountain to deliver the awkward load to the professor. He watched the others unpacking the cable car with deep suspicion and left worrying that these fanciful men would never survive a winter in the harsh environment of Northern Norway, particularly considering their "unholy" mission to study the Lights. When the postman arrived the following week, Birkeland was at the foot of the summit adjusting the base of the cable car. He put Hætta's sack into it and began to turn a large wheel. Effortlessly the car started its ascent and Hætta's cynicism turned to joy when he understood that this invention would save him, and his reindeer, many hazardous climbs up to the summit of the mountain.

On the last day of October Hætta arrived, two days before his usual weekly delivery, with a letter from Hammerfest. It was dictated by Hansen who was convalescing in a hospital after an operation to remove the tips of all his fingers, some to the first joint, others to the second. He planned to return to Christiania as soon as he was well again and wished them all good luck. The men fell silent at the thought of Hansen's suffering and the loss of his future career. That the mountain had claimed a victim so soon shocked Birkeland, who hoped that his small group would survive the Arctic winter with no more casualties.

3

The Castle

November 1899
Auroral observatory, Haldde Mountain

*As I looked, behold, a stormy wind came out of the North and a
great cloud with brightness round about it, and fire flashing forth
continuously and in the midst of the fire, as it were gleaming bronze like
the appearance of the bow that is in the cloud on the day of rain, so was
the appearance of the brightness round about.*

The Book of Ezekiel in the Old Testament, c. 593 B.C.

LIFE IN "The Castle," as the observatory had been christened due to its resemblance to the mythical abodes of troll giants, began smoothly. From 1 November, when observations began in earnest, Sæland's timetable became the group's bible, giving structure to their days and guidance on the freezing nights when they followed the schedule like sleepwalkers, too cold to think for themselves. One man would do the morning measurements, another the afternoon's and another the night's. Sæland, alone on Talvik peak, took all the meteorological and auroral measurements himself.

The tour of duty at the main observatory began by winding up the automatic recording devices in the instrument room, changing the photographic paper, and developing the exposed rolls. It had taken several days for Birkeland to trust Boye and Knudsen to fulfill this task without disturbing the magnetometers. Next, layers of reindeer skins, hoods, mittens, and boots were donned in order to record wind speeds, air humidity, temperature, and air electricity, and to note in ledgers any auroral activity, weather formations, and particular cloud shapes during Northern Lights displays. They did not see auroras every night; in fact, they appeared infrequently and a whole week could pass without a sighting. Sometimes cloud cover hid the sky; sometimes the moon was so bright the Lights were hard to discern against it; sometimes the night was as clear as a new window but only the stars could be seen. On nights when auroras blazed across the heavens, the man on duty would wake up his colleagues, phone Sæland, and carry the photographic equipment outside. Glass plates were inserted into the back of the camera and a view of the Lights fixed in relation to the stars in the sky. The position was then relayed to Sæland, who arranged his own camera. At a certain signal the operators of both cameras would open their shutters, usually for ten seconds or more. The plates were then stored in the darkroom to be developed the following day. As the men curled into their bunks at night, it was not the biting cold that made it difficult to sleep but the excitement of seeing the auroras and hoping that soon they would have scientific explanations that were every bit as dramatic as the old Norse fairy tales.

Birkeland usually offered to do the night-time readings. He had been plagued with insomnia since his student days and remembered lying in bed as a child listening to the city fall silent. Now he used his sleeplessness as an opportunity to work through the night. He would putter around the instrument room making tiny adjustments or watching for movements in the mirror of the magnetometer as each minute twist showed that out in space the magnetic field was pulsating. When the instrument moved more strongly he would pull on his reindeer skins to see if the aurora had appeared. If the weather was clear, the sky would be filled with mysterious, luminescent streamers more brilliant than any fireworks or electric lights.

Although Birkeland regularly sat in temperatures of −20° Celsius to watch the light displays, he was oblivious to the cold. He agreed with folklore that the lower the temperature, the brighter the Lights, although he could find no explanation for this. Their arrival, heralded by rapid movement in the magnetometers, was perfectly silent as the first sinuous streak of light appeared above the distant mountain peaks and arced slowly across the sky, from horizon to horizon. They would sometimes form translucent curtains, blowing like gauze across the darkness. Birkeland was increasingly convinced that they must appear above the height where any wind could catch them, and he certainly did not witness them touch the ground.

He would lie flat on the roof of the tower and gaze at the shooting lines of light wrapping their brilliance around the crown of the Earth, like a ribbon shot through with iridescent metals, tracing distant mountain peaks and valley troughs, filling the night with shimmering threads. From his vantage point, Birkeland could see for about one thousand kilometers from horizon to horizon, but he knew that the Lights continued beyond his line of sight to create a dazzling crown around the magnetic pole of the Earth. These "auroral glories," as they were christened due to their similarity to haloes, were first surmised in the middle of the eighteenth century, when a Swedish professor, traveling around North America to collect seeds and plants, also noted the dates and positions of auroral displays. When he returned to Sweden this information was correlated with local observations of the Lights and it became clear that the same display had been seen. In the years following this discovery, other observations of the Lights across the globe proved that they occurred in an oval around, but rarely over, the pole. Captain Cook had witnessed that the Lights also occurred around the South Pole in 1770 during the voyage of the *Endeavour.* He christened them the "aurora australis." As Birkeland watched the Lights, night after night, he realized that if his theory was correct the Lights seen around the two poles would be a mirror image of each other. He did not have proof for this, but his intuition told him it must be true.

The weather proved the little group's main challenge as autumn became winter. Birkeland's notes express disbelief in the violence of the storms:

> The wind sometimes roars so against the house that you would have thought you were sitting at the foot of a waterfall; and the floors tremble and everything shakes. We are able to gauge the storm outside by the noise within. Often we cannot get out of the house ourselves for several days and it takes three strong men to shut our little door. One strong anemometer was blown apart in the course of a few days and we found pieces of it 50 to 100 metres from the place it had been put up.

The telephone cable was as vulnerable as the instruments on the observatory roof. In nine or ten hours of bad weather the cable could become as thick as a man's arm with ice and frequently snapped under the weight. Knudsen and Boye would set out with ladders and rubberized sheathing as soon as the winds died down.

> We have seen a layer of snow a metre thick and so hard you could jump on it without sinking in, practically disappear from the summit in the course of a few hours. It may be imagined what a whirling and drifting there is in the wind, when the snow is comparatively fresh and not pressed into a compact mass. Even indoors the situation is not always comfortable. Water freezes a couple of feet from the stove and the lamp is often blown out on the table in the middle of the room, although in a general sense the house is well-enough built.

It was hard to tell when one day ended and the next began, and the logbooks were marked "a.m." and "p.m." to prevent confusion. Long days of work were punctuated by brief moments of excitement—when the aurora twisted over the distant mountains, or on the occasional mornings when Hætta appeared with the post or Sæland arrived with his measurements and to pick up supplies. The days were busy with taking recordings, mending the instruments outside, keeping warm, and reading. Despite the intense cold, the little sunlight, and the monotonous diet of meat, there was rarely any tension in the observatory. Boye, in particular, used the time for almost constant questioning of Birkeland, trying to cram the contents of a science degree into a crash course of a few months. The professor was a patient and inspiring teacher, grabbing any available object or drawing simple diagrams to make abstract concepts visible. Although he admired all the men on his team, it was the irrepressible Boye to whom he became most attached. When not on duty, the two would often sit around the stove, discussing basic concepts such as gravity and electricity, Boye benefiting from the most contemporary and profound understanding available in Norway and Birkeland enjoying the intelligent and often surprising questions Boye asked. For Birkeland, the expedition had an unexpected and pleasant side effect: he felt happy. He enjoyed being surrounded by intelligent young graduates whose enthusiasm and energy matched his own, their banter and practical jokes alleviating the bone-aching cold. Far from being depressed by the weather and diminishing daylight, Birkeland was enjoying the challenge that the location and the scientific puzzle presented and the camaraderie that resulted among the closely knit team.

There had been several times in Birkeland's life when he had not been so contented—he had blamed these episodes of "nervous freezing fits," when he lay incapacitated in bed, on overwork, physical illness, or homesickness if they occurred while he was traveling, but the truth was that he had suffered from mild mania and depression since his student days.

3, rue Casimir Delarique
Paris
5.2.1893

Dear Bjerkenes!
Thanks for your letter; you can't imagine how timely it was.
I have been in bed for four days without sleeping after a
tremendous nervous freezing attack caused by too much
work. Now I am up again and feel relatively well but I think it
is necessary to proceed more carefully.

Now about the Carnival fun. Yesterday was the first day
I could think of going out after my illness and I decided
to watch the parades and spectacles in the grands boule-
vards . . . as you know, confetti plays a large part in these and
I bought a large bag for fifty centimes to return fire from
sweet young ladies! . . .

Best wishes to you
Kristian

His prodigious talent had a cost in that it was fueled by an appetite
for work that his body could barely cope with; he became lost in the
puzzles he found and time ceased to exist, tiredness and hunger
evaporated. Newton had once replied, when asked how he managed to conceive of gravity, "by thinking continuously upon it";
Birkeland did the same, driven to explore the ideas that arose in his
mind. His acute scientific intuition was born of a young life devoted
entirely to "thinking continuously upon it." Here on the mountaintop Birkeland was free to spend every minute on his work: there
were no other demands upon his time and the act of living, though
strenuous due to the conditions, was simple.

On most days Birkeland would spend several hours with the
magnetometers. Before entering the room he emptied his pockets
of pens, penknife, keys, and any other object that might contain
magnetic materials that would disrupt his results. All the buttons on

his clothes had already been replaced with bone, his glasses were rimmed with gold, a nonmagnetic metal, and he wore reindeer slippers that enabled him to tread softly among the instruments. His three magnetometers were in constant use, writing a map of the magnetic field for every second of the day. The first showed the direction of the field, the second its horizontal strength, and the third its vertical strength, from which calculations could be made to map its position overhead and note any changes that occurred. They had been made in Germany by the best instrument manufacturer in Europe, Otto Toepfer, and were about the size of large shoeboxes. In one side of each instrument a hole was pierced, six centimeters in diameter, through which a quartz thread could be seen hanging, like the workings of a grandfather clock. Attached to the bottom of the thread was a tiny magnet that sensed changes in the magnetic field caused by electric currents flowing overhead at least a hundred kilometers above the Earth's surface, possibly as far as 100,000 kilometers away. A continuous recording was made automatically using a narrow beam of light from an oil lamp, focused with the use of a lens, beamed directly at a small mirror attached to the front of the magnet. This tiny mirror reflected the beam onto a long roll of photographic paper that scrolled by clockwork at a steady pace. As long as Birkeland remembered to wind up the recording machine every day and refill the oil in the lamps, the beam of light would create a continuous line on the photographic paper that fluctuated as the magnet responded to changes in the magnetic field. If there was no magnetic activity, a straight line would be produced. The scrolls would be developed every morning in the darkroom and hung up to dry. By comparing them with visual observations of auroral activity, Birkeland would soon build up an accurate picture of how movements in the magnetic field related to the occurrence of auroras.

Birkeland first became fascinated by the force of magnetism at school when his math teacher, Elling Holst, had persuaded him to buy a magnet with the money Birkeland made from teaching math to his less talented peers. Rapidly he learned what his magnet could do by experimenting with it and reading all he could about magnetism. He became fascinated by the Englishman William Gilbert, who in 1600 wrote a book called *De Magnete* (On a Magnet). Not only was it the first major scientific book published in England, but in it Gilbert established that "the Earth itself is a giant magnet." In Gilbert's time bar magnets, such as Birkeland bought as a child, did not exist. The only naturally occurring magnetic materials were iron and "magnetite" or "lodestone," a rare rock that had magnetic properties and was quarried, with iron, along the coasts of the Aegean Sea, on the Mediterranean islands, and near Magnesia in Asia Minor, whence the name derived. An ancient Greek fable explained the name: a shepherd, Magnus, was walking on Mount Ida in Crete when the tacks in his sandals and the iron tip of his staff became so strongly attracted to Earth that he could not move. He began digging to ascertain the cause and found a wonderful stone—which he called after himself, magnetite. As it was not possible to dig into the core of the Earth, the mechanism that created the magnetic field was still one of the greatest unsolved scientific mysteries of Birkeland's day, along with the Northern Lights and what powered the sun.

For his experiments, Gilbert made spheres of lodestone turned on a lathe, a difficult task in itself due to the hardness of the material, and called them "terrellas," little Earths. Placing iron needles that could pivot freely around the terrella, he noticed that the needles all pointed north. When he put terrellas on cork floats and let them move freely in water, he saw that they circled each other for a while before coming together—for the north pole of a magnet is only attracted to the south pole of another magnet and vice versa. Gilbert discovered not only that the Earth was a magnet, but also that it had two poles, north and south. When iron filings were sprinkled around a magnet, they spread out furthest at the poles, forming a shape like an apple cut in half with the magnet, or the Earth, being the central pip. The strength of the field was at its greatest at the poles because the lines of force were more concentrated there. As Birkeland and scientists before him had understood, the auroras were mostly seen in the polar regions of the Earth—where the lines of magnetic force could reach great distances into space. Birkeland also saw, from studying the magnetometer readings, that the auroras appeared only when the steady magnetic field was disturbed and "storms" could be detected. What force was creating these storms was the question Birkeland sought to answer.

Gilbert had realized that magnetism was a force related to but separate from electricity, he was the first to use the words "electricity," "electric attraction," and "electric force." He took the terms from Thales of Miletus, who, in the sixth century B.C. in ancient Greece, noticed that rubbing amber gave it the power to attract light objects. This phenomenon, later known to be static electricity and produced by many materials when rubbed, was named after the Greek word for amber, "electron," the root of the terms Gilbert coined.

It took more than two hundred years from the publication of *De Magnete* for the connection between magnetism and electricity to become clear. In 1820, the Danish natural philosopher Hans Christian Ørsted set up an electric circuit and held a compass near the wire. When the current was flowing, the needle of the compass was deflected. Ørsted realized that the electric current caused this magnetic disturbance and that an electric current must therefore have magnetic effects. Eleven years later, Michael Faraday, a research assistant at the Royal Institution in London, demonstrated that when a copper wire was subjected to a changing magnetic field— the opposite of Ørsted's experiment—an electric current began to flow through the circuit. Magnetic forces, he observed, gave rise to electric currents—a discovery he called "electromagnetic induction." This discovery led to the invention of dynamos and generators that in turn led to electric lights, the telegraph, the telephone, and other technological developments that Birkeland had witnessed changing the world around him during his youth. Faraday realized that light must also be a form of electromagnetism, an idea later proved by James Clerk Maxwell, a Scot, in his *Treatise on Electricity and Magnetism* (1873). Maxwell tied together the work of Ørsted, Faraday, and other experimenters in a series of equations that contained the fundamental laws of electromagnetism: that an electric current was always accompanied by a magnetic field and that a varying magnetic field created an electric field. The equations also stated that a varying electric field gave rise to a magnetic field and thus the two kinds of fields could create each other in an endless loop. The result was a wave of electric and magnetic fields inextricably tied together and emanating outward in space. Maxwell called them "electromagnetic waves" and proposed that waves with a length of about a thousandth of a millimeter corresponded to visible light, but he also showed that waves with much greater or shorter lengths were possible. This was proved experimentally in 1888 by Heinrich Hertz, who generated radio waves, and in 1895 by Wilhelm Roentgen, who discovered X-rays. Birkeland himself had used Maxwell's equations to study mathematically the propagation of such waves under certain conditions and was the first to do so successfully—a feat that had propelled him into the first rank of mathematical theoreticians at the age of twenty-eight. Now he intended to use this knowledge to unravel the complicated physics behind the aurora.

Once Birkeland understood what Gilbert had achieved, he was surprised how few people had heard of him. Queen Elizabeth I had recognized his talents; he was the only person to whom she paid a retainer during her reign and she made him her physician. Newton and Galileo also admitted their debt to him, but few others had understood his ideas because he had been too far ahead of his time to be appreciated.

It was totally dark in the instrument room apart from the strings of light bouncing between the small paraffin lamps, the magnetometers, and the recorders. Only the steady clicking of the mechanisms told Birkeland that the Earth was turning on its axis and day was melting into night. A knock on the door announced dinner and he emerged blinking into the kitchen, a studious mole. He had become used to just three of them sitting down for dinner since Sæland took a sled and left for Talvik peak on the last day of October. The first night without him, they had telephoned and told him to look in a rucksack where Birkeland had secreted a small bottle of *akevitt*. In unison, across the dark, icy peaks standing sentinel over the mountain slopes, the men raised their glasses and tossed the burning spirit into their mouths.

Only two days varied much from the usual pattern. The first was 24 November, when Birkeland asked his companions to wrap up and accompany him outdoors. The wind was bitter but the cloud was broken and patches of clear sky could be seen. At twenty minutes past eleven the pale, glowing orb of the sun appeared over the low ridge of the Finnmark plateau in the south. The sun grazed the horizon for nine minutes before dropping below it once more. It was the last sunlight they would see for two months; from then on their world would be pitch black except during the three or four hours of twilight around midday. Such deprivation had been known to depress the sturdiest of men, but Birkeland reminded them that the perpetual darkness gave them perfect conditions for studying the Lights round the clock. Every man was on permanent watch for auroral activity.

The second unusual day was 13 December. After delivering the post, Hætta was invited to stay for breakfast and Sæland traveled over from Talvik peak. The kitchen table was loaded with plates of waffles, cloudberry jam, slices of meat and cheese, flasks of coffee, and a small pile of packets, letters, and telegrams. Birkeland was bewildered by the activity until Sæland reminded him of the date. It was Birkeland's birthday.

Among the messages of congratulation Birkeland received was one from Anders Quale, director of the copper mine in Kaafjord. He and his wife had invited Birkeland and his team to spend Christmas with them. The men were delighted at the prospect of fresh food, warm baths, female company, and soft beds. Birkeland was keen to visit for quite another reason.

On Christmas Eve, Boye harnessed the reindeer. Hætta had brought three more the previous day so there would be enough animals to pull the sleds and riders down to Kaafjord. Then the sleds had to be packed. They were made of thin strips of wood, designed for pliability rather than balance so that they would not shatter on hitting hard stumps, ice packs, and rocks. Their single hull meant they tipped to one side when stationary, particularly when full of heavy objects or people. The only way to start a journey was to leap into the sled just as the reindeer began to move. The forward motion kept it from tipping to the side and throwing the rider out. Unfortunately, reindeer were only semidomesticated and always outraged at the inconvenience of pulling sleds, so the necessary coordination was difficult to attain. Being so low to the ground, the occupant was constantly showered with the snow, grit, slush, and stones thrown up by the high-kicking reindeer, who leapt wildly to left and right and never in a straight line. There was no brake other than arms and legs, and when the path was downhill the sled often descended faster than the reindeer, usually ending with the occupant being thrown out at high speed. As Birkeland wrote in his account of the expedition:

> The journey with fresh reindeer was the wildest piece of driving one could imagine and the most exciting couple of hours I have ever gone through. The animals flew like the wind, and galloped along in places where a horse would have gone carefully step by step. We had five reindeer fastened together in a *raide,* and I sat in the last sled, firmly lashed to it. Occasionally the sled was thrown over the edge of the slope, notwithstanding that I put on all the brake that I possibly could with my elbows. I'm not sure I care to repeat it but I can certainly recommend sled-driving for excitement.

The Castle

On the edge of the fjord conditions were mild and calm compared to those on the summit of the mountain: Kaafjord was the most northerly point in the world at which wheat ripened and was largely protected from the fierce storms that blew through the mountains. The sleds crossed the town on their way to the director's house near the copper mine that had been established by the British in 1826, the most northerly industrial enterprise in Europe. From a tiny hamlet, Kaafjord developed into the largest town in Finnmark over the fifty years that copper was drilled out of the seams, then sifted and smelted by hand on the shores of the fjord. Influenza struck the town, and a third of the children and many adults, including the former director's wife, died. The following year the world prices of copper slumped, the director returned to England, and the mines were closed. The town shrank back to a small village as nearly half the workers and their families emigrated to America, settling in a small corner of Michigan that became known as Little Norway. Those who stayed returned to a semi-nomadic life in Finland and northern Sweden or to farming in southern Norway. The mine was deserted until 1896, three years before Birkeland arrived, when copper prices recovered and it was bought by a Swedish ore millionaire, who sent Anders Quale, accompanied by his wife and four children, to manage the business.

The group received a warm welcome, despite the tensions that existed between Norway and Sweden in the Union. Their house, decorated simply in the Swedish style of pale wood with bright yellow–and–blue painted details, was large, comfortable, and warm. Outside, the layout of the formal garden could be discerned beneath the snow but only the old wooden skittle run and the tennis court had been excavated. Boye and Knudsen spent the afternoon playing friendly matches with the mine engineers, while Birkeland, Sæland, and Quale walked along the Alten fjord until they reached the hydroelectric plant Quale had just finished constructing. This was the real motive for Birkeland's descent from the peak. He wanted to inspect the hydroelectric plant on a waterfall with the longest usable drop in Europe: 370 meters, a full seventy meters higher than the Eiffel Tower. The plant, which Birkeland had seen being built ten years before, was the highest manmade structure in the world. This far north, it was a remarkable engineering feat, and Birkeland wanted to see how it worked in practice.

The men spent several hours walking among the massive turbines that converted the energy of the water, falling through hundreds of meters of steel pipes, into electricity. Birkeland was particularly interested in the problems Quale reported about mechanisms to turn the current on and off quickly: they had no switching mechanism able to do that, and if something malfunctioned in the plant it was an ordeal to cut the power. It was during the hours spent with Quale at the power station that Birkeland first realized that his knowledge could be combined with his love of inventing machines to help improve the hydroelectric power industry and aid the process of Norway's transformation from a remote, rural dependency into a fully industrialized power. He decided to spend some time trying to solve the switching problem on his return to Christiania. If successful, he might earn money with his invention that he could put toward further research into the aurora.

On Christmas morning the bells of Kaafjord church called the faithful to prayer and the small wooden building reverberated to the sound of more than two hundred voices, caroling in unison. On either side of the promontory on which the church stood sentinel, the frozen water reflected the singing voices for many kilometers along the fjord. When the singing stopped, the silence echoed against the mountains. In the midday twilight the windows sparkled with candlelight and cast flickering shadows onto the snow-softened graves outside. The congregation was too large to be contained in the simple building and spilled out of the church onto the path. As special visitors, Birkeland and his expedition members were invited to sit in the front pew beside the Quale family. The ceiling and walls were freshly painted in glowing blues and yellows, a renovation paid for by the mine and gloriously incongruous in a sunless landscape of muted whites and deep grays. The most eye-catching feature of the new decor was the barreled roof on which gold stars speckled a deep blue heaven.

After the service a small group stood on the jetty at the end of the Quales' garden, waiting for the mine steamer *The Fortuna* to arrive with guests for Christmas lunch. The ship sailing toward them was the brightest object for miles around, dazzling in the night waters with small electric bulbs strung the length of the deck and the portholes blazing with light. The captain, Richard Lange, was a short man in his fifties with strong, rough hands and a short beard that began high on his cheekbones and continued to his cravat. His expression was usually serious and alert, that of a man who had lost several close relatives and friends to the sea. Lange had abandoned fishing for his living when the mine reopened and a steamer was needed to bring people and supplies up the fjord. It was not a more reliable job—copper prices were as unpredictable as herring shoals—but it was a less hazardous one as fishermen were killed every year along the coast, particularly those with their own small, open boats. Lange had been a baby when his father drowned in the notorious storm of 1848 that took the lives of more than five hundred fishermen during a single night. Lange and Birkeland spent many hours discussing the *vindlys,* the windlights or weatherlights, as the auroras were referred to along the coast by seafaring Norwegians and the Lapps, and the ways in which they could predict the weather. Birkeland was interested in the *vindlys* because the search for an accurate method of weather forecasting had been uppermost in successive governments' objectives for decades—to save lives and benefit fishing and agriculture, Norway's most profitable industries. The Northern Lights had been used to predict weather in the north for centuries and a surprising similarity in their interpretation existed—Scandinavians and Greenlanders used the Lights in similar ways as the Cheyenne Indians of Wyoming and Colorado and the Penobscot of Maine.

Birkeland was convinced that there must be a scientific explanation behind these folkloric predictions and, as no one had yet scientifically observed the weather and the Lights in parallel, he had stressed to Parliament that his expedition would be the first and best situated to do so. Even though proving the link between weather and auroras was not crucial for his theory about how the Lights were created, it was important for attracting funding and was given equal prominence in the title of the expedition manifesto, "Expedition to Study Aurora, Geomagnetism, and Cloud Formations."

Another tactic Birkeland used to squeeze money out of Parliament was to play on national pride:

> *15 January 1899*
> There is, of course, the option of collaborating with foreign scientists and thus continuing the Expedition without further grants from the Norwegian State, but I hesitate to do this because I regard the investigations to be of such importance that I prefer them to be Norwegian.

This tactic had proved fruitful: the Ministry for Church and Education, responsible for research projects, granted Birkeland 12,000 crowns for building and equipping the two observatories, more than twice Birkeland's annual salary. They realized that it would be a disgrace if a Norwegian did not receive the honors for solving a centuries-old mystery for want of a few thousand crowns.

However, Birkeland was already in trouble for overspending and failing to keep proper accounts. Since the early summer he had been receiving complaining letters and telegrams from the ministry, demanding that he send accounts and justify all future expenditure to the finance committee. These Birkeland had largely ignored, other than sending replies requesting yet more money and giving the reasons for needing it. On 22 December he had received a telegram informing him that all monies would be frozen until he sent full accounts as the expedition was already overspent by 16,000 crowns, nearly one and a half times the original budget. Birkeland usually recorded expenses on scraps of paper that he then lost, making accurate accounting a difficult task, but two days before Christmas he sent a telegram in reply saying that he had posted his accounts on 22 October along with a request for another 1,000 crowns.

> I cannot believe that they have not reached the ministry. Everyone is asking me for money every day. I used one thousand crowns of my own pay for the transport up the mountain, to keep everyone quiet until parliament has handled my request for more money. When I receive it I will be able to pay the wages.

It is unlikely the accounts were ever sent. Birkeland simply did not think about expenses and budgets when he was preoccupied with science, and he hoped to distract the ministry and cajole Parliament into granting extra money by reporting progress on the question of weather prediction.

Captain Lange himself did not know whether the Lights created cloud but he was quite sure they predicted weather. If the Lights moved to the south, the weather would turn milder, especially if the Lights were bright. If the Lights were red it would rain or snow very hard. If the Lights made an archway between northwest and southeast without much motion then the conditions would be cold and clear, but if there was much movement the forecast was for windy weather. The more the rays were playing, igniting and extinguishing, the stronger the wind expected. If there was a very dramatic show of Lights fishermen would avoid going to sea the next day, for a storm would be expected. Birkeland paid particular attention to Lange's observation that there had been fewer auroras over the past two or three years and that the weather had, by and large, been milder.

With only three months left on the mountaintop, if Birkeland did not soon find solutions to the questions he had set the expedition, the whole enterprise would be condemned as a failure, Norway's pride would be dented, and the country's reputation as a scientific backwater confirmed. Birkeland's own standing as a scientist might be diminished to such an extent he would find it hard to obtain funding for any future research. Too many sacrifices had already been made, including Hansen's career as a surgeon, for failure to be entertained as a possibility. Although he enjoyed the Christmas celebrations and fruitful conversation with Lange, Birkeland was keen to return to the mountain as soon as he could.

4

A Warning

New Year, new century 1900
Auroral observatory, Haldde Mountain

*The scientist does not study nature because it is useful to do so. He
studies it because he takes pleasure in it and he takes pleasure in it
because it is beautiful. If nature were not beautiful it would not be
worth knowing and life would not be worth living.*

HENRI POINCARÉ (1854–1912), *Science and Method*

*I*T WAS THE last day of 1899. The wind whipped around the
observatory, brushing spumes of powder snow from the
summit until the mountain range looked like a string of
smoking volcanoes. Not a crack of light escaped from the sturdy
building, every source of drafts having been blocked up and
papered over in an attempt to keep warm.

Birkeland's hope for the coming century was that the value of
their work would be recognized by the government and that the
observatory would become permanently manned, the auroras and
magnetic field recorded every day for a number of years. A more
comfortable house could be built on the flat ground at the base of
the final peak and a group of scientists, or even a family, could live
all year round on the mountain. His personal dream was to earn
enough money to build his own observatory and laboratory, staff it
with young, talented scientists, and follow his ideas in complete
freedom, released from teaching duties, beyond the confines of a

conservative university and without having to beg the government for every thousand crowns or fill in pages of paperwork to account for it. At five to twelve Birkeland rose unsteadily to his feet and reminded the small group that they were the first men in history to celebrate New Year on that remote corner of the Earth. He raised a toast to the twentieth century and the men drained their glasses of *akevitt* as the clock chimed.

The first ten days of January were cloudless and intensely cold with temperatures down to −25° Celsius. For three nights in a row the auroras danced from six in the evening until two or three in the morning. Their beauty alleviated the continuous dark of the polar winter and the group understood why the Lapps believed God gave them the Northern Lights to compensate for the disappearance of the sun. Birkeland noted in the ledgers that, when the Lights were at their brightest, he could read print of about this size. The men never grew accustomed to their beauty, blasé about their arrival, or tired of watching their sensuous, fluid flames traversing the heavens. They took readings round the clock, free from all distractions, and a new sense of purpose set in. The phone line between the observatories was always open for the two stations to make simultaneous observations and take simultaneous photographs. Several answers to the minor questions Birkeland had set the expedition were already clear. The auroras did not touch the ground and therefore could not singe hair or burn flesh. Birkeland's opinion was that the lowest edge of the auroras was about a hundred kilometers above the ground. None of the group had suffered headaches while the Lights snaked across the sky, nor had they heard any of the crackling and hissing noises several eminent observers had noted.

On 11 January the honeymoon came to an abrupt end. Cirrus clouds appeared during the afternoon and rapidly built up into a huge bank, the length of the eastern horizon. Hætta, who had delivered the post that morning and stayed for lunch, took one look at the sky and rushed to harness the reindeer. The animals were skittish, nipping each other and chewing at their tethers, sensing the need to find shelter from the coming storm. Hætta gathered the reins into his hands and the animals careered down the hill before a command was out of his mouth. Boye nailed planks to the outside of the windows and let loose the reindeer to fend for itself, making sure its bell was firmly attached, in the hope of finding it again once the storm had passed. He brought in all the food he could carry from the larder and stacked it in the vestibule. Knudsen climbed onto the roof to dismantle the instruments, leaving only the strongest anemometer to measure the wind speeds. Birkeland called Sæland to warn him of the approaching weather.

Within an hour of Hætta's departure the wind on the summit was too strong to stand in. The men inside the observatory grew tense as the screaming air ripped at the boards on the windows, forcing its way around the frames and under doors. Despite the sturdiness of the building, they felt small and vulnerable in comparison with the might and ferocity of the hurricane outside. It was like being in a tiny fishing boat facing towering waves. They had to raise their voices to make themselves heard and lean against the stove to keep warm in the drafty building. The candles in the lanterns were blown out so frequently that Boye filled the paraffin lamps instead— no one liked the smell but they were less easily extinguished. Despite Boye's best efforts to seal the outside door, the wind and snow forced their way inside. The floor of the tower was covered in powdery snow, which formed small drifts in the corners as well as around the drums of oil and paraffin. Every hour Birkeland put on his reindeer jacket and left the kitchen to check that the magnetometer recordings had not been disrupted by the sudden gusts of wind that blew under the doors. With such events outside, Birkeland expected to see the magnetometers in motion, but the beam of light shining on the photographic paper was as straight as a ruler, an instance of serenity amid chaos. By eight o'clock the phone line to Talvik peak was severed and the group in the main observatory prayed Sæland would be all right; memories of Hansen's mutilated hands were still fresh in their minds. The Talvik observatory was less substantial than their own, and without the phone Sæland would be utterly alone.

The three men went to bed but no one slept. The thick walls shook with the blasts and the timbers in the roof made alarming snapping sounds. The steel guy ropes holding the roof to the house strained in the heaviest gusts; the men were aware that, if the ropes snapped, their shelter would be sucked into the storm as if it were made of straw. A plank was ripped from the window between the bunks and there was an immediate increase in the freezing air forcing its way through the frame and into their beds. Boye nailed a reindeer skin over the window, but it had little effect. Around midnight one of the guy ropes snapped and ricocheted against the building, and the men listened in fear to hear if the others would follow suit. They held. After a while exhaustion lulled the men into fitful sleep until three in the morning when the outside door burst open and a jet of wind, ice, and snow overwhelmed the tower and slammed the kitchen door back against the wall. Papers, pans, books, lamps, crockery, and chairs were hurled around the room by the spiteful blast. Dressed only in woolen pajamas, Knudsen tried to push the door closed, but twice it was blown from his hands and thrown back against the wall. Boye went to his aid, crawling across the floor, but even together they could not force it shut against the wind. Only with the combined strength of all three men was it eventually closed and nailed shut. With their escape route thus blocked, Birkeland feared they could burn to death as the winds gusting down the chimney forced smoke and hot ash into the room.

The savage storm blew for twenty-one days without a break. They were completely cut off from the outside world, from newspapers, post, people, doctors, food, and fuel, even from the landscape; all that existed was the weather. The group became disoriented at first: with the windows boarded up and the storm obscuring the twilight of midday, there was nothing to indicate the passage of time. On the fourth day, during a brief lull in the storm and desperate to leave the cramped observatory, they launched one of the kites for taking measurements of air electricity and wind velocities at high altitudes. The wind gusted and the kite dragged Boye to the edge of the cliff until he was forced to let it go. The three men watched in dismay as the small point of white was swallowed by the mass of dark, scudding clouds and was lost forever.

They seized any moments of relative calm to climb onto the roof to repair the anemometer or note the outdoor temperatures. Birkeland decided that a second ethanol thermometer and anemometer should be placed away from the shelter of the observatory to obtain truer readings. While Knudsen was attempting this task, a sudden squall hit the summit and he was blown down the steep incline by the cable car into deep snow forty meters below. Boye crawled to the observatory and called to Birkeland for help. The professor roped himself to the ring by the door and Boye clung to him as the gale, with renewed force, tore at their hair and Birkeland's glasses. Knudsen would die of exposure if they did not find him quickly. When they reached the cable car, Boye tied himself to the metal struts, but before he could descend a gloved hand came over the lip of the slope and grabbed at his foot. Boye and Birkeland dragged Knudsen over the edge, put his arms round their shoulders, and helped him back to the hut. Birkeland broke the ice on a bucket of water and pushed Knudsen's hands into it. His eyes were half-shut, his face white with frostbite and his lips a purple blue. They sat him next to the fire, standing beside him to keep him upright. Knudsen had fallen only a few meters onto a narrow ledge and was bruised and winded but nothing seemed broken and the frostbite soon receded. They decided that the next time anyone ventured outside they would rope themselves to a metal ring that had been set into the wall beside the entrance by the builders, who knew better than Birkeland how violent the weather could be.

The wind on the summit seemed to defy all the natural laws they had ever observed. At times, the storm grew so violent that the men were afraid the little building would lose its battle and be hurtled from the summit into the jaws of the valley below. Enormous snowdrifts that threatened to block the door or chimney would be blasted away in hours when the wind changed direction. The lack of sunlight and the claustrophobic effect of being trapped in the dark hut began to exert a depressive influence. There seemed little they could do and conversation began to lag.

"You need a sanguine temper to be a physicist," Birkeland reminded them when the difficulties imposed on their work by the extreme weather led to frustration and bad moods. Despite his brave words, the strain was beginning to show on him too. Pressure from the government combined with his own high hopes stopped him sleeping. During the first week of confinement he worked through the night with the 250 rolls of automatic readings from the magnetometers that had been amassed since 1 November. They were the shadows of invisible forces raging overhead, and they allowed Birkeland to see what was happening to the magnetic field above their observatory. As the lines on the rolls wavered, they revealed when the field increased or decreased, turned east or west. In this way, Birkeland was soon able to build up an accurate picture of how the magnetic field changed during the course of a day, a month, two months. Studying the magnetograms with his understanding of Maxwell's electromagnetic equations and other experiments by Ørsted and Ampère, Birkeland became convinced that the magnetic disturbances were caused by electric currents in the atmosphere, although he was still not sure where these massive currents came from. Was it something limited entirely to the Earth, like a form of lightning, or was it something entering the Earth's atmosphere from space, a cosmic force? He worked feverishly, often all night, sensing he was on the edge of a breakthrough.

He roused the others from their torpor and set them the task of creating small maps out of the recordings and equations. Boye, who could draw well, was in charge of tracing the outline of Finnmark over which Knudsen and Birkeland would mark arrows of different lengths to represent the direction and strength of the magnetic storms above their heads. As currents were known to run at right angles to the magnetic field, Birkeland's assistants were also able to plot the direction and strength of the electric currents that were causing the storms. The field was usually quiet until about six o'clock in the evening when the first small variations in the recording line appeared. On some days there was no variation at all, but on others the line began to veer a great deal across the page, creating peaks and troughs that mirrored the changes in the field. Birkeland quickly confirmed the reports of earlier observers that the auroras appeared only during magnetic disturbances.

In many ways it was satisfying that the storm outside seemed a permanent accompaniment to the storms the men were plotting. Had the weather been better, perhaps they would not have spent such an intensive period thinking and analyzing results. Night after night Birkeland would sit up and furiously scribble equations. On 17 January the men recorded in the ledgers that the sun had returned—according to their charts it would rise over the mountains that day for six minutes—but the weather was too bad to risk opening the door to see if there was any perceptible change. It seemed unlikely that it could shine through the dense, swirling snow that wrapped itself around the summit like a snake around its prey.

Once Birkeland had firmly established that auroras did not appear without magnetic disturbances, he turned his attention to what caused these storms. The beginnings of a theory had occurred to him as early as 1896, and an extraordinary event two years later had led him to write about his ideas in the newspaper *Verdens Gang*. On 9 September 1898 a huge auroral storm could be seen in startling red and brilliant orange over the skies of Europe as far south as London, Paris, Vienna, and Rome. As in previous centuries, the red auroras were popularly interpreted as portents of war, famine, and strife. Many scientists, including Birkeland, scoffed at the notion that they were a celestial warning, but as the Lights evaporated in the dawn of 10 September, a horrifying tragedy rocked Europe and echoed across the world in thousands of telegraph wires and newspaper headlines. An Italian anarchist, Luigi Luccheni, assassinated the empress of Austria and Hungary, once regarded as the most beautiful princess in Europe and much loved for her charitable work. She was stabbed in the chest with a stiletto knife.

Because auroras occurred in southern Europe only a few times in a decade, to see an extraordinary red light on the eve of an assassination caused many to believe that the scientists were wrong and that the Lights were indeed some form of message. Birkeland, however, considered the tragedy to be an unfortunate coincidence—unfortunate indeed for the empress and her family but also for a scientific explanation of the auroras. He started to research what was known about auroras and read that they frequently coincided with the appearance of sunspots. He had immediately sent a telegram to an acquaintance, the famous Parisian astronomer Camille Flammarion, at the Paris Observatoire, requesting information about sunspot activity around the time of the assassination. Flammarion had confirmed that there were several unusually large sunspot groups passing the sun's meridian three days before the massive auroras were seen over Europe.

The connection between sunspots and auroras was mentioned by Birkeland in the article he wrote following the assassination, entitled "A Message from the Sun." The title was a direct reference to Galileo's *Starry Messenger*, published in 1610, in which the famous astronomer promoted the heliocentric concept of the solar system first suggested by Nicolaus Copernicus a hundred years earlier. In this system, the sun, and not the Earth, was at the center of the solar system, and Birkeland believed the sun's importance in the phenomenon of the aurora was greater than anyone had so far imagined. Sunspots were not the only event on the sun related to auroras. In 1859 Sir Richard Carrington of the Kew Observatory was the first to observe a flare coming from the sun—"two patches of intensely bright and white light broke out." He noted that this "conflagration" was followed eighteen hours later by a great magnetic storm that disrupted telegraphic communications and coincided with tremendous auroras seen in Hawaii, Jamaica, Chile, and Australia. Despite this seemingly direct correlation, Carrington "would not have us suppose that he even leans towards hastily connecting" these events; "one swallow does not make a summer." Many scientists dismissed the connection between activity on the sun and auroras because there were often sunspots without auroras, or vice versa, and because they did not believe that charged particles could reach the Earth from such a distance. Birkeland, however, was becoming more and more convinced of a solar-terrestrial relationship.

Stranded in the darkness on the mountain in howling gales, Birkeland thought continuously upon the connection between sunspots and the auroras. The sun had been systematically studied in Europe since 1610, when Galileo trained his telescope on it and first noted that the glorious golden orb was, in fact, spotty. In 1843 a German pharmacist and amateur astronomer, Heinrich Schwabe, showed that the sun was not constant in its activity, that it passed through an eleven-year cycle. For many years he had studied the number of sunspots on the face of the sun and realized that their number increased for just over five years then decreased for another five or so. When Captain Lange mentioned that the incidence of auroras had been lessening in recent years, Birkeland had been delighted because he knew the year 1900 was at the least active part of the sun's cycle, resulting in fewer auroras to watch. This was useful for his research because too many or too complicated auroras would be hard to decipher and render repeating patterns difficult to discern.

Birkeland had brought with him the available records of auroral displays. These were nowhere near as complete as the sunspot records, the Lights being a more elusive phenomenon and a greater challenge to study, but there were some useful observations—particularly from the Polar Year 1882–3, the first international attempt to obtain regular observations of the Lights and related magnetic disturbances. For many nights Birkeland pored over these books and his own results, comparing all the work that previous scientists had done with his own observations, puzzling over the connection and the imperfect coincidences among the sunspots, the magnetic field, and the auroras. He remembered his days in Paris when he had worked on Maxwell's equations with the eminent Professor Henri Poincaré, Birkeland's mentor, who was greatly admired for his advanced understanding of mathematics, physics, mechanics, and astronomy and his philosophical and popular expositions on science. He thought of Quale's hydroelectric power station and of electric currents until he became so tired that the elements of his past melded into one. Without warning, one evening suddenly the muddle cleared and the pieces came together to form a solution.

He became convinced that his initial hunch was correct: the force disturbing the magnetic field came directly from the sun in narrow beams of electrically charged particles called cathode rays. Cathode rays were first noticed at the end of the 1860s when mercury pumps were developed that were able to create vacuums in glass tubes. Experiments with electric currents in these vacuum tubes revealed that, under certain circumstances, they produced glowing rays. In 1876 the German physicist Eugen Goldstein named the rays after the cathode, the negative terminal in the tube, from which they appeared to be emitting, although it was not understood how or why these rays were formed. Only in 1897 did the British scientist J. J. Thompson show that cathode rays consisted of high-velocity streams of negatively charged particles: electrons. Birkeland was sure that the sun emitted similar beams that were narrow and focused and often missed the Earth completely, which was why sunspots did not always result in auroras. Birkeland surmised that sometimes these active particles hit the magnetic field of the Earth and followed the field lines down toward the poles, where they struck atoms in the atmosphere and the energy created by the collisions was emitted as light—the Northern Lights. That explained why they appeared only during magnetic storms: the cathode rays from the sun were moving beams of electrons that created electric currents; these, in turn, made their own magnetic fields, which were recorded by the magnetometers. These same beams of charged particles, on reaching the upper levels of the atmosphere, created the auroras. Birkeland never gained any significant readings of air electricity near the ground because the force that disrupted the magnetic field did not come from Earth, as so many scientists believed, but from space, from the sun. His theory also explained why on one or two occasions that winter, similar auroras appeared at twenty-seven-day intervals: the sunspots took twenty-seven days to make a complete circuit of the sun and often made two or three circuits before disappearing. In effect, the sun was creating the magnetic storms and was the original source of the auroras.

Birkeland sat for a while before turning to the others, who had been working on the charts, to tell them his ideas. The long days of calculations, mapping, and observations had taken their toll. Knudsen had slipped into his bunk and Boye was fast asleep at the table. Sæland, the one who would have understood Birkeland best and would have been most excited, was less than four kilometers away but might as well have been on the moon.

Two days later the wind dropped as suddenly as it had arrived. The cloud cover broke and revealed small patches of twilight blue between the gray. The men emerged from the hut like bears out of hibernation. Birkeland's first concern was to ensure Sæland was safe. Boye volunteered to go over to Talvik peak and left with a large saucepan on which he banged to attract the reindeer and pockets stuffed with dried moss, perfect reindeer bait. Hætta had taught him that trick which Boye hoped would work—it was a long walk to the summit of Talvik. He returned after two hours, hoarse from shouting but triumphantly leading the reindeer and they left almost immediately. Birkeland and Knudsen assessed the damage inflicted on the observatory by the storm. Several of the steel guy ropes had snapped, the wooden rail on the roof of the observing tower was gone, the anemometer was smashed to pieces, and the wooden casing that protected the winding mechanism of the cable car had completely disappeared. The larder had been blasted to nothing and the crevices and hollows of the summit were filled with little offerings of food and shards of timbers. In the back of Birkeland's mind was fear at what Boye might find on Talvik peak.

At five o'clock Birkeland heard shouts and out of the darkness trudged Boye and Sæland. Sæland had seen the storm hit the Haldde peak and the whole mountain disappear in snow. He had just had time to take down the electrometer, put the reindeer behind the tower for shelter, and bring in supplies. By the time Sæland ventured outside after three days trapped in the hut, the reindeer was dead, which saved him from having to slaughter it himself. He used every part of the animal, blocking drafts with the fat and covering the door with the skin. There was not enough fuel to keep the fire going, but once the drafts were tackled the temperature inside was bearable. Sticking to the timetable for readings had kept him sane. That night, the first clear night for three weeks, the sky blazed with the brightest auroras they had seen since arriving. The men were too tired to stay up watching until they faded; only Boye had the energy to sit on the tower and write notes in the ledger.

Two days after the storm abated Hætta arrived, so covered in ice that he was unrecognizable and too cold to move the muscles in his face. They put him by the fire to thaw out and unpacked his bags— fresh milk, eggs and bread from the Quales, who had been anxious about the men on the peak, a few letters and a telegram for Birkeland from his brother.

FATHER DIED THIS MORNING. FUNERAL 5 FEB. PLEASE RETURN. TØNNES.

Birkeland was saddened but not surprised by his father's death. When Kristian left Christiania, his father had been unwell, feverish and coughing, although the doctor had said he would recover. Reinert Birkeland had been a farmer in southern Norway until he married and moved with his bride to the capital, using the proceeds from the sale of his small farm to set up a small import-export firm and a shop. For a decade business had been reasonable and the family comfortable but his father had lost most of his business during the depression that struck when Sweden imposed a number of trade sanctions. After that he had become very withdrawn and Birkeland grew closer to Elling Holst, his math teacher. Spending most of his time at the university, Birkeland rarely saw his father.

Once Hætta was warm enough to leave the stove and return along the icy, twilit route to the fjord, he gabbled a short speech to Birkeland, expressing regret about the death of Birkeland's father but claiming it was a warning that they should leave the mountain. The terrible storm, the dramatic Lights that shone afterward, and then the death of Birkeland's father—these were bad omens. Hætta feared the scientists had angered the Lights with all their measuring and photographs and that they would take their revenge. Birkeland assured Hætta that they would leave the following month; they needed just a few more weeks of observations. After that, every week that Hætta arrived with the post he repeated his warning, until the morning of 15 March when Birkeland suggested that one member of the group return with Hætta to collect sleds and extra reindeer for their descent from the summit. Knudsen volunteered. Deciding he would enjoy another fast sled ride, Boye joined them at the last minute. They arranged to return to the observatory the following afternoon.

Birkeland and Sæland were nailing lids to the last packing cases the next day when they heard shouting from below. Two men were struggling up the mountainside as fast as possible. Birkeland and Sæland almost fell down the slope in their haste to reach them. It was Quale and Knudsen, panting so hard they could barely speak, the frozen air spiking their lungs. Quale and some friends had asked to join Knudsen and Boye on their return journey in order to visit the observatory and help with the removal. As they climbed, snow had fallen away from the road under their feet and taken some of the group with it. Knudsen had been swept under in the avalanche but had found a branch and managed to pull himself out. Two were dead. Knudsen explained that he had found Boye within minutes of his own escape but all attempts to revive him had proved futile. Captain Lange's lifeless body was discovered later by men from the village who had come to help. Boye and Lange were carried to the church where they were laid under the blue roof studded with golden stars.

5

"Riddle Solved!"

April 1900
Christiania, Norway

In such moments solitude also is invaluable, for who would speak or be looked upon, when behind him lies all of Europe fast asleep, except the watchmen, and before him the silent Immensity and Palace of the Eternal, where our Sun is but a porch-lamp?

THOMAS CARLYLE (1795–1881)

21 April 1900
To Boye's parents,

I will not make any excuses about why I have not written before as there really aren't any. It is not because I am indifferent but because I too have been mourning his death. His touching goodness, open heart, his faithful companionship and the eagerness he showed carrying out everything I asked, all this made me appreciate him very much and I feel his loss like the loss of a dear friend.

I never watched him on the mountain without enjoying his youthful energy which made everything go at full speed—I admired his strength, his courage and his scientific abilities that were developing fast. He was also very kind. I was once so touched by his manner that I took his arm and called him "posen" [a term of endearment]. He was astonished, but that name is what my father used to call me.

Allow me to tell you how I met your son. I was in need of help to perform some calculations and was therefore looking for some science students as assistants. When your son turned up he told me he was a Latin student but it may help to know that he had two "1s" in Mathematics. I looked him in the eyes a second and immediately realized that I really liked him a lot. I said aloud, "It could be useful to have some Latin input" and thus he was hired before anyone else. From the first time I saw him until his death, I have always had the same impression of him. The image in my mind just became more detailed and nicer. This image of him will always stay with me.

Kristian Birkeland

Captain Lange was buried in Kaafjord on 22 March at 3 p.m. Boye's body was shipped back to his parents. Boye had been insured for 10,000 crowns and Birkeland was required to fill in many documents explaining the circumstances and details of the tragedy before he could leave Finnmark.

He eventually boarded one of the new steamers that plied up and down the long western coastline, and docked in Christiania harbor in early April. He engaged two porters to supervise loading a large wagon with the boxes of instruments and to deliver them to his office in the university. Then he hailed a smaller carriage to take him to his parents' home, where he still lived. It was virtually a straight road all the way across the capital from the south, where the harbor was, to the north, where the large state hospital was just being built and his parents' apartment was situated. The weather was gray and cloudy, with a bitter wind that made women pull their shawls closer round their necks and men hold on to their hats. There were still patches of slush pushed up against the curbs and between cobbles and the sky threatened rain or snow. After the vastness of Haldde Mountain with its unobstructed views, Christiania seemed cramped, noisy, and brash.

As they passed out of the harbor precinct and crossed the central square, he saw that the trees in the gardens were still barren. Children skated on the oblong pond. To his left, the National Theatre building was nearly finished and only the roundels and the decorative friezes had still to be attached. Across from the theater, the university looked just as it had when he left in October, with groups of students sheltering under the imposing portico, smoking and laughing. At the end of the east wing was the clock by which Ibsen checked his watch every day. Birkeland would see his large, slightly stooping figure stop before his windows on the dot of twelve. Satisfied that he was as punctual as ever, the great playwright would then carry on along Carl Johan Gate, the main route connecting east and west Christiania, to the elegant portals of the Café Grand, where he sat at the same small marble table by the door. Perhaps due to Ibsen's presence, the Grand had become the focus for Christiania's artistic and intellectual élite, who gathered there every day except Sunday.

Up the hill on Birkeland's left, beyond the theater and the university, stood the Royal Palace. Built in the 1840s, at the same time as the university, it had a similarly institutional air. There were no ornate gates or railings around it; it stood blind-windowed and empty on the hill, deserted the year round by King Oscar, who preferred his residence in Sweden. Out of Birkeland's sight, beyond the palace hill, lay expensive avenues where large houses were being built for the new class of entrepreneurs Norway was creating in international trade and communications, industry, and shipping.

The carriage was held up for a few moments as the tram crossed their path along Carl Johan Gate. A new department store had opened in his absence but many small specialist shops had shut in the past decade, unable to compete as Norway's investors aggressively bought out or undersold their smaller competitors. The few that survived were struggling in the recession following the Christiania Crash of 1899, a spectacular financial disaster that had occurred in June, just a few months before Birkeland left on his expedition. The crash started with a young messenger boy who overheard one of the most important financiers in the capital say that this was the last time he could pay off all his creditors. His next delivery was to another large business where he relayed his information. Panic set in. Credit was withdrawn from the first company, despite the chairman's protests that the news they had received was incorrect, and the bank supporting him was forced to close. Other companies heard of the extraordinary move and began clawing back money from their own creditors; businesses collapsed, particularly in construction and banking; and the speculative boom of the previous five years ended almost overnight. Far too much had been built during the last years of the century and Christiania had an enormous surplus of housing. Birkeland had hoped the situation would blow over quickly, but the newspapers he had received in Haldde revealed that the crisis was deep and would continue for several years—gloomy news for Birkeland, who knew that this would inevitably affect funding at the university and make his budgets even stricter.

Passing through the central square and into the streets leading north, the carriage climbed gently uphill toward the State Hospital and Vår Frelsers Gravlund, the cemetery where Norway's most eminent citizens were buried. As the carriage continued into the part of town in which Birkeland lived, he saw that new apartments were standing half-finished in the northern districts. A thin layer of stone and plaster dust covered the streets and mixed with the slush to form slippery yellow mud. The carriage crossed the square on which his old school, Aars and Voss, was situated and turned left onto Langes Gate. When Birkeland's parents had moved here thirty-five years before, theirs was the only block in a street surrounded by fields, but Birkeland had spent his childhood playing in the building sites that sprang up across the district as more families renounced farming and fishing to take jobs as clerks, telegraphists, and shop assistants. He had seen the capital grow at an incredible pace as new residential and mercantile areas ate up the countryside in all directions except south, where the waters of the fjord halted their encroachment. Those who did not come to the city crossed the Atlantic to find work in America, some moving there permanently, others making the journey only when work failed in Norway. The country came second only to Ireland in rates of emigration; a quarter of its two million population had left over the previous half century.

Langes Gate consisted of three- and four-story apartment buildings designed for the emerging middle class, with no separate servants' quarters. Birkeland was born in an apartment on the second floor of number 6, a four-story, white-plastered building that formed the corner of Langes Gate and Nordal Bruns Gate. It was built around a small courtyard that was mainly used for hanging laundry, as no one in the building owned a carriage or a horse. The main entrance was not imposing—only a simple wooden staircase connected the floors—but the apartments were light and modern, with electricity and indoor plumbing.

Coming home was like returning to the whole building, not just his parents' flat. Birkeland knew his neighbors well; they had all moved into the building when it was brand new and very few had left. He looked at the names on the post rack in the hall. Johan Meinich, a telegraph inspector, was still there with his wife and four unmarried children, all of them around Birkeland's age. Birkeland had gone to school with Meinich's sons and loved to be invited back to tea so he could ask their father about the telegraph. The blacksmith was still there too, but with few exceptions the building was a refuge for single women. He knew best those on his own floor, Widow Olsen and her three unmarried daughters in their fifties and the one married daughter who lived across the landing with her husband and another of her single sisters. On the floor above lived the old Brown sisters and Widow Amundsen and her forty-year-old daughter; next to them was Widow Fritzner, her two single daughters in their forties, and her ward. This flock of unmarried or widowed women had made a great fuss of Birkeland when he was a child, and he had spent many afternoons in their apartments, waiting for his mother to return from the shop, being fed delicious biscuits that the women took turns baking.

He climbed the familiar stairs to his own landing. Birkeland had been so shaken by the death of Boye and Lange that he had not even thought of the consequences of his father's death. On entering the apartment he was shocked to find it barely recognizable; even its smell had changed. The hall was littered with packing cases, most of the familiar furniture had gone, light patches on the walls marked where pictures had been removed, and rolls of rugs and carpets were stacked in a corner. His mother was in the dining room, surrounded by piles of papers, old books, and china. Ingeborg Birkeland was a short woman, small-boned but strong, sporting wire-framed spectacles that gave her the look of a severe teacher although the dark eyes behind them were often full of humor. Her thin, graying hair was pulled tight into a bun and covered with a small piece of black mourning lace. Turning sixty that year, she had been the family's main breadwinner for most of the previous decade, keeping the much-reduced import-export business going and working in the small shop in which they sold their goods. With her husband Reinert dead at only sixty-one, she had decided to close the shop and spend her remaining years with Tønnes, Birkeland's only sibling, who was three years older. Tønnes, who had a wife and eight children with another expected, lived in Porsgrund, a growing town on the southern coast of Norway about half a day's boat journey from Christiania, where he ran a busy doctor's practice. In preparation for the move she had sold most of the furniture, carpets, and the few paintings they owned. She told her newly returned son that if there was anything he wanted, he was welcome to have it as long as all his things were out of the apartment within a fortnight when the lease on the flat expired. Ingeborg planned to leave as soon as the apartment was packed up.

Uncle Andreas, his father's younger brother, was a ship's captain and had left that morning, gone to sea with no plans to return. The maid, Karoline, who was in her early fifties and had been with the family since Tønnes was born, would have to find another position, as there was no room in his house.

During the following weeks Birkeland found a place to live in the lively quarter of Lysaker, about five kilometers west of the center of Christiania. His belongings were moved from the old apartment, his mother took the boat to Porsgrund, and all links with his childhood were severed. He spent most of his time at the university, working alongside Sem Sæland, who had become his assistant. The two men passed many intense hours poring over the recordings from Haldde and putting them into a form that could be published. Sæland was delegated the unenviable task of writing accounts for the expedition, a laborious task because Birkeland had lost, or never received, most of the receipts.

Bjørn Helland-Hansen came to visit them at the university and reassured Birkeland that he was coping well, despite the loss of his fingertips. He had decided to enter the field of oceanography and meteorology and had been given help by the great explorer Fridtjof Nansen. Along with several colleagues in Norway and Sweden, Nansen was trying to establish an international group to study unusual ocean currents that he had observed during his three years trapped in the polar ice. He wanted to send Helland-Hansen to Stockholm to study with Wilhelm Bjerkenes, Birkeland's great friend and schoolmate. Bjerkenes had moved to the Stockholm High School, a private university for graduate studies in science, in 1893 to pursue his interest in understanding the physics of the atmosphere in order to make accurate weather predictions. Bjerkenes had developed a theory of air circulation that, for the first time, gave a three-dimensional picture of how weather systems developed, including the potential effects on the weather of ocean currents. He was pleased to have help with the oceanographic aspect of weather forecasting and had invited Helland-Hansen to come to Stockholm early in 1901. The meeting with Helland-Hansen cheered Birkeland, as the young man seemed undiminished by his terrible experience on Haldde Mountain and in Hammerfest Hospital.

The rest of Birkeland's time was spent settling into his new apartment in Lysaker, an area that was home to several of Norway's leading intellectuals, explorers, artists, and scientists, including Fridtjof Nansen, who shared a radical, democratic, nationalist outlook and called themselves the Lysaker Group. Their aim was to combine traditional Norwegian folklore and culture with modern art and science, to promote a Norwegian identity distinct from that of any other Scandinavian country, particularly Sweden, and to prove Norway's "fitness" to take its rightful place among the civilized nations of the world. Nansen had written to Parliament in 1899 that "to me it seems important that a small country like ours should assert itself in as many cultural fields as possible to prevent it being treated as a quantité negligéable by the great powers." He had already made his political opinions clear in a number of fiery columns to *The Times* in Britain that denounced the Union as "a constant source of hatred and separation . . . which irritates and humiliates every Norwegian who has a sense of honour in his breast."

Birkeland was passionate about helping to achieve independence for Norway and promoting his country's right to stand alone. He believed that his auroral research provided an avenue for advancing national honor as well as developing the role of science in the country—particularly that of physics, defined at the time as the study of heat, electricity, and magnetism. It was important that both the scientific establishment and a popular audience be exposed to his ideas as soon as possible to show that a Norwegian had formulated the most advanced explanation for the aurora borealis. He decided to publish the manuscript he had been preparing about the Haldde expedition and made an appointment to see his acquaintance Jacob Dybwad, editor in chief of a small publishing house in Christiania, mentioning only briefly what the book was about. Birkeland had not written a book before but many of his colleagues at the university had been published by Dybwad, who was often the only editor prepared to find the resources to produce scientific texts. They rarely had a large readership and relied on grants rather than sales to cover the costs of printing and publication.

Dybwad, a tall man who stooped as low as possible to talk to people on their own level, had a habit of repeating the final words in his sentences; this lent him a mantle of eccentricity behind which hid a considerable intellect. He was delighted to deepen his acquaintance with Birkeland and ushered him into his cramped office in a building behind the university. Every surface in the room, including the floor, chairs, table, and two desks, was covered in piles of manuscripts, proof copies, and plate illustrations. Birkeland handed over a slim parcel wrapped in brown paper and tied with a piece of wire (he had been unable to find any string in his office). When Dybwad unwound the wire, the paper fell open and on top of the eighty sheets of hand-written manuscript were a photograph and a drawing of the Haldde observatory. The editor held the photograph close to his shortsighted eyes. It was a portrait of a young man, under which was written "In Memoriam. Elisar Boye. Buried by an avalanche at the age of twenty-two on 16 March 1900." Birkeland explained that his assistant had been tragically killed at the end of the expedition and that he would like to honor his memory and his contribution by including the photograph. Dybwad nodded, then held the drawing close to his nose. Made by Boye days before he died, the colored-pencil sketch depicted the Haldde observatory perched on the mountain with the smaller Talvik building in the foreground.

Dybwad carefully studied the stone buildings that had been erected with great difficulty to shelter Birkeland and his researchers in the notoriously fickle and violent storms on the sub-Arctic peaks of Finnmark. They were the perfect symbol for Norwegian scientific, cultural, and political aspirations. Dybwad was thrilled at the thought of the dramatic frontispiece to the book that the photograph would make, while the drawing could be featured on the cover. The scientific monographs he published did not usually have special covers but in this case it would be worth the extra cost. The photograph and the drawing encapsulated a sense of the dangers involved in the quest for scientific knowledge and the sacrifices that had been made so that this book could reach the reader.

Looking closer at Boye's drawing, Dybwad noticed that the flag flying from the observatory was a pure Norwegian one, without Sweden's insignia, and he thought for a while of the consequences of publishing it. He could be reprimanded for doing so by the Swedish government, he might even lose a few readers across the border, but his sympathies lay with Birkeland and his desire for an autonomous Norway. So he said nothing about the flag, simply praising the quality of the drawing. He hoped that, rather than being censured, the book would attract comment in the newspapers not only for its contribution to science but also for its contribution to the cause of independence. The title of the book was to be *The Norwegian Expedition of 1899–1900 for the Study of the Aurora Borealis.*

Dybwad quickly read the introduction and paused at the key paragraph, Birkeland's summary of his research:

> It emerges from our results, that the magnetic perturbations and the aurora borealis are secondary and local phenomena attaching to the same cosmic phenomenon. This primary phenomenon consists, there is no doubt, of electric currents in the upper levels of the atmosphere; in the polar regions, where they seem to have their point of departure, these currents are fairly well defined and concentrated. The currents pass, on average, at a height of approximately 100 km above the terrestrial surface and can cause strong magnetic perturbations of a total intensity above 400,000 amperes.

Dybwad was intrigued and wanted to know what the "cosmic phenomenon" was that could cause electric currents to flow above the surface of the Earth, but he realized that he should perhaps read the book first. He told Birkeland that he would look for funding and apply for a grant to the Fridtjof Nansen Foundation set up by Waldemar Christopher Brøgger, a prominent academic at the university and acquaintance of Birkeland's. Brøgger had telegraphed Nansen as the explorer was sailing triumphantly down Norway's coast after the *Fram* expedition in 1896, asking if he could use his name to start a foundation to publish academic books on science and letters and give financial aid to new expeditions. Nansen, himself an excellent biologist and talented also in other scientific fields, had readily agreed. As Brøgger's father owned a printing company, he was able to keep down the costs for such publications while also providing his father with steady work. Dybwad told Birkeland that he was awaiting the foundation's reply but hoped that the book could be published soon—he wanted to capitalize on the exploration fever that still gripped the country in the wake of Nansen's return from the Arctic.

As the foundation would only provide money for the book to be published once, the two men had to decide in what language it should appear. The Norwegian audience for the book would be tiny: the population was very small, science education was poor except in the best schools, and only those who had passed through the university would be likely to read it (a very small number indeed and most of those would be fluent in another language). In order to transmit his ideas to a wider Norwegian audience, an aim close to his heart, Birkeland planned to write popular articles in newspapers, but there was little point in using Norwegian for the book if he wanted to convince the world, particularly the scientific world, of his arguments. The second language most Norwegians spoke was German. There were many cultural and economic links between the two countries because many Germans had emigrated to Norway in previous centuries and become eminent burghers. But Birkeland's German was not fluent and he had not enjoyed his stay in Bonn, nor did he feel it was the best language for a wide readership.

English was widely read but he did not speak it well and had no particular links with any British scientists, although he admired many of them. For him, the language of science was French. At the turn of the twentieth century, French was still the language of diplomacy and was spoken across the European continent as widely as English. Birkeland spoke and wrote it fluently; his mentor, Poincaré, lived in Paris and the French Academy of Science frequently published his papers. Dybwad and Birkeland agreed the book should be published in French.

From the editor's office, it was not far for Birkeland to walk to the university along Carl Johan Gate. This gracious avenue, always bustling during the day except in bitter weather, began at the foot of the Royal Palace and stretched eastward for a mile, past the new Parliament building to the railway station. The Royal Norwegian Fredrik's University was the largest building on Carl Johan Gate, with an impressive façade of columns and shallow steps, flanked by two stories of tall windows. Birkeland could see the windows of his office to the left of the main portico, on the raised ground floor. He walked up the broad stairs and turned left through the double doors, into a corridor lit by narrow windows. The first double doors on the left opened into his large office, which was crammed from floor to ceiling with papers, books, instruments, electric cables, maps, globes, and unidentifiable pieces of dismantled equipment. Three tall windows looked onto the square in front of the university and beyond to the street.

Sæland, at his desk in one corner of the office, was pleased to hear that Dybwad wanted to publish the book. It was a relief to have some good news. Since Boye's death Birkeland had been easily distracted, jittery and short-tempered, particularly in the mornings; he frequently complained of insomnia, and he ate little. After the informal camaraderie of the mountaintop observatory, Birkeland felt uncomfortable in the formal, hierarchical atmosphere of the university, a highly conservative institution with a history of upholding anachronistic opinions and rituals even against its own best interests. A key example of this had come while he was a student, during the 1880s, when a debate raged between the Norwegian Parliament and the Swedish king over the sovereign's power to elect the government of Norway, regardless of which party was voted in. During this furor, the university had sided with the king against the forces of democracy in Norway. When the king backed down and agreed to appoint only the leader of the main elected party, the university's credibility was severely damaged; it was perceived in Norway as antidemocratic and élitist, and Parliament reduced its funding. By the time Birkeland was elected a professor in 1898, some members of the university were trying to improve its image, among them Waldemar Brøgger, dean of the Science Faculty. Brøgger arranged for Fridtjof Nansen, the most famous man in Norway after his attempt to reach the North Pole, to be granted a professorship not only in acknowledgment of his extraordinary achievements but also to allow the university to benefit from association with the great hero. Brøgger's was a slow and difficult struggle though, and the unapologetic conservative professors clung to their power within the institution.

Like Brøgger, Birkeland was a reformer and therefore not universally popular. His drive and energy exhausted or irritated many of his colleagues, who were resigned to the university's reputation as an intellectual backwater. As a student he had realized that the science teaching was parochial, and when he returned from a three-year pilgrimage to the greatest scientists and laboratories of Europe, he endeavored to implement many of the practices he had seen abroad. Until the Faculty of Mathematics and Science was established in 1862, the only natural science degree available at the university was in "mining science." When Birkeland was appointed professor, it was the first time that the university had had two professors of physics simultaneously. Determined to drag the science department into the twentieth century, he acted as the grain of sand in the oyster, slowly producing a pearl by the use of friction against those who considered his science too controversial and his dislike of tradition unsettling. Since his return from the expedition to Haldde, opposition against him had hardened. Among certain professors there had been criticism of the enthusiastic physicist whose foolhardy schemes had led to the death of a talented young man. His grand ideas were also a drain on the annual science budget of 500 crowns, a meager amount that would not have covered even the cost of installing the telephone between the observatories on Haldde Mountain.

Although Birkeland attracted criticism, he also enjoyed a degree of admiration from those with a more modern outlook. One of his greatest friends was Amund Helland, an eccentric but brilliant geologist working on an encyclopedia of *The Land and People of Norway* in thirty-nine volumes, who wrote in the newspaper *Dagbladet,* "I love everything Norwegian—from Amund Helland to herring and cod." He spoke Old Norse, excelled in Norwegian history, but was also blessed with a cosmopolitan outlook, having traveled after graduating to Greenland and Shetland and throughout mainland Europe to study mines and glaciers. Twenty years Birkeland's senior, Helland spoke to everyone in the same manner, regardless of age, rank, or sex. He was a committed socialist, renowned throughout Christiania for his extreme views, which were regularly expressed through his column in *Morgenbladet,* the most left-leaning paper of the time. He would attack any public figure he felt deserved a good drubbing by writing three highly critical pieces and publishing them week after week without paying any heed to the victim's response. When granted a decoration by the king, he sent it back. Helland was not made a professor until 1885, many years after he had become eligible, due to his outspoken politics, and even then it was an "extraordinary" professorship, narrowly voted in by the government. Christiania was a conservative town.

Birkeland frequently left the university with Helland in the evenings and repaired to Helland's house on Drammensveien, where he held an informal salon, attended by politicians, newspaper editors, and scientists. At these evenings, Birkeland was nicknamed the "Boy Professor"; he looked so young and sweet compared to his colleagues, most of whom were of Helland's generation. Women were encouraged to attend, and Helland favored those who were intelligent and independent—journalists and writers. He was unconventional in his approach to women, forming friendships with widows and divorcées, and even the occasional wife—though all his approaches were platonic. He would dispatch sacks of potatoes to any woman he admired (he did not approve of fancy gifts), and his most loving gesture was to send dried flatfish. He himself adored dried fish and would use it as a bookmark in case he became peckish while reading. On one sack of potatoes he sent to a young assistant in a perfumery he attached a note: "These potatoes are for your fair mouth only. Do not let your husband eat any."

Whiling away evenings with Helland provided comfort to Birkeland, who was suffering from the loss of Boye, his father, and his family home in the space of a month. His eating became so erratic that his friends began to invite him to dinner to ensure that he ate well at least occasionally. Birkeland's mother had charged Professor Henrik Mohn and his wife, Julie, with keeping an eye on her son once she left. The Mohns had been near neighbors of the Birkelands at 8 Nordal Bruns Gate and Henrik Mohn had encouraged Birkeland's desire to follow a career in science. He was patient at explaining scientific concepts to the young Birkeland and would allow him into his office, a secret world adorned with mysterious instruments and incomprehensible charts covered in arrows and figures.

Mohn was the founder of meteorological science in Norway and had become the director of the Meteorological Institute, where he organized systematic weather observations as a foundation for the world's first forecasts—particularly storm warnings. He had encouraged international cooperation for meteorological observations, realizing early that the weather was a worldwide phenomenon, not a national one, an ambitious and cosmopolitan attitude that influenced Birkeland greatly in his student days. Mohn was also interested in the effects of the aurora borealis on the weather. He had sent Birkeland several papers and cuttings while he was at the observatory and they frequently discussed the matter. Mohn and his wife had only one child, Louise, named after his first wife, who had died at the age of twenty-nine. He had given his daughter a thorough science training and subsequently employed her to make calculations for weather predictions. Although Birkeland spent more time in the Mohn house than his own as a young man, he had taken little notice of Louise. She was six years younger than he was and perpetually surrounded by an endless stream of cousins, having ten uncles and aunts on her father's side and seven on her mother's, most with children.

When Birkeland was invited to dinner with Henrik and Julie, a few weeks after his mother had left for Porsgrund, he noticed how much Louise had changed since he had last seen her. She was now twenty-six and able to converse with him about the complexities and difficulties she and her father were facing in developing a science of weather forecasting. Birkeland's attention, however, was drawn to another of the guests, a niece of Mohn's whom he did not recall meeting before, Ida Charlotte Hammer. Ida was the daughter of Mohn's next youngest sibling, Justine, born the year after him. Ida explained that she had five sisters and therefore it was understandable if Birkeland had no recollection of her but she remembered him because he had let them experiment with his new magnet when he was twelve or thirteen. She had been sixteen then; now she was thirty-seven but with the air of a younger woman.

Ida wore subdued colors and simple clothes that suited her small frame and unadorned face. Her black silk dress, pulled in sharply at her tiny waist, emphasized her narrow shoulders but was softened at the neck with a striped purple and gray silk cravat, carefully tucked into the bodice of her dress and held in place with a modest silver brooch. Her chestnut hair was parted in the middle, twisted and pinned to the crown of her head with two wooden hairpins, each tipped with a carved flower. The style was severe, but a few fine hairs refused to be smoothed into place and curled around the nape of her neck. Her pronounced earlobes were ornamented with small pearl studs set in silver and she wore several narrow gold bracelets, a surprisingly Bohemian touch to an otherwise somber outfit. Her large eyes protruded a little either side of the narrow bridge of her nose and her lips were very thin. A tiny pointed chin gave her an appealing, elfin grace but the overall effect was neat and kempt rather than pretty.

Birkeland entertained the group with tales of life on the mountain peak, the reindeer rides and the wind strong enough to blow a man off his feet. Julie Mohn asked him many questions about Alten, a small town at the foot of Halldde Mountain, where she had been born and brought up. No one mentioned the tragedy of the avalanche. Ida also had stories to tell of adventurous travels. She had recently spent several months in America and England studying the cooking and customs of those countries. On her return she had found a new position at a school just east of Christiania, and she was living with her uncle and aunt until she could find an apartment of her own nearer the school. Ida's family lived in Raade, a small rural community south of Christiania near the coast, where her father was the vicar. Ida was clearly intelligent, independent, and stubborn when convinced she was right. Probably a kind teacher, she was not an immediately warm presence, fair rather than friendly. Although she was plainer than Louise and more than a decade older, Birkeland was intrigued by Ida and was pleased to find himself seated next to her for the meal. For several hours he thought and talked of things other than science. At the end of the evening he shook her hand warmly and expressed his pleasure at renewing their acquaintance after so many years.

DYBWAD CALLED Birkeland with the news that the Fridtjof Nansen Foundation would fund publication of the book and Birkeland took Sæland out for a celebratory drink. He confided in the younger man his hopes that the published work would find its way to the desks of the world's scientists, that his theories would be understood and appreciated, and that Norway's reputation in the scientific community would be greatly improved. Sæland had no doubt that the professor's hopes would be realized. Meanwhile, they continued working on the recordings from the Haldde and Talvik observatories and began to look further afield for magnetograms with which to compare their results. In the manuscript of the book they had used results from Potsdam, an observatory at a lower latitude, but Birkeland really needed figures from other areas within the auroral oval. At the back of his mind was growing an idea that he had first had during his captivity in the observatory. He wanted to launch a new expedition, four times more ambitious than the last, with observatories spread around the Arctic Circle within the auroral zone. For the time being the idea remained a daydream.

Birkeland's only distraction from his magnetic recordings was the time he spent in hydroelectric plants around the southern half of the country. His vow to help develop the hydroelectric industry in Norway, made while visiting Anders Quale in Kaafjord, had borne fruit sooner than anticipated. On his return to the capital the government had asked him to sit on a committee discussing the state of the industry and searching for ways of developing the production of electricity from waterfalls. Birkeland realized that the position would give him carte blanche to experiment with new technology and tremendous voltages in the country's emerging power stations. He jumped in with alacrity. Several days a month Birkeland examined different plants, rapidly developing such expertise in the practical challenges of hydroelectricity that he was asked to work as a consultant for private hydroelectric firms.

One of these companies was Christiania Lightworks, established in 1891 by Thomas Nordberg-Schultz, who soon became a good friend of Birkeland's. Only six months older than Birkeland, Nordberg-Schultz was a pioneer of the practical possibilities of electricity in Norway: he had set up the country's first electric power plant in 1889, with the financial backing of a powerful Norwegian shipping magnate, Gunnar Knudsen. The two men spent many hours bent over circuits and switches, Birkeland benefiting from his friend's practical experience and Nordberg-Schultz from Birkeland's theoretical knowledge. As Birkeland had noticed at the hydroelectric plant in Kaafjord, the major difficulty engineers experienced in the power stations was breaking the current once it was flowing— switching the power on and off. Back in his office, he began doodling ideas for a switching mechanism in the margins of his manuscript. Even in the street, he would be utterly preoccupied with this technological challenge, walking absentmindedly between his tram stop and his office.

When Birkeland's book was published in the late spring of 1901, it made the front pages in Christiania under headlines such as "Riddle of the Aurora Solved!" Birkeland's photograph was captioned "brilliant scientist," "brave explorer." Birkeland wrote elegant and entertaining popular articles for the daily papers that explained in lay terms the complicated events happening in space that were invisible to Earth dwellers but were hinted at by the mystical Lights. In Scandinavia and continental Europe his stock rose rapidly. He gave lectures to general and scientific audiences at the university and the Academy of Science, was feted at dinner parties and grilled constantly about the Lights, space, the sun, and how the elements fitted together. For the first time, listening to Birkeland's explanations, people began to understand the intimate connection between the sun and the Earth and to realize that the stars in the sky are other suns. The university officially allocated the basement below his office for his use. Only one cloud obscured Birkeland's contentment. At first it was a minor disappointment.

In England, reviews of Birkeland's book were few and unfavorable. As it was published in French, a number of journals did not even review it, assuming their subscribers would not be reading it. Those that did, particularly the *Philosophical Transactions* of the Royal Society, attacked the book as fundamentally flawed. British scientists had one very strong belief: that space was an empty vacuum. This uniformity of opinion of the British scientists was in part due to the hegemony of the Royal Society over scientific institutions in Britain. The Royal Society, once chaired by Sir Isaac Newton, vetted scientific papers, awarded prizes, and conferred influence upon those with whose theories the chairman and his committee agreed. Election to the Royal Society was a great honor and a badge of approval for the work of the new member. By the time Birkeland published his book, the Royal Society was fast becoming the most influential scientific institution in the western world and the man elected its president was treated with awe. Until recently, the position had been held by Lord Kelvin, a very great mathematician and physicist, whose work in thermodynamics helped to develop the law of the conservation of energy and the absolute energy scale, from then on measured in degrees Kelvin. He also presented the dynamical theory of heat, developed theorems for the mathematical analysis of electricity and magnetism, and investigated hydrodynamics, particularly wave motion and vortex motion. Birkeland had enormous respect for Kelvin, but the great man had made an almost throwaway remark in 1892 that had been slavishly followed ever since. The *Proceedings of the Royal Society* published in May that year reported Kelvin's statement that the sun could have no effect on geomagnetic activity and that the correlation between these storms and sunspots was illusory.

> There is absolutely conclusive evidence against the supposition that terrestrial magnetic storms are due to magnetic actions of the sun; or to any kind of dynamical action taking place within the sun, or in connection with hurricanes in its atmosphere, or anywhere near the sun.
>
> . . .
>
> The supposed connection between magnetic storms and sunspots is unreal, and the seeming agreement between the periods has been mere coincidence.

Given the esteem in which Kelvin was held, few scientists were prepared to stand up against such an unequivocal statement. It was doubly ironic that Kelvin was, inadvertently, the source of his present woe because it was Birkeland who had been instrumental in Norway's being represented at the celebrations to mark Kelvin's fiftieth year in science. Because of Kelvin's pronouncement on the matter, the British had thrown out Birkeland's entire thesis and he was bitterly disappointed at their offhand and negative reception. He suspected that in Britain, Norwegians were thought of as the poor relatives of Vikings, fisherfolk with a quaint attachment to skiing and polar exploration, and that he himself was regarded as just a small man, in a tiny physics department, from an unremarkable university in a diminutive colony of Sweden. As he saw it, the argument between him and his British colleagues was a perfect reflection of Norway's and Britain's relative positions in the world. He perceived the Earth as a small planet, part of a huge solar system, under the influence of a much larger force—the sun—but with its own protection and independence in the form of the magnetic field. For the British scientists, as far as Birkeland could tell, Earth stood in splendid isolation in empty space, impenetrable to outside cosmic forces other than that of gravity, which, after all, was British.

It was obvious that he would need to make a much greater impact to be noticed in Britain. He returned to the idea of mounting a more ambitious expedition, establishing four observatories around the Arctic Circle. By gathering data simultaneously from different points along the auroral oval, he could build up a picture of how and where magnetic storms started and abated and where the auroras appeared. By adding to this data recordings taken at observatories in lower latitudes, he would be able to create a global map of magnetic storms. Then, Birkeland was convinced, the weight of evidence would prove that such storms could not originate on Earth but only from a body as powerful as the sun. The British would be forced to reconsider his theory.

Characteristically, Birkeland became consumed by the idea of a new expedition, but there was one major obstacle in his path: lack of money. He was out of favor with the government, despite the success of his book in Norway. He had acquired a reputation for being cavalier with budgets and a hopeless financial organizer—accusations, Birkeland knew, that were probably true. When it came to science, money was simply a means to an end. He frequently became so absorbed in what he was doing that he would forget to eat, sleep, change his clothes, or pay his bills. He was careless not only with government money, but also with the university's and his own. He frequently spent his salary on new instruments without giving it a thought. While lecturing he would blow expensive fuses with complete abandon, pushing the equipment to its maximum to see what would happen. His students loved his approach, but the administration did not.

Funding for the new expedition was going to be a major hurdle. At the same time as Birkeland's book was published, another work of tremendous effort was sent to the government: the accounts Sæland had been preparing for over a year. At the bottom of the meticulous calculations Birkeland wrote, "Mainly correct. The smaller details I cannot remember." The figures showed that Birkeland had spent three times more than the amount originally allocated to his expedition. The final sum was 38,297.02 crowns instead of the original budget of 12,000. The government had already paid 31,100 crowns but still owed Birkeland 7,000—more than a year's salary. He knew from talking to politicians at Helland's salon that individual members of the government appreciated his work but that many members of Parliament did not understand it and knew only that he had spent three times more than he should—an inexcusable lack of economy in a country that prided itself on financial prudence.

He would have to find the money himself. The only potentially lucrative work Birkeland engaged in was with the hydroelectric industry. If he could design and patent a switch that would allow the huge currents in power stations to be switched on and off quickly, then he might be able to earn the funds he needed. He asked Sæland to start exploring suitable locations for the new expedition and the equipment and resources that would be necessary, while he spent many hours at Christiania Lightworks. As when he had worked beside Dr. Quale in the Kaafjord hydroelectric power station, Birkeland felt at home surrounded by engineers and technicians in the massive turbine rooms of the plants. He began experimenting on a new design for a switching mechanism. Although he made rapid progress developing the idea, his experiments did not always go according to plan. He learned how unpredictable electricity can be when, on several occasions, he was thrown high into the air by a massive spark that jumped between the main conductor of the switch and the bar he pulled out to break the current. He would cheerfully point out as he picked himself up, "You learn more from your mistakes than your victories."

By late autumn, Birkeland thought he had ironed out the problems with his new circuit-breaker switches and was ready to experiment with an emergency stop procedure at the ten-kilovolt station at Maridalshammeren. His colleagues in the hydroelectric power committee gathered to watch the demonstration. Events did not go quite as planned. When Birkeland pulled out the metal "knife switch" that should have broken the current, a huge arc of electricity jumped from the circuit to the metal switch in Birkeland's hand and gave him a shock powerful enough to throw him across the engine room. All the fuses were destroyed, the circuit board broke in half, and the entire power station was plunged into darkness and began to burn. While the members of the committee and the employees ran for their lives, Birkeland sat on the floor laughing until his sides hurt and the fire was extinguished.

"It was the most cheerful moment of my life!" he said to Sæland the next morning when recounting the extraordinary events. Birkeland believed that he had found the answer to his prayers. The switching device he had been working on turned out to have another use entirely. The experimental switch used a solenoid, a large coil of metal connected to an electric circuit. Birkeland noticed that when he switched on the power, two metal screws were sucked into the solenoid with great force. When he reversed the current, they were ejected from the solenoid so violently that they had given him two little bruises on his hand. When he showed the effect to the engineers, they said they had seen it before but it was rare enough not to be a problem. For Birkeland it was not a problem but rather the solution to his funding worries. In a moment of intuitive brilliance he had glimpsed a use for the solenoid that everyone else had missed. Leaving Sæland puzzled as to his meaning, Birkeland hurried upstairs to his office, sure that he would now find the means to finance his great expedition.

6

The Cannon

Early September 1901
University of Christiania, Norway

"Mother, give me the Sun."

HENRIK IBSEN (1828–1906), *Ghosts*, 1881

*F*OR TEN DAYS passersby on the Carl Johan Gate saw flashes of light and heard loud bangs emanating from Birkeland's office. Groups of students bunched below his windows trying to guess what strange activities were taking place within, and on several occasions the law professor had to dispatch a student to request silence as the explosions and crackles were distracting attention from his lectures. Oblivious to the curiosity he was arousing, Birkeland worked furiously on hundreds of equations and detailed plans for currents, switches, circuits, and barrels. He set up a large solenoid coil on his desk and looped electric cable across the ceiling, down the far wall, and through a hole he had drilled in the floorboards to the cellar, where he had installed a generator. Three bangs on the floor and Sæland would start the generator to power up the solenoid. Birkeland tested different strengths of current to see which forced the metal out of the solenoid at the greatest velocity, and soon the plaster on the far wall of his office began to look like the last retreat in a shoot-out. Sæland asked Birkeland several times how these experiments would help develop the switching mechanism he had been asked to create for the hydroelectric industry but the professor would purse his lips, gently shake his head, and say nothing.

One afternoon in the middle of September, Birkeland threw down his pen, pulled on his coat and hat, rolled up several large sheets of plans, drawings, and equations, and left the university, walking east toward the Parliament. Just to its right, on Carl Johan Gate, was a large, brown-brick building with ornate cream pediments above the windows. Birkeland barely altered his pace as he burst through the heavy entrance door past the sign:

Alfred Bryn
Patent Office

From that day on Birkeland's life took a different turn. Alfred Bryn, the most important patent issuer in Norway, could see that the plans Birkeland was showing him were extraordinary. He had first met the professor nearly six years before, in January 1896; Bryn remembered the date well as he had gone to the university to watch Birkeland give a demonstration of X-rays just days after Roentgen first announced their discovery. The professor had set up the X-ray equipment in his office and a long queue of people had formed in the narrow corridor outside, all wanting to be the first in history to see the bones in their own hands, or the coins in their closed purses. Birkeland claimed then to have been experimenting with X-rays before Roentgen's announcement. Whether or not that was true, Bryn had admired Birkeland's performance at the demonstration and felt sure that one day the professor would walk through his doors with an idea every bit as revolutionary as X-rays. Maybe that day had arrived. Bryn could see that what set Birkeland above his peers was his ability to extract big ideas from tiny seeds of chance. He seemed to have an intuitive understanding of events that allowed him to push them instantly to their limits while other people were trying to categorize, regulate, repeat, systematize, and render "scientific" their experience. Birkeland was so instinctive a scientist that he had the confidence to use his imagination like an artist; he could picture what space must be like because he understood so well the essential forces that kept the world turning. In the same way, he had seen a radical new use for a solenoid.

Bryn carefully registered Birkeland's drawings in his Patents Pending ledger, wrote the date in the margin, 16 September 1901, and next to them put the patent number 11201 and, finally, the title: "Birkeland's Electromagnetic Cannon." Looking at the plans, Bryn saw that this strange object, the first gun he had seen to utilize the power of electricity, could revolutionize weaponry in the way gunpowder had in the sixteenth century. If that were the case, this single invention might alter forever Norway's role as a subsidiary state and put it on the map as a major power. Birkeland hoped that it would solve his financial problems and allow him to fulfil his dream of building a laboratory and observatory for the sole purpose of pursuing his scientific quest to reveal the cause of the Northern Lights and to understand the message of the sun.

Once Bryn had agreed to draw up the patent diagrams for the electromagnetic cannon, Birkeland went straight back to his office to write four rather cryptic invitations to a secret demonstration the following evening. Two were addressed to high-ranking military officers, Colonel Krag and General Olssøn, and two to heads of industry, the director of Christiania Lightworks, Nordberg-Schultz, and engineer Gunnar Knudsen, owner of an important shipping company. Knudsen was unable to attend but the other three were ushered into Birkeland's office once the university professors and students had left for the night. Birkeland explained to his distinguished guests that they would be the first to witness a potentially revolutionary instrument of war. His reputation as a scientist in Christiania was sufficient to put the men in a high state of excitement. He then banged on the floor to Sæland in the basement who started the generator while Birkeland loaded a projectile into the barrel of the gun and placed a thick wooden board on a chair at the other end of the room. Once Birkeland was satisfied that sufficient electricity was reaching the cannon from the generator, he flicked a switch (of his own design), and before his guests could blink, a loud bang announced that the projectile had hit the target. The board had been struck with such force that the chair slammed against the back wall and fell over. Several seconds of complete silence followed the demonstration after which Birkeland was heartily congratulated. He explained to the men that the gun was powered by electricity, would be silent when fired, had a potential range several times that of any conventional weapon, and could be operated at the flick of a switch and coordinated with several other guns connected to the same generator. Understanding that the design was indeed revolutionary, the army officers invited Birkeland with Nordberg-Schultz back to their club to discuss the future of his invention. Over whiskies and cigars, they pledged financial support for the construction of a prototype.

Directly after this meeting Birkeland wrote to Gunnar Knudsen, whom he had met several times at the salons of Amund Helland. Knudsen was a member of Parliament with ambitions to lead the party he supported, Venstre (the Left), and it seemed likely that his political hopes would be fulfilled. It was important for Birkeland to attain his support for the gun project; if it was successful, Knudsen might also persuade Parliament of the merit of Birkeland's new expedition.

September 1901, Christiania

Dear Engineer Knudsen,
I have just recently invented a device that uses electricity instead of gunpowder as a propellant. With this device it will be possible to shoot large amounts of nitroglycerine over long distances. I have already partly secured priority on a world patent.

Colonel Krag has proposed that a company be formed, consisting of a few men who will furnish capital to build a small gun according to my plans, at a cost of approximately 4,000 crowns. This gun will then—if it works properly—be demonstrated to Krupp and other weapons forgers.

It is a lottery, but the contribution would be comparatively small while I believe the chances are good for significant gains. Those who have seen my experiment, Colonel Krag and Director Nordberg-Schultz and General Olssøn, will participate in the company.

Naturally this must be kept a secret.

With kind regards, yours sincerely,

Kr. Birkeland

Two days after sending his letter, Birkeland received a telegram from Knudsen.

I ACCEPT WITH PLEASURE YOUR INVITATION TO PARTICIPATE IN YOUR INVENTION AND PROMISE, EVEN IF THE BIG LOT DOES NOT COME OFF, TO KEEP SMILING.

By November a joint-stock company was formed called Birkeland's Firearms with 35,000 crowns as capital divided into thirty-five shares; Birkeland received five free shares as payment. Given that his annual professorial salary was 5,000 crowns, his cannon had already been successful in expanding his purse strings. Birkeland worked on improving the design of the gun and by December the first small prototype had been forged by Engineer Jacobsen at his firm, Jacobsen Elektro. The cannon was capable of shooting a half-kilogram projectile at 80 meters a second. In early spring 1902, a larger model was built and tested in Christiania before a number of Norwegian dignitaries and European journalists. As was reported in the journal

English Mechanics and World of Science, "shells have been hurled much further than by old-fashioned methods and Birkeland's experiments will be followed with great interest."

In May the board of directors of Birkeland's Firearms decided that the cannon was ready for a demonstration in Berlin, where they hoped to attract the interest of Armstrong and Krupp, the largest weapons maker in Europe. Although Birkeland would have preferred the invention to remain purely Norwegian, there simply was not enough money in the country to make the development of the cannon possible. Norway had a tiny army already struggling on the small budget allocated to it. Due to the extreme tensions between Norway and Sweden in the Union, both sides were preparing for military conflict should matters deteriorate. The government could not afford to develop experimental weapons and industrialists needed to be sure of a large enough market for the cannon. Birkeland resigned himself to accept foreign investment in the company, although no Swedish interests were invited to his demonstrations.

He traveled to Germany in May to demonstrate the latest gun. It was four meters long, fired ten-kilogram projectiles, and had a potential range of 100 kilometers. The cost of forging the gun was 10,000 crowns, twice his annual salary, but the demonstration in front of a large committee of technical and firearms experts in Berlin was so successful that Birkeland returned to the board with offers to purchase the invention. Many newspapers reported the demonstration, including the *Daily Mail* and *English Mechanics;* the latter concluded that many of the experts on the committee believed Birkeland's electromagnetic gun would revolutionize modern warfare. The *Daily Mail's* concluding paragraph revealed the suspicion already present between the British and the Germans: "I hear that the military reports about this remarkable gun have excited the Kaiser's deepest interest."

Knudsen, who by early 1902 had become Secretary of Agriculture in the government, informed the Swedish-Norwegian king,

Oscar II, of Birkeland's electromagnetic gun and explained the principles on which it operated. The king asked about its maximum range and Knudsen replied, "Birkeland says that the projectiles can reach Stockholm," the king's permanent residence. Seeing the look of horror on the king's face, he quickly added, "or from Stockholm to St. Petersburg." The king cheered up considerably at that news although, since the distance between the two was more than 700 kilometers, Knudsen had exaggerated by a factor of seven the potential range of Birkeland's gun.

The board of Birkeland's Firearms decided to allow more time for Birkeland to develop the cannon, after which it might fetch a higher price. Although Birkeland's first foray into the technical application of his scientific knowledge was proving a success, his sole aim was to achieve financial backing for his scientific research and the cannon was not yet profitable. It had, however, added to his reputation as a scientist of note, following closely on the successful publication of his book on the aurora. Hoping this would be enough to convince the government of his worth, Birkeland requested a grant of 38,000 crowns to fund his expedition. He stated his objectives clearly: "To study magnetic disturbances and formation of cirrus clouds and auroras and their relation to a huge system of electric currents parallel to Earth's surface at high altitude." Clearly hoping to impress the government with his connections, Birkeland enclosed with the application translations of letters he had received from six of the world's foremost geophysicists, giving him their support for his planned expedition, and a separate list with their names and positions:

> *Geheimrath von Bezold,*
> *director of the Royal Prussian Meteorological Institute*
> *Professor Mascart,*
> *director of the Central Meteorological Bureau of France*
> *General Rykatchev,*
> *director of the Central Physical Observatory in St. Petersburg*

Professor Wild,
former director of the previous observatory
Professor Adolf Schmidt,
director of the Educational Institute in Hamburg
High Admiral Neumayer,
German Naval Observatory, Wilhelmshaven

The foreign scientists all stressed the importance of Birkeland's mission to resolve the puzzling variations in the Earth's magnetic field as well as the magnetic storms that accompanied the Northern Lights. No British scientists endorsed the venture.

Letters of support from Nansen, director of the Norwegian Meteorological Institute, Professor Henrik Mohn, and Professors Geelmuyden and Schiøtz from the Christiania observatory were also included, as was a warm statement of approval from Waldemar Brøgger, dean of the Science Faculty at the university, who stressed Norway's "duty to participate, a duty, which especially because of its location, certainly cannot be evaded." Birkeland added to the end of the application that his friend Joergen L. W. Dietrichson would voluntarily cover his lectures for the term. Sixty-two-year-old Dietrichson was a passionate and brilliant constructor of instruments and an excellent lecturer. For most of his life he had been a grammar school headmaster but he had also invented a special thermometer to prove that the temperature at the bottom of fjords was constant. He had introduced himself to Birkeland in 1901, when he moved to Christiania after retiring from Skien grammar school, and Birkeland saw immediately how talented and helpful Dietrichson could be.

With a little persuasion from Knudsen, the government agreed to the sum Birkeland requested and put forward an application for the money to Parliament under the title "An Expedition for Investigation of Terrestrial Magnetism, Aurora Borealis, and Cirrus Clouds." In the ensuing four-hour debate, a great deal of dissent was voiced. Memories of Birkeland's large overexpenditure on the last expedition were still fresh in the minds of many members who represented the unemployed and other disadvantaged groups and who thought that Birkeland's ever more grandiose schemes should be a low priority in the government's spending plans. Birkeland was held personally responsible for the financial fiasco: "the main cause seemingly being a lack of foresight and practical sense in the erudite observer." Other members were concerned that the government was poor and the benefit of this huge expedition with rather abstract aims was dubious. At least with polar explorers, such as Nansen, there was always a clear goal and a single victor. Birkeland's project required international cooperation, expensive equipment, and time to collate the results, and the victory, should there be one, would be understood by very few.

Others argued that it was important that any possible glory involved in this expedition should fall on Norway's shoulders. It would be shameful if Birkeland had to find sponsors from abroad. His supporters claimed that internationally prominent scientific activities—such as Nansen's expeditions and now Birkeland's—had an impact that was "recognized by the entire civilized world and have gained our country yet further right to be named as one of the civilized nations." Norway also wanted to promote its economic and political interests in the Arctic. There had been several scuffles between countries with Arctic coasts over fishing and trading rights in the waters and islands of the Arctic Ocean. A "neutral" scientific expedition would establish a Norwegian presence in places where there had previously been little or none. Birkeland's intimations that the expedition would advance the embryonic yet crucial science of weather forecasting were also highlighted by those in favor of the expedition. Passages from his application were quoted for their positive implications for marine commerce, fisheries, and agriculture, vital Norwegian economic activities.

The energy of the electrical discharge of the Aurora, the intensity of which reaches at times hundreds of thousands or even millions of amperes, seems sufficiently large as to provoke or unleash profound meteorological changes. This current is measured by its magnetic effects and it is therefore eminently possible one day, that magnetometers will become as indispensable to meteorologists as barometers and humidity measurers.

The result of the parliamentary debate was that the government's proposal to fully fund the expedition was defeated 65 votes to 46. However, a proposal to grant a more modest 20,000 crowns was approved by 90 votes to 21.

After hearing the results, Birkeland called on Gunnar Knudsen to thank him for his efforts to persuade Parliament of the merit of his expedition. Knudsen was saddened that Parliament had been so belligerent and gave Birkeland 6,000 crowns, a generous contribution but not nearly enough to make the expedition viable. He also suggested Birkeland contact his friend Johan Fabricius, a landed proprietor. Fabricius matched Knudsen's donation with 6,000 crowns of his own.

Birkeland then called at the imposing offices on the busy square near the Parliament building of one of Norway's most influential citizens, to whom he had been introduced by Amund Helland: Amandus Theodor Schibsted, owner and editor of Norway's most widely read paper, *Aftenposten*. Although *Aftenposten* was a conservative paper, Schibsted was a great philanthropist and particularly enjoyed supporting ventures that would reflect glory on Norway. Schibsted was in his early fifties, tall, with a bullish neck and very fine handlebar mustache that reached beyond the dimples in his cheeks. His piercingly blue eyes had faded only a little with age, their sharp appraisal softened somewhat by the smile lines that curled up at the corners. Birkeland excited the newsman with the ambitious aims of his plan to mount an observational expedition on a grand scale to some of the harshest environments on Earth, one that would be undertaken by scientists rather than experienced explorers. It was scientifically daring too. Continuous, simultaneous measurements of magnetic disturbances would allow the polar skies and near space to be mapped for the first time. It would be possible to plot the movement of magnetic storms over the Arctic Circle; assess their speed, strength, development, direction, points of arrival, and points of departure; and discover the conditions necessary for auroras to appear and whether they induced any meteorological effects, such as cirrus clouds. Schibsted also pledged 6,000 crowns and plenty of publicity. Birkeland was delighted. Eighteen thousand crowns richer in the space of a week, he wrote in *Aftenposten:*

> It may safely be said that economy is one of the virtues of Norwegians as a nation, perhaps one may say a virtue of necessity; but the nation's idealism often turns the balance in delightful nonconformity with economy. The grants to my aurora expeditions are an instance of this.

He still needed up to five thousand crowns for contingencies but this he decided to borrow from a bank against his interest in the firearms company. It was a huge financial gamble to borrow the equivalent of a year's salary against a company that consisted only of prototypes and promises, and all for a project that itself was potentially disastrous.

While Birkeland had been improving his cannon and chasing funding for the expedition, he had also been working with Sæland on the final locations for the observatories and the simultaneous recording methods they would use. His plan was to put four teams of scientists around the Arctic Circle, with 1,000 kilometers between them, using already extant buildings wherever possible to avoid the costs and delays he had encountered with the Haldde observatory. As Birkeland had determined during his first expedition that auroras occurred at about a hundred kilometers above the surface of the Earth, there was no need for observatories to be placed on mountains. He planned to use the Haldde and Talvik peak buildings for some measurements, but the Finnmark team of scientists would be able to perform most of their duties along the banks of the fjord in Kaafjord and Bossekop. Birkeland had originally planned to site one team off the coast of Greenland on Jan Mayen Island, but Fridtjof Nansen warned him that they were unlikely to survive a winter there and building an observatory from scratch would prove too expensive. He settled instead on Dyrafjord, in western Iceland, where the scientists could be supported by a Norwegian whaling station. The third team would be situated at Axeløen in the southern part of Spitsbergen, an island nearly 900 kilometers to the north of Norway in the Arctic Ocean, where they would live with hunters from Tromsø. After negotiations with the Russian authorities, Birkeland was granted permission to send the fourth team to Matotchkin Schar on the island of Novaya Zemlya off the north Russian coast. He wrote to the Russian painter Alexander Borisoff about the possibility of using the house the artist had built there, in Pomorskaya Bay, and to which he retired occasionally to paint Arctic landscapes and glaciers. Borisoff not only loaned Birkeland the house, he also told him to make full use of the food supplies kept there. The Russian authorities were efficient and helpful to Birkeland and sent a letter to the governor in Archangelsk, from which the team would set sail to Novaya Zemlya, requesting that he afford them all possible assistance.

Birkeland also wrote letters to observatories around the world asking for measurements to be taken at specific times on certain dates in order to build up a global picture of magnetic activity in the layers between the Earth's atmosphere and space.

> I now take the liberty of asking all those who are in the position to do so, to give or lend me copies of photograms of magnetic disturbances that may occur on the thirty days denoted above and urge them, in the interest of science, not to mind facing the considerable amount of trouble which must be taken to fulfil such a request.

With such evidence Birkeland was convinced that his detractors would have to concede that his Northern Lights theory was correct.

BIRKELAND had very little time to socialize during these months of frenetic activity. He thought nothing of working fourteen-hour days, including on the weekend. Only Amund Helland was his equal in industriousness. Consequently, Helland was the one best able to coax Birkeland away from his office for the occasional evening gathering at his home, because he did not expect formal attire or follow complicated and time-consuming rules of etiquette. Birkeland could arrive when he wished, empty-handed and casually dressed, speak or not speak once there, and leave when he felt tired. The Mohns, due to their lifelong friendship, were also expert at persuading Birkeland to spend an evening with them. His visits to their house were rare at this busy time, but he would see them every three or four months. On most of these evenings, Ida would also be invited and the two would sit near each other during dinner. At times their conversations were quite heated, as when Birkeland explained that he had invented an electromagnetic cannon. Once Ida had understood the full implications of the machine, she was appalled and told Birkeland so without demur. Ida was a devout Christian; her father was the priest for several parishes, and she had been brought up with an unquestioning faith and a strong belief in doing unto others what you would have them do unto you. So emphatic was her disapproval of Birkeland's plans that the meal was rather awkward and the next time he dined with the Mohns, Ida was not present. Birkeland did not comment on her absence although it was clear to Henrik and Julie that she was missed.

When Birkeland told Mohn that he had received sufficient money to make the expedition possible, the meteorologist was delighted and asked him to come by to discuss his plans for meteorological observations and the instruments he would need. On the appointed day in late March Birkeland arrived straight from his office, covered in a thin layer of chalk. The two men closeted themselves in Mohn's office among the maps and globes and instruments, until Julie called them to eat. When they arrived at the dining table, they found Ida sitting next to her aunt. During the evening Mohn carefully described to the women Birkeland's plan to mount a year-long expedition to dangerous climates in the cause of science. Perhaps Mohn was trying to rehabilitate the friendship between Ida and Birkeland by obliterating memories of the cannon; if so, the tactic worked. Birkeland enjoyed talking to Ida again after so many months; her thinking was uncompromising and independent and, because she had met him as a young boy, she was a rare link with his past. She treated him as a younger brother, part of the family, and was not intimidated by his intelligence or greatly interested in his researches. The Mohns clearly thought that Ida would be pleased to receive attention from a gentleman with prospects, particularly at her age, but she seemed unconcerned with such matters. She appeared fulfilled by her work as a teacher at a school in Lillestrøm, just east of Christiania. As only one of her sisters, Julie, was married with children, Ida felt no sibling pressure to find a husband, and her parents certainly implied that it was better to remain a respectable spinster than to marry unsuitably. Julie's marriage had caused a number of unspoken but serious rifts in the family. Ida's parents had moved to Raade in 1888, just at the time when the daughters were looking for eligible suitors; Ida was twenty-five, her oldest sister, Caroline, was twenty-seven, and the youngest, Helga, fifteen. Raade was an agricultural area and the Hammer children were better educated than their peers. To be the vicar's daughter also conferred a degree of social elevation far above that of a farmhand—they were as close to an "aristocracy" as Norway possessed. Julie had married a farmer who, despite a comfortable income, was not considered a suitable match. She now had five children while her sisters had abandoned hope of marriage and had forged careers for themselves as teachers and nurses or had stayed home to look after their parents.

When Ida rose to leave at the end of the evening, Birkeland offered to accompany her to the tram stop and, for the first time since they had met on his return from Haldde Mountain, nearly two years before, they left the house together. As the tram pulled into the stop, blaring bright with electric lights and bells, she shook Birkeland's hand and wished him a safe trip.

7

Mad Dogs

July 1902
Archangelsk, Russia

*The scientist is a builder. Collecting scientific data can be compared to
gathering stones for a house; a stack of data is no more "science"
than a heap of stones is a house. Unstudied scientific results are just
a dead heap of stones.*

KRISTIAN BIRKELAND, letter to the Ministry of Church and
Education, 26 September 1903

O N 1 JULY 1902 Birkeland boarded a train at Christiania's
new railway terminus, bound for Sweden. He was waved
off by a small crowd of well-wishers including Helland,
the Mohns, Ida, and Sem Sæland. The three men chosen by Birkeland and Sæland to run the observatory on Novaya Zemlya had left
two weeks earlier and Birkeland was joining them in Archangelsk,
from which a steamer would take them on the seven-day journey to
the remote island of Novaya Zemlya. Once satisfied that the observatory was running smoothly, Birkeland would travel by steamship
from the White Sea along the Kola Coast to Varanger in eastern
Finnmark, to the base in Kaafjord, where he would lead the observations.

After a day's journey by rail across southern Sweden, Birkeland
arrived at the Stockholm rail terminus, built by the same engineer-

ing firm as the Christiania station, S. Eyde's Engineering Office. He could imagine he was back home, so similar were the two buildings with their iron-girded green-glass roofs and soaring arches. He took a cab to the harbor, then caught a ship for the twenty-four-hour journey across the Gulf of Finland to Helsingfors, capital of the Russian dependency of Finland, and on to St. Petersburg.

He was met at the ferry dock by the two scientists of L'Observatoire Physique Centrale who had written him letters of recommendation for the expedition, General Rykatchev and Professor Wild. On the way to the observatory their carriage trundled along the embankment of the Neva River until they reached the Winter Palace, where the carriage paused for Birkeland to look at the ornate, baroque building decorated in pale green and white with double-headed gilt eagles, symbol of the imperial czar's mastery of east and west. Across the Neva River from the palace stood the Peter and Paul Fortress, within which the cathedral, the tallest building in the city, marked Russia's exit to the Baltic Sea. One hundred twenty-two meters high, its gilded spire glowed in the midday sun like a column of fire. As he watched, a cannon was fired from the fortress walls and the professors (and nearly all the men Birkeland could see near their carriage) checked their pocket watches. Wild explained that his observatory gave a signal to the fortress every day at noon so the guardsmen knew exactly when to fire the gun. The whole city now relied on the gunshot to set their timepieces.

Across the expansive, colonnaded Palace Square, the carriage continued into the city. All horsecab drivers in St. Petersburg had to pass a two-year course in navigational astronomy, French, geography, history, and polite manners before they were allowed to accept passengers and Birkeland's driver volunteered a smattering of historical facts as they passed important monuments. The carriage took them along the grand shopping street of Nevsky Prospect, across canals and through vast squares with monumental equestrian statues of czars and generals, sharp and perfect under the pale splendor of the afternoon sunlight. Birkeland was struck by the gold onion domes of the Orthodox churches, the like of which he had never seen before.

St. Petersburg enjoyed "white nights" around the summer solstice, when the night sky never grew dark as the sun dipped only a few degrees below the horizon. The phenomenon was receding by the time Birkeland reached the city, but the day was still around sixteen hours long and it was not until late afternoon that the professors took Birkeland to their observatory. Over dinner, the three men discussed the expedition. The two Russian professors had supported Birkeland's project with letters of recommendation without being wholly convinced by his theories. After meeting Birkeland, though, Wild and Rykatchev were almost won over by his arguments, which were based on a brilliant understanding of the forces of electromagnetism far exceeding their own. They offered him every assistance for his expedition and gave him the names of two friends in Archangelsk who would help him in any way possible.

After a few days Birkeland left St. Petersburg for the 3,000-kilometer journey to the White Sea. He caught the night train to Moscow, which arrived around lunchtime the following day, then traveled across the city to the northern terminus to catch the connecting train. The railway to Archangelsk had opened four years earlier. The sleeper carriage allocated to Birkeland was fitted with hot and cold taps and small electric lights by which he could shave and read.

The following morning the train pulled into Vologda station, the halfway point, after which the view from the windows was of forests, broken occasionally by rivers flowing to the White Sea. The main river in the area was the Dvina, a major transport route that took wood, flour, pearl barley, leather, linen, wool cloth, and various Russian household articles, including wooden spoons and lacquered boxes, to Archangelsk, the main port in northwest Russia. Here, the Pomor, Russians who lived along the White Sea coast, enjoyed a lively trade with northern Norway, sending at least three hundred ships a year to the ports of Tromsø, Vadsø, and Hammerfest; these returned with full loads of fish and fish oil.

Archangelsk station was one of the few stone buildings in a city with the largest number of timber structures in the world. Forests surrounded the city and there were no local quarries for stone. At the platform, Hans Riddervold, the man he had chosen to lead the expedition to Novaya Zemlya, met Birkeland. A twenty-six-year-old science graduate from Christiania University, Riddervold was tall and slim with tightly curled blond hair and a wispy mustache and beard. His unusually long, delicate fingers looked like those of a pianist rather than those of a hardy Arctic researcher. Two assistants, Hans Thomas Schaaning and Johan Koren, who were close friends, accompanied him. They had spent two years in the remote forests of Pasvik on Norway's border with Russia, collecting birds and animals for museums. Both had been engaged on the understanding that they could speak Russian, although in fact neither of them could. Koren had bought a phrase book and was practicing a few sentences with enthusiasm, but Schaaning planned to make up for his linguistic shortcomings with his culinary skills. Though he was the youngest of the group, the twenty-two-year-old Koren had already taken part in an expedition to Antarctica from 1897 to 1899, aboard the *Belgica*. The crew, among whom was Roald Amundsen, were the first to overwinter in such southerly latitudes.

Archangelsk was a cosmopolitan town where people of many nationalities, including Germans and Norwegians, had their own quarters, newspapers, and clubs. In the middle of July the city was teeming with merchants and tradesmen from many different countries, as most trading took place in the summer months. The harbor, at the heart of Archangelsk, bustled with vessels being loaded and unloaded while a bevy of small boats scuttled between them with goods and passengers. As the carriages carrying Birkeland and his entourage crossed the waters of the Dvina to the pension where

they would be staying, great rafts of logs were steered to the waiting boats by women in ankle-length skirts and headscarves who
wielded long punts. The wooden Pomor houses lining the streets
were adapted to withstand the harsh winter climate, with living
areas on the second floor so that doors and windows wouldn't be
blocked by high snowdrifts and the main entrance to the side of the
house, for protection from the wind that whipped down the
Archangelsk thoroughfares. Birkeland was surprised at the grandeur of many of the houses; the business possibilities in the town
were clearly more favorable than he had imagined.

The governor, Rimski Korsakoff, invited Birkeland and his assistants to his house, where they were joined by Surkow and Makarow, the two men recommended by the St. Petersburg scientists.
Birkeland explained his scientific mission to the Russians as a silver
samovar brewed tea and rich fruitcake was passed around. Surkow
was an influential merchant and factory owner who had been born
in Moscow and kept a house there but ran his business from
Archangelsk. He was educated in technology and basic scientific
principles and enjoyed the opportunity to discuss scientific matters
with the eminent professor. Makarow, his friend, was also a trader
and the only one to have been to Novaya Zemlya. He had links with
a small group of Samoyed there, hunters from whom he bought
seal pelts and polar bear skins. The Samoyed had been forced to live
there by the authorities to reinforce Russian ownership of the
island, over which erupted frequent disputes with Norwegians who
were able to hunt there earlier in the spring than Russians, because
the little ice formed in the Barents Sea melted sooner than the thick
ice of the White Sea. Makarow seemed personally unconcerned by
the situation and was friendly toward the Norwegian scientists. He
described the barren island and warned them about the ferocious
and changeable weather. Tea became dinner and not until the early
hours of the morning, after many shots of vodka, did the four Norwegians stumble back to their pension. Birkeland later wrote in his
account of the expedition:

The governor, Rimski Korsakoff, has shown us great good-will in many ways and has arranged for us to be carried free of charge, with all our baggage, in the steamer *Wladimir*. We have received permission, if necessary, to make use of a depot that is intended for shipwrecked sailors who may come ashore there. There is already a weather-vane hut and a thermometer hut so all we will have to do is put in the thermometer-screen. The weather is inclement, rarely more than ten degrees, almost always cloudy with the sun seldom visible . . . and this is high summer.

On the morning of their departure to the island, a young man from the Samoyed family living on Novaya Zemlya arrived at Birkeland's pension. Makarow had found him trading in the Pomor market the day before and had suggested that he be their guide. He stood at the foot of the steps beside a large sled loaded with odd-shaped bundles and parcels. Seeing the young man dressed in the traditional Samoyed clothes of reindeer skin gave Birkeland the idea of having a group portrait taken together with his assistants and their guide in full Arctic clothing. Birkeland was thinking of the interest the expedition would attract if he could show that the intrepid scientists faced climates and landscapes just as dangerous as those faced by the more famous "pole chasers." They went to Mr. Litovsky's studio, near the harbor, where the photographer arranged the five men against a backdrop of stormy clouds. Birkeland had not equipped himself with Samoyed clothing and wore instead a good suit and hat, tipped at a jaunty angle. He was seated on a bench while behind him stood his three assistants and guide, clad in skins and furs from head to toe.

As the group left the photographer's studio they did not at first notice the stray dog struggling through the mud with its head strangely bent forward. Riddervold nearly tripped over it as he crossed the road and the dog began to snarl viciously, pulling back its lips to reveal yellowing teeth, a few of which were streaked with blood. There were many dogs in Archangelsk that belonged to the Samoyed, who used them for driving their sleds, but this one had no mark of ownership, its coat was matted and its expression odd. The Samoyed guide spoke quietly to the animal in the same way he spoke to his own dog team but the creature seemed not to hear him and was fixated on Riddervold. Without warning it lunged at the young man, who lashed out with his thick reindeer boot. The dog then went for the one member of the group not protected by reindeer skin. Sharp teeth penetrated the fine material of Birkeland's best suit, deep into his calf. Litovsky, who had seen the commotion from his window, ran toward them with a pistol and fired into the body of the dog. Birkeland's assistants helped him back to the pension while Litovsky phoned the doctor and the governor.

Within an hour the doctor arrived. He swabbed Birkeland's wound with iodine, then dressed it with lint. Once the governor and Surkow arrived, the doctor explained that, in case the dog was rabid, Birkeland should travel immediately to Moscow for treatment at a small outpost of the Pasteur Institute that had been established there. The governor and Surkow left immediately to obtain Birkeland's train ticket. Surkow also arranged for Birkeland to stay in his own house and instructed his servants to take care of him. Riddervold volunteered to accompany him, but the professor protested that all three men were needed to set up the observatory on Novaya Zemlya and that he did not want to cause delay, particularly as the sea between Archangelsk and the island could freeze any time from mid-September on. He told Riddervold to leave that afternoon, as planned, but to send a telegram to Sem Sæland, asking him to go to Novaya Zemlya in Birkeland's stead to check that the station was properly set up. That evening Korsakoff and Surkow put Birkeland on the train to Moscow. Riddervold, Schaaning, and Koren had said goodbye a few hours earlier and were now on the *Wladimir*, leaving the port to steam north across the White Sea.

Birkeland had a contradictory attitude toward his health. On the one hand, he did nothing to preserve it, eating and sleeping little, working too hard and exposing himself to dangerous substances such as radium and mercury. On the other hand, he bordered on the hypochondriacal when suffering from headaches, colds, or ear infections. These frequent afflictions would send him to the State Hospital Pharmacy on St. Olav's Place, round the corner from his old apartment in Christiania, where he would describe his symptoms to the pharmacist in minute detail. Rest and nourishing food were never a satisfactory remedy for him; he always wanted a pill or potion to aid his recovery. But, despite the numerous colds and bouts of insomnia he had suffered since childhood, Birkeland had never been in as potentially serious a situation as he was then.

As he tried to make himself comfortable in the sleeper carriage, he thought about Louis Pasteur, to whom he had been introduced by Marie Curie when he lived in Paris. Pasteur had vividly described the symptoms of rabies and the difficulties of creating a vaccine for it. After someone was bitten by a rabid creature, it could take up to six weeks for the first sign of the disease to appear, although usually the onset was much quicker. Delirium, hydrophobia, and convulsions invariably resulted in death within four or five days. Patients usually died of a broken neck caused by the violence of their spasms. Birkeland himself was eighteen in 1885 when Pasteur first used the anti-rabies vaccine on a human. Every detail had been reported in the Christiania press. A woman had brought her young son, Josef, to Pasteur's laboratory begging for help after a rabid dog had attacked him. Pasteur had agonized over the ethics of testing an experimental vaccine on a human being but it became increasingly clear that it was the child's only chance. The boy was put to bed in an anteroom of the laboratory and syringes of vaccine were drawn from small flasks of yellow liquid that Pasteur had been distilling over the past year. Each was carefully labeled with its strength, and the boy was injected first with the weakest and then gradually the strength was increased. In order to dilute the virus sufficiently to make it safe, Pasteur had infected rabbits with the disease, and when they died he reduced their spinal cords to powder and passed a solution of this material into other rabbits and so on until the virus was sufficiently weak. After being given the vaccine, the young boy made a full recovery and Pasteur became a hero.

When Birkeland arrived in Moscow, he was met on the platform by Surkow's butler and helped into a carriage. His leg had grown very stiff and was red and hot around the bite. Surkow's house was in the northeast of the city, on the borders of the new industrial areas growing up beyond the Sadovoye Kol'tso. Until the turn of the century foreign investors had controlled much of Russian industry; Birkeland saw the names Bromley and Goujon on factory walls. However, in recent years there had been substantial growth in the Russian bourgeoisie and their homegrown industries, especially in Moscow. Surkow was an example of successful Russian business acumen. His house was large and imposing; it formed the corner of two streets with gardens behind it. An ornate glass and wrought-iron portico covered the stone steps up to the front door. The butler helped Birkeland up the grand polished staircase to a gallery landing and into a spacious sitting room that led to a bedroom and a bathroom. A fire had already been lit in the rooms. Birkeland settled down in the stiffly upholstered chair to eat the meal that was brought to him. He was tired and shivery, suspecting every twinge and twitch of his wound to be the onset of the ghastly disease. The butler informed him that Governor Korsakoff had arranged for him to visit the Pasteur Institute in the morning.

Birkeland slept fitfully, the sheets rubbing on his injured leg. In the morning, he refused breakfast. The carriage took him to the Pasteur Institute, which was beside the main hospital in a street northwest of the Kremlin. The carriage driver explained that he could not wait directly outside the hospital as security was tight near the Kremlin, but he would return every half-hour to see if Birkeland was ready. Since Czar Alexander II's assassination in 1881, security measures to protect the imperial family had been increased. With the emancipation of the serfs and the industrialization of the country, numerous anti-royalist groups had emerged and Czar Nicholas II and Empress Alexandra Feodorovna were attempting to clamp down on revolutionary fervor. Birkeland waved agreement to the driver and limped toward the laboratory. A blue and white enamel plaque announced that what looked like the hospital laundry or boiler house was really the Pasteur Institute. Birkeland entered a small vestibule with coat pegs and shoe lockers covering two walls and a large samovar pushed against the third. Within a few minutes, a French doctor wearing a laboratory apron appeared with Korsakoff's telegram alerting them to Birkeland's imminent arrival. The doctor showed him into a small room and asked questions in French about the incident, Birkeland's general health, and the behavior of the dog. Birkeland was told that the vaccination process would take at least twenty days and that he might experience unpleasant side effects such as flulike symptoms, headache, nausea, insomnia, and stomach cramps. The alternative, Birkeland knew, was to experience one of the most unpleasant deaths possible. He felt great relief as the first dose of vaccine was administered.

For the next three days Birkeland was obliged to visit the laboratory every morning and late afternoon for inoculation. He would spend the rest of the day sleeping or working. On the fourth day he developed the flulike symptoms he had been warned about, which made leaving the comfort of the house to drive through the dusty August streets of Moscow a torture. After the sixth injection Birkeland had to return once a day for the last seven doses. When the course was complete, he was told not to leave Moscow, but to return in ten days to confirm that the vaccination had worked.

Birkeland was not well enough for work or ill enough to sleep all day. He sat for many hours in the garden, scribbling occasionally in his notebook but otherwise just thinking. The dog bite had made him realize how difficult and unpredictable, as well as expensive, his expeditions were. Although he felt sure that the results they achieved would be worth the difficulty, he began to set his mind to thinking of other ways to study the Earth's magnetic field and the auroras. The forced rest allowed him to brood upon the problem, without distraction, and an idea began to formulate in his mind of a way to bring the Lights indoors, to re-create them in a laboratory.

On the tenth day Birkeland returned to the institute. The doctor warned him that, although it was extremely unlikely after vaccination, rabies could return at any time within eight years and he should be vigilant for symptoms. For the time being the treatment appeared to have been successful. Birkeland sent telegrams to Korsakoff and Surkow relaying the cheerful news and thanking them for their help. He decided to write to the king as soon as he returned home, recommending that they be awarded medals for their services. As soon as he felt completely recovered from the side effects of the injections, he returned home by train and steamship, arriving in Christiania at the beginning of September.

After only two weeks in the capital, Birkeland left again for Kaafjord in Finnmark, to check the auroral station he was supposed to be in charge of. In his absence it had been managed by Richard Krekling, a science graduate, with the assistance of Olaf Egenæs, an engineer. When Birkeland arrived, Krekling and Egenæs were achieving good results with the magnetometers and meteorological instruments. Two tasks not required of them were to take photographs of the auroras and to measure air electricity. Attempts to triangulate the height of the auroras during the previous expedition had not been successful, as the photographic plates had been too blurred to find exact matching points between plates taken from Haldde and those from Talvik peak. Birkeland deduced by other means that the auroras occurred at about a hundred kilometers above ground. The air electricity meters had recorded almost nothing either, as the electric currents causing the auroras did not come from the ground or the lower atmosphere. One of Birkeland's great strengths as a scientist was the rapidity with which he drew conclusions from data that more detailed analysis later confirmed, an ability that saved him and his researchers much labor and bore witness to his complete grasp of a subject.

As Birkeland noted later in his account of the expedition in Kaafjord:

> The aurora of 24 November in particular was one of extreme beauty. It developed into an auroral corona, which lasted some minutes, then dissolved into a great number of intensely brilliant, red streamers. These moved backwards and forwards across the heavens for some time, making the sky glow with red. The violent storms experienced on former occasions up at the mountain we, that winter, escaped by keeping down in the valley at Kaafjord.

Although the Kaafjord team observed twenty-seven auroral phenomena that winter, cloud cover obscured many more. Particularly in February, large variations in the magnetic needle indicated that auroras were extremely likely, but overcast weather for a week kept them hidden. Birkeland became even more convinced that his plan to bring the Northern Lights into the laboratory, where he would not need to worry about clouds or storms, was necessary to continue his research. As he could not go into space, he would bring space to him and re-create the universe in miniature. He had been a mathematician, a theoretician, and an observer in the field, and now he needed to become an experimenter. Without waiting for the cloud to clear, Birkeland returned to Christiania, leaving Krekling to manage the auroral station for the next five months.

Dietrichson, who had volunteered to give Birkeland's lectures for one year, continued to do so even when Birkeland returned, allowing the professor complete freedom to research his new idea. Soon after Birkeland's return from Kaafjord, Henrik Mohn visited him in his office to hear news of his adventures in Russia and to invite him to dinner with his family and niece, Ida. Birkeland was happy to be among close friends again—it had been nearly eight months since the last time—and the evening went well. He again walked Ida to her tram stop and this time, as she shook his hand goodbye, he asked her to accompany him to a Sunday lunchtime lecture to be given by his friend Jens Lieblein, professor of Egyptology, who had recently returned from Egypt with some unusual artifacts. Birkeland hoped Ida might be interested in seeing them and she agreed. For the following months the two attended lectures together every few weeks and took tea afterwards at the Grand. Helland, the only person to whom Birkeland could mention such things, approved of his growing friendship with Ida, but advised him strongly against making the relationship more than platonic. Although Helland enjoyed flustering women with his gifts of potatoes and dried fish, his dalliances were always chaste, as he believed steady emotions were conducive to happiness and productivity. He was virulently against the institution of marriage, believing that it brought out the worst in people and prevented a man from pursuing his work. Helland preferred the companionship of women uncomplicated by any sexual tension, and Birkeland assured his friend that Ida seemed as uninterested in marriage as he himself was.

After his return from Kaafjord, Birkeland received more evidence of the limitations and dangers of observation in the field. His teams in the Arctic Circle were all experiencing great difficulties completing research in the face of terrible weather conditions. Because Birkeland had been unable to accompany Riddervold and his team, Sæland had traveled to Novaya Zemlya to inspect the auroral station in his place, arriving on 28 September and leaving again three days later, on the *Wladimir*. The need to visit the Russian station had hindered his departure for Iceland and he encountered atrocious weather trying to reach Dyrafjord on the west coast of the island. He described his journey in a letter to Birkeland:

> The station in Iceland was established much later than we had hoped. On the journey to Scotland we were delayed due to bad weather and again at the Faroes for another couple of

days. By the time we reached the first stop in Iceland we were very late. We rushed around the Icelandic ports and saw the sun for the last time for a couple of months. More fog. More delays. On the last day of October a very heavy snowstorm began and we were forced to stay in Reykafjord for five days. It snowed non-stop and so thickly you could only see a couple of ships' lengths ahead. When we finally arrived at Captain Berg's whaling station the wind was so fierce that a portion of the roof was blown off even though it was covered in gravel and earth and tied down with steel wires. The Whaling Station is situated near the isolated promontory I have chosen for the measuring stations but the weather is creating great difficulties—overcast, deluges of snow and rain, high winds. It is the most remote place possible.

A letter also arrived from the team on Novaya Zemlya. Johan Koren had made great efforts to get to know his Samoyed neighbors: he learned their language and came to understand that they were unhappy under Russian rule. They asked Koren to write a letter on their behalf to King Oscar of Sweden and Norway, requesting him to take the islands from the czar "since we Samoyeds are suffering, lacking flavor, sugar, tea, everything . . ." The researchers promised to pass this on to the royal household at the end of the expedition, and, in return, on their hunting trips the Samoyeds carried letters from the Norwegians to their relatives. In this way Birkeland received a letter in Christiania, several months after it had been written, that contained alarming reports of the conditions on the inhospitable island. The weather was utterly unpredictable. Temperatures were often in the minus thirties Celsius and could reach as low as −42°C. Strange effects in changing wind or barometer pressure meant the ice floes in the straits would freeze and flow again with great rapidity and no warning. Sæland had narrowly missed being trapped on the island because only a few days after he sailed away the straits froze over during a snowstorm. When their supplies of fresh food ran low, the three men decided to go hunting, a decision that nearly cost them their lives. The team leader wrote:

> We left in a rowing boat and landed on the far side of a little river that could be easily waded. The boat was moored to the bank. Within hours and without warning a terrible storm broke out, with thunder and lightning which was very unusual in those parts. On returning to the boat several hours later the effect of the storm was frighteningly visible. The small stream had become a veritable foaming torrent and the entire tongue of land on which the boat had lain had been washed away.

Birkeland was appalled at the danger the men had put themselves in for the sake of a more varied diet. Memories of Boye's death made him pray that the young men had not hurt themselves.

> It was clear, however, that we must at all costs manage to get home. The fare was not first-class, it consisted of one dish— raw bird. With some old rope and driftwood we made a kind of raft and also found some boards that could be used as oars. It was an exceedingly poor vessel; even when we all three rowed with all our might it made only the slowest progress. When we got into the river current we were carried rapidly out to sea and were soon several kilometers from shore. The worst of it was that the raft began to fall to pieces, so that one man had to hold it together with his feet and hands while the others rowed. After a hard struggle we reached an iceberg that was at least grounded and did not drift. Once more we took the oars and were fortunate enough to get into the counter-current, which carried us shoreward. Once we reached terra firma we saw how great the danger had been, for a fog as dense as a wall came pouring down from the north. If this had come a little sooner,

while we were rowing, it is highly probable we would have rowed in a circle while the current took us farther and farther out.

Birkeland wondered whether the young men were paying enough attention to the scientific goals of the trip or only to hunting and befriending the Samoyeds. The polar bear would arrive in late February and he suspected there would be gaps in the recordings for those weeks. He was correct in his hunch. When the team eventually returned from Novaya Zemlya, Schaaning had amassed a huge collection of rare Arctic birds, eggs, and polar bear hides that he started selling to museums across Europe. Birkeland told him that he could either receive his wages or the income from hunting, but not both. Schaaning opted for the latter and made a great deal of money.

Facing even harsher weather conditions was the group in the station at Axeløen, southern Spitsbergen. The leader of the team was Nils Russeltveldt, who had been recruited from the Meteorological Institute in Christiania and who was managing to obtain excellent results from his instruments despite the climate. It was impossible to send a letter from the island but Russeltveldt wrote a report upon his return:

> It must be in great measure due to the tremendously varying conditions of weather that the immense loss of life on Spitsbergen is due. It is no exaggeration to say that all round about our station is one great graveyard. It is for this reason that no one of late has ventured to winter in Spitsbergen; it is only during the last three or four years that it has been done once more, for the polar bear hunting. While we were building the instrument house a hurricane blew up so strongly that it was impossible to stand upright. It was a regular Spitsbergen storm in all its wildness and greatness. We were awakened by the roar and noise occasioned by wind, ice and rain. The

wind varied incessantly; at one moment there was none, or a slight breeze, the next it was blowing the wildest hurricane. It was these fearful gusts of wind that were dangerous to anyone going out, for it was impossible to keep one's balance and gravel, snow and stones were whirled about.

Although we managed to finish it, the hut was torn to pieces and a huge wooden panel hurled a hundred meters away. It will be easily understood that weather such as this places enormous difficulties in the way of observation.

Birkeland's teams in the field were the human link in the chain of instruments around the Arctic Circle. They did not interpret the results, but their dedication and tenacity in the face of extreme conditions determined how successful the different stations were. They made the bricks, foraged for the stones, and brought them to the building site where Birkeland would use them to construct his theories. If there were too many blocks missing, the house would be prone to collapse. Birkeland believed that observing nature should be the starting point of any investigation into the Earth's mysteries and that the expedition would provide him with all the details he needed as long as his teams could work accurately under the difficult conditions.

Although Birkeland was proud of his men and of the scale of this expedition, he knew it was time to test his theories experimentally. He needed to build his own laboratory to see if he could discover the scientific formula that defined the drama and beauty of the Northern Lights. To build a laboratory from scratch would require a huge amount of money, more than he would ever be granted by Parliament, the university, or private donors. He would have to raise the money himself, a daunting task for a professor on a modest salary. Birkeland, however, had one opportunity to raise a significant sum: his invention of the electromagnetic cannon. He began to plan how the gun could make his fortune.

PART II

The Terrella

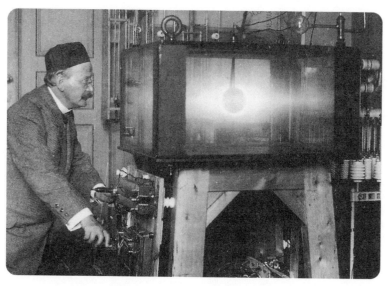

Kristian Birkeland with his terrella machine simulating the Zodiacal
Light in the laboratory at Christiania University, around 1910

8

Explosion!

6 March 1903
University of Christiania,
Festival Hall

They have driven me almost mad
And forced me to curse my fate,
  Some of them with their love,
  Some of them with their hate.

They have poisoned the cup I drank,
They have poisoned the food I ate,
  Some of them with their love,
  Some of them with their hate.

HEINRICH HEINE (1797–1856), C. 1827

OR THREE DAYS, *Aftenposten* had been running advertisements for an unusual gala lecture to be held on the evening of 6 March in the university's Festival Hall. There were few attractions to rival such entertainment, for although Christiania was developing quickly, its cinema would not be finished until the following year and the choice of evening amusement was limited to musical recitals, the theater in season, and occasional séances. Now the trampled snow outside the building was illuminated in squares by light escaping through the blazing windows. Figures in top hats and wasp-waisted skirts were silhouetted against the light as they mounted the flight of steps to the columned entrance. Christiania's elite was in attendance—men from shipping, mining, the railways, the telegraph, politics, banking, and newspapers in a sea of black and white punctuated occasionally by their more decorative wives. Professor Birkeland had arranged this unusual lecture to unveil to a waiting public his electromagnetic cannon. Although there had been many articles and even drawings in the press about his invention, only his shareholders and a few weapons makers in Europe had so far been able to see it.

Birkeland's prime motivation in demonstrating the cannon was to obtain the funds to turn his dream of "domesticating" the aurora into a reality. He needed money to build and equip a modern laboratory as the only facilities in the entire country were at the university; they were used solely for teaching and contained only rudimentary equipment. His plan was to raise 50,000 crowns from the lecture to build a longer gun that would send larger missiles, up to two tons, shorter distances but at faster speeds, turning the cannon into an electromagnetic torpedo to be fired from a ship just above the surface of the water. Birkeland was aware not only of the escalating naval arms race between Germany and Britain in particular, but also of the limitations in his design—which necessitated a large power source nearby. In a land battle this would be difficult, but on a ship it would be much simpler to connect the torpedoes to generators in the engine rooms.

Although several companies had shown interest in buying his patent the previous year while the gun was still in an early phase of development, he could not have commanded a high enough price to be able to fund his scientific research. The board of Birkeland's Firearms agreed to postpone selling the patent until the torpedo design was ready for demonstration, but they were not in a position to fund its development. So Birkeland had decided upon this lecture to promote the project; he was convinced that if the gala proved successful, he would solve his money worries for years to come. Looking around the rows of dignitaries, Birkeland felt sure he would have pledges for 50,000 crowns by the end of the night. The front row alone included Gunnar Knudsen, the minister of defense, the head of the army, the head of Coastal Artillery, the commander in chief of Central Operations, members of Parliament, several Danish military officers, and representatives of the companies who had already shown interest in the cannon, including Armstrong and Krupp. Behind them sat a number of university professors and Birkeland's friends and supporters—Amund Helland, his cousin Richard, his old math teacher Elling Holst, several of the women with whom he grew up in Langes Gate and for whom he was a prodigal son, the Mohn family, and, despite her dislike of weaponry, Ida.

To create more space for the audience, Birkeland had put the large generator needed to power the cannon in the university gardens behind the hall, and had cordoned off a narrow corridor between the gun and the thirteen-centimeter-thick wooden target, although Fridtjof Nansen placed himself within the danger area and refused to move. When the ornate lecture theater and balcony above were full to capacity, Birkeland instructed Sæland to close the doors and took his place before the audience. As he looked down to collect his thoughts, Birkeland noticed that he was standing in the heart of a mosaic of the sun, set in gold tiles into the floor. He was not a superstitious man, far from it, but seeing his feet haloed by rays of light filled him with hope for a successful evening. After welcoming his audience to the demonstration, he briefly explained the principles of the cannon using a large diagram. An instinctive showman when demonstrating scientific devices, Birkeland built up the tension by reassuring the gathered audience that they would neither hear nor see anything except the noise of the ten-kilo projectile hitting the target, so they should not be afraid.

Birkeland took his time walking from the podium to the gun, building up an atmosphere of anticipation. With one final look around the audience, he repeated that the gun would be totally silent and that there was no need for alarm. He then pulled down the starting switch on the cannon. Chaos ensued. An almighty roar filled the hall, a large flame issued from the mouth of the cannon, and a deafening hiss accompanied a huge arc of brilliant light that shot out toward the audience. The 3,000-amp current had short-circuited in the gun with the most dramatic results. Several people in the audience panicked and the hall emptied in a few minutes, despite Birkeland's shouts that there was no danger. As he related to an assistant later, "It was the most dramatic moment of my life. With this missile, I shot my stock down from a value of 300 crowns to zero, although it did hit the bull's-eye!"

Overnight, Birkeland became the talk of the capital, though not in the way he intended. The cannon had been a potential source of huge wealth, not only for the original investors but also for the nation that would have manufactured it. The spectacle of Birkeland's grandiose scheme backfiring was less than welcome for the numerous dignitaries gathered in the front rows: any event that made Norway a laughingstock was regarded as a major setback in the struggle for independence. It was also a huge blow to Birkeland's hopes of building his own laboratory.

Birkeland transported the burnt-out gun back to his office and retired to think. Sæland expected him to sink into a black mood but the professor seemed more intrigued by the event than depressed and appraised the whole debacle with good-natured calm. Many of his colleagues kept away, embarrassed for him. Others were secretly pleased by the failure of his latest enterprise. His commercial aspirations for the technological inventions that sprang forth from his unusually broad scientific abilities created resentment among less resourceful professors who had no such opportunities or who failed to spot them. It would have been a simple task for Birkeland to modify his gun to prevent the short-circuits, but the explosion helped him to make a decision. The cannon was not the only application for this technology—there was another use for it that might prove more lucrative, if more time-consuming.

An idea had taken shape the previous month during a dinner party to which Gunnar Knudsen had invited Birkeland upon his return from the auroral expedition in Kaafjord. Sitting opposite him was a man Birkeland was intrigued to meet, Sam Eyde, about whom he had heard a great deal through his work with the hydro-electric industry. Eyde had established a company to buy Norwegian waterfalls on which to build hydroelectric power stations, in collaboration with Swedish financiers whom he had met through his very advantageous marriage to a Swedish countess, Anna Ulrika Morner of Morlanda. He had bought two of Norway's major waterfalls the previous year, the Rjukan Falls on the upper course of the Skien River and the Vamma Falls on the Glomma, Norway's longest river. Birkeland had heard that Eyde intended to use these massive sources of cheap electricity to power new industrial enterprises and had been working on furnaces for iron or aluminum production. He was a man of broad vision with an American attitude to time and talent; he promoted young engineers, was the first to chant "time is money," and had no patience with old-fashioned bureaucracy or traditional niceties.

Although he was only a little taller than Birkeland, Eyde was powerfully built, with plump cheeks, dark almond-shaped eyes, an olive complexion, and a large mustache that curled up at the ends. He was graying at the temples but the rest of his curly crop was combed back from his forehead and held approximately in place with hair oil. He smoked slim cigars; on his left hand he wore a large gold wedding band and on his little finger a chunky signet ring. Eyde exuded an air of charm and unshakable confidence. In between courses, a conversation began among the landowners, shipping magnates, politicians, and other distinguished guests around Knudsen's table about the crisis looming in Europe over the shortage of fertilizer. At that time the sole agricultural fertilizer available in Europe was a natural sodium nitrate mined in Chile called "Chile saltpeter." In 1898 Sir William Crookes, an eminent scientist and president of the British Association for the Advancement of Science, had drawn popular attention to the "near exhaustion of the world's stock of fixed nitrogen," the rapid emptying of the

Chilean mines, and the impossibility of feeding the world's population without fertilizer. He noted that demand for saltpeter had increased fourfold in the previous twenty years to 1.5 million tons annually and added that "at the rate required to augment the world's supply of wheat to the point demanded thirty years hence, it will not last more than four years."

Throughout the previous decade knowledge that the sources of natural fertilizer were running dry had sparked off an intense search to find alternatives. It was well known that ordinary air contained nitrogen and oxygen, which, when combined using high temperatures, became the main components of fertilizer, but furnaces to extract them in a usable form were proving difficult to develop. Birkeland had followed the process with interest. He explained to the dinner guests that all attempts to produce fertilizer on an industrial scale had failed. Eyde, whose interests were in construction and industry, not agriculture, remained silent until Birkeland mentioned furnaces. He inquired what type of furnace was required and Birkeland explained that it should be capable of reproducing the power of lightning on Earth. The strange smell left in the air after a lightning flash was of nitrogen being oxidized by the intense energy of the bolt—exactly the process needed to make fertilizer.

Eyde had been planning to develop smelting furnaces that needed very high amounts of energy, which he could provide with his waterfalls. If Birkeland's explanation was correct, the same was true of artificial fertilizer production. Producing gold from air was every businessman's dream, and Eyde, who more than most had his sights firmly on economic and social success, understood that finding a solution to the fertilizer crisis would bring him fame as well as profit.

When the ladies retired to the drawing room and the gentlemen stood around the fire, drinking whisky and smoking cigars, Birkeland approached Eyde and said, "I have the solution." He explained that his cannon, of which Eyde was already aware through Knudsen, produced high-energy electric arcs if it short-circuited during testing—arcs exactly like bolts of lightning. Birkeland believed this faulty element of his gun design could be combined with electromagnetic furnace technology to ionize air and produce nitric acid. Eyde listened intently, knowing that his ownership of two of Norway's largest waterfalls gave him the leverage to persuade investors to support the development of a furnace to create fertilizer. Both men fought off the temptation to leave the dinner party immediately to inspect Birkeland's cannon; a meeting was arranged for Monday morning, in Birkeland's office.

Birkeland stayed at the university all weekend, looking at the patents for his cannon and sketching new designs that would deliberately create the electric arcs that accidentally occurred during tests. He already had a small electric furnace that he had bought with Brøgger five years before to do some experiments with the composition and formation of rocks in order to find traces of radioactivity and the possible effects on crystal formation of electric currents in the earth. They had not had an opportunity to use the furnace, and it was still in its box with the company name on the side, Wiesenegg of Paris, and the price tag attached—128 crowns. Birkeland hoped it would help him make a great deal more money than that. The furnace, although small, was already equipped with the electrodes needed to make an arc of electricity. He had the weekend in which to design a mechanism that would allow air in and out of the furnace and to retrieve the large electromagnets in the physics laboratory to place around it. His idea was that the electromagnets would draw the arc of electricity into a wide semicircle, much larger than would occur without magnetic influence. He was surprised that he had not thought of using the electromagnetic technology he understood so well to create a fertilizer furnace before. It was not a new idea. Two British scientists, Priestley and Cavendish, who produced tiny amounts of "nitrous acid" using electric sparks, had made the first attempt in 1780. More recently, two Americans, Bradley and Lovejoy, had built a small factory beside Niagara Falls to produce saltpeter at the end of 1902, but their attempt had proved too inefficient to form the basis of a new industry. A description of their furnace had been included in the first edition of a Norwegian scientific publication, *Electrochem Industri*, launched only the previous month; Birkeland studied the drawings in the new magazine to check that his idea was different, and therefore potentially more rewarding, than theirs. He saw that they had made a myriad of tiny arcs in their furnace, while Birkeland was planning one large arc, repeated at a high rate and swept sideways by the magnetic field to make contact with as much air as possible. It would look like a circle with the shape and heat of the sun.

The following Monday Eyde and Birkeland spent the morning together at the university, inspecting the strange-looking furnace and weighing each other up as potential business collaborators. The first prototype, cobbled together in a few hours, beautifully demonstrated Birkeland's idea of using magnetism to make large electric arcs and the tremendous noise and smell it produced were persuasive testimony to its potential. Birkeland was wary of telling Eyde too much about the principles upon which the design was based as Eyde was trained as an engineer and could potentially steal his ideas. Eyde had less to fear from the professor—no one could appropriate his waterfalls or business contacts—but he wanted to be sure Birkeland was not bluffing. Birkeland's main preoccupation, until Knudsen's dinner party, had been with weaponry, not fertilizer, and his collaboration with Eyde could be a ruse to interest Eyde's commercial contacts in the cannon. Equally, if Birkeland was happy to swap from one idea to another so easily, he might do the same later if a seemingly better invention occurred to him. The hours passed in cautious and provisional exchange, the professor answering some of Eyde's questions about the method of creating the electric arcs and in turn asking Eyde about financing, power provision, and how a company could be organized. By lunchtime, they decided to sign an agreement to take out a joint patent the following day.

As soon as Eyde had left the university, Birkeland called Gunnar Knudsen and asked to meet him that evening. He needed to know more about Eyde before collaborating and sharing the profits with him on an idea that was entirely his own. When he arrived at Knudsen's house, he did not tell him exactly what he and Eyde were considering working on, as Knudsen was one of the main shareholders in the cannon and Birkeland did not want him to think he had given up on that project. Knudsen seemed content with Birkeland's evasive explanations and told him what he knew about Samuel Eyde. They had first met when Eyde moved to Christiania from Lübeck in Germany in 1898 and set up S. Eyde's Engineering Office, which soon became one of the largest in Scandinavia with thirty full-time engineers. Eyde and his German colleague, Gleim, had won the contract to build the new railway stations of Christiania and Stockholm, worth nearly 53 million crowns. However, the economic crash of 1898 had badly affected the construction industry and, as soon as the stations were finished the previous autumn, Eyde had been forced to lay off all his engineers. Birkeland now understood the reason for the urgency Eyde had demonstrated to make progress on the fertilizer furnace: his business was in crisis. Eyde's father had gone bankrupt when Eyde was a schoolboy and Knudsen felt that his tremendous ambition was partly due to not wanting history to repeat itself. Knudsen would not have picked out Birkeland and Eyde as potential collaborators but each man held vital cards and a trade was the only way forward. He advised Birkeland to proceed with the venture, exercising caution to ensure his interests were secured.

The following afternoon Birkeland went to Eyde's office at 20 Rådhus Street, next to the National Bank of Norway and close to the harbor. Although the large sign above the entrance announced "S. Eyde's Engineering Office" and another "Gleim and Eyde Construction," the office was empty except for his secretary, an attractive woman in her late twenties whom Eyde introduced as Tara

Kjørstad. Birkeland was shown a legal document that Eyde had drafted, a formal agreement in which credit for inventing the furnace was given entirely to Birkeland, who was named as "inventor," but both Birkeland and Eyde were named as owners of the invention.

> Mr. Professor Kr. Birkeland, Christiania
> According to our agreement today I confirm with this, the agreement between us, that we together shall apply for patent for the process invented by you [Birkeland] to, by means of electric arcs, produce nitrogen compounds or other chemical compounds of air or other gas combinations.

Birkeland was deeply unhappy about having to share credit with Eyde, who had no part in the technical development of the idea, but he was forced to collaborate because only Eyde had access to the huge amounts of electric power that would be needed to run the furnaces. Birkeland knew his position as inventor was tenuous. With Eyde's name on the patent as well as his own, and Eyde's money and contacts in the business and banking worlds, Birkeland knew he would be easy to sideline once the furnaces were developed and his expertise was no longer needed. Eyde himself was well aware of this and believed he could nudge Birkeland into a nominal consultative role as soon as the furnaces were productive.

The two men shook hands and Birkeland agreed to submit his designs to Alfred Bryn for a joint patent on Friday, 20 February. He asked Bryn to keep quiet about the application as he did not want rumor spreading that he was working on a furnace for fear of inciting competition. He also still had hopes for the cannon and did not want his shareholders to suspect him of divided loyalty, but for the time being the furnace seemed more likely to provide him with the resources he needed to build a laboratory. With some misgivings he asked Bryn to lodge the application with the Christiania Patent Office.

Explosion!

On the back of his copy of the agreement Birkeland wrote:

This contract states that Eyde is joint-owner of the invention
but that I am the sole inventor. This document is for historical interest in case Eyde tries to take the whole credit. Kr. B.

From the start, the collaboration between Birkeland and Eyde
was riddled with suspicion and doubt, and it proved to be more
damaging than Birkeland ever imagined.

9

The Furnace

7 August 1903
Frogner Bay factory, West Christiania

I have never known any other man so engaged with science with such reckless devotion. His capacity for research was part of his innermost mind, it fascinated him and made him work far beyond the resources a human constitution can tolerate without being worn out too early.

SEM SÆLAND, memorial address, 22 September 1919

IRKELAND marched around the edge of the fjord, west of Christiania, oblivious to everything around him except the rays of the August sun warming his body, which ached from months spent in a cramped workshop. It was the day of the first official trial of the fertilizer furnace. If the furnace produced saltpeter, the project would continue; if not, there was no further money to develop it and the attempt would have to be abandoned. Everything rested on this test. Birkeland, whose nerves were already strained from the heavy workload, could not bear to stand and watch while his assistant engineer, Eivind Næss, ran the furnace.

Birkeland looked very different from the man who had submitted the first patent for the furnace in February. The past six months of intense pressure had taken their toll on him: although only thirty-five, he looked ten years older. He was pale and drawn, and his clothes were baggy on his weak frame as he rarely left the workshop in time to enjoy the summer sunshine or to exercise. At weekends, he went to his university office to continue work on the gun or on switching mechanisms for the power stations, neither of which he felt he could abandon until he achieved positive results with the furnace. One of those ideas had to bear fruit, and allow him to pursue his science beyond debilitating financial constraints.

Birkeland decided that he no longer had time to attend the Sunday lectures with Ida. He explained to her that, for the next few months, he would be completely preoccupied with a project to avert the agricultural crisis in Europe. He emphasized the importance of his task in the hope that she would understand that he had no choice but to stop seeing her for a while. In the face of such a mission, Ida knew she could not make claims upon his time. She took the tram and train back to Lillestrøm, twenty kilometers east of the city, to her school, wondering if this was merely an excuse to terminate their friendship. Birkeland was aware that this was how it must seem to her but he believed he had to choose between his work and seeing Ida. It never occurred to him not to concentrate wholly on his work.

In late February Eyde and Birkeland had set up an unlimited company, Birkeland's Risk Venture, under the aegis of which Eyde would finance experiments conducted by Birkeland to develop the furnace. During March and April Birkeland began small-scale tests with the furnace design at the university but soon his office became too small and hot to work in. Carl Anton, father of his childhood friend Wilhelm Bjerkenes, told him about a group of warehouses and small factories producing electrical equipment on the western side of the city, by the fjord's edge, called Frogner Bay. Carl Anton had himself established a makeshift laboratory there a few years before and thought it would suit Birkeland's needs. Birkeland moved his prototype furnaces there at the end of May and was joined by Eivind Næss, who had worked on the Christiania railway terminus but had been laid off with all the other engineers at the end of the project. Eyde had told Næss to call on Birkeland, but had given him no details about the task he was needed for. When Birkeland asked Næss whether he was an electrician, Næss confessed that he was only an ordinary construction engineer. "No matter," Birkeland replied, and in that way Næss came to be Birkeland's chief assistant at the Frogner Bay factory.

"Factory" was a grand name for what was essentially a large wooden shed in a junkyard. It had been hurriedly erected in cheap timber planks with a rusting corrugated-iron roof and Birkeland had to pick his way past piles of splintered wood, broken chairs, old packing cases, and anonymous pieces of rusting metal to reach the factory door. A wooden pole lashed to one side of the building supported the electric cables and white enamel insulators that brought power from a small electricity plant nearby. On warm days the sun's rays beat down on the iron roof and combined with the heat from the furnace to broil the two men inside. Birkeland wore a straw boater to work and kept it pushed to the back of his head throughout the day, refusing to remove it because he felt it protected his head from the heat. Both men wore suits, stiff white collars, and cravats in the workshop despite the dirty, sweaty work they had to do.

The interior was as makeshift as the rest of the building. The walls were unplastered, the roof not insulated, and bare wires ran across the roof joists and hung down into the room like black vines. The furnace was in the center, attached to pumps, magnets, and generators, like the heart of a living organism. Næss had never worked with an experimental physicist using high voltages before. Birkeland warned him of the dangers; he described how flames shot out of the mouth and stomach of an electrocuted person and their insides were liquefied. The guilt and loss he felt over the death of young Boye had instilled in Birkeland a need to keep people safe in his hazardous domain. After the stern advice, Birkeland explained the principles of the design.

The furnace would use a 50-hertz alternating current between two electrodes to produce electric arcs that moved outward in a semicircle under the influence of a strong magnetic field created in the furnace by a number of large electromagnets. These arcs formed, spread sideways, broke, and reformed fifty times a second or more. The alternating current caused the polarity of the electrodes to change, making the arcs flip from one side to the other so fast that they seemed to create a continuous glowing disc with a temperature of 3,000° Celsius. Once the furnace was working properly, ordinary air containing 79 percent nitrogen (N_2) and 21 percent oxygen (O_2) would be pumped over this disc, the heat of which would force the molecules to move about so fast that they would collide and cause the usually stable N_2 to combine with oxygen to form nitrogen oxide, NO_2. The resulting gas would be mixed with water to create nitric acid (HNO_3) and trickled over limestone (calcium carbonate, $CaCO_3$) with which it would react to make $Ca(NO_3)_2$, calcium nitrate, called saltpeter by Birkeland, although that term usually referred to potassium nitrate, an important component in explosives. Schoolboys knew the components of air; the brilliance of Birkeland's discovery lay in the use of large electromagnets to force the arcs of electricity outward so that they created a disc of sufficient size to make potentially profitable the ratio of energy used to saltpeter produced. To the eye, the disc would glow with the constancy of the sun; only the loud, pulsating roar made as each arc formed would reveal that the disc was an illusion created by rapidly moving individual arcs. The disc would be fully enclosed in firebricks and a metal case, although their working model was protected only by a wall of firebricks that had to be removed and replaced every time an alteration was made.

There were a number of problems with the design that needed to be solved and the two men worked from early in the morning until eleven or twelve at night and occasionally for thirty-six hours at a stretch. They would build, test, and dismantle the 28-kilowatt furnace each day, having to develop from scratch not only every component, but whole new systems and methods. They had no predecessors to guide them; everything was new and unknown. Many nights they locked the factory, disappointed that no progress had been made other than that of eliminating failed possibilities. On other days, a new part or arrangement bore fruit and took them one step closer to a finished design.

Næss and Birkeland were very different in character. Birkeland arrived most mornings with new ideas to try and tremendous enthusiasm for the pure science they were witnessing. Næss was more pragmatic, testing each idea thoroughly and recording the results before moving on to the next, like a policeman eliminating suspects one by one rather than using his intuition to find the culprit. Although Birkeland found Næss's attention to detail a little frustrating, he realized it had value and the two coexisted contentedly although without the trust and camaraderie Birkeland had experienced during the winter with his assistants on the Haldde summit. Næss was Eyde's employee, loyal to Eyde, not motivated by Birkeland's inspirational science.

During these months of trial and error, Eyde managed to finance the cost of the premises, electricity, and materials, though he did not tell Birkeland how. He traveled abroad nearly every month to develop contacts and keep his name current among the financial elite on the continent. He would work on the train, ship, and carriage and late into the evening if necessary, frequently calling his lawyer, Birkeland, or Næss after dinner and demanding that they come for a meeting immediately. Birkeland complied initially, believing the calls to be urgent, but he soon learned to ignore the phone in the evenings when he realized that Eyde simply expected others to be working if he was. To the great irritation of his wife, Næss regularly had to leave the dinner table to respond to the summons. Eyde came to the factory weekly to inspect their progress and never failed to tell them not to spend more than was necessary. Birkeland was not being paid and Næss's wages were terribly low, although he did not complain: jobs for engineers were very scarce and he was happy to have work at all.

Eyde put tremendous pressure on Birkeland to get the furnace working fast. He had heard through his contacts in Germany that Badische Annilin und Soda Fabrik (BASF) was also developing a design for a nitrate furnace that the engineer Otto Schönherr had been working on since 1897. BASF was a large company, founded in 1861 to produce artificial indigo, with ample funds for research and development, an industrial giant compared to the tiny Birkeland's Risk Venture, into which Eyde poured the meager sums he was able to find; Birkeland used the funds immediately for developing the furnace.

Closeted in the dark and steamy factory that made his head and lungs ache, Birkeland was working so hard that he did not even stop to welcome back his teams from the Arctic Circle in late July. Sæland had to find him at Frogner Bay to tell him everyone had returned safely. Though desperate to hear their news, look at the results they had achieved, and start using them to develop his theories, Birkeland had to test the fertilizer furnace ten days later. The furnace had to take priority, so there was no choice but to make the huge sacrifice of postponing seeing the expedition members.

The sacrifice, however, was worth it. On the test day Birkeland entered the dark, intensely pungent workshop and saw Næss swirling a milky white solution around a shallow pan, grinning broadly. Birkeland stared at the evil-smelling liquid and shouted, "Good! Now we are getting rich." He telegraphed the news to Eyde, who was in Stockholm visiting his wife's family:

7 AUGUST 1903. CHRISTIANIA. SALTPETRE PRODUCED.

The news came just in time, as there was no more money to fund the research if the trial failed and Eyde was dependent on the fertilizer furnace to keep him from bankruptcy. As soon as he received the telegram, he telephoned some of the influential Swedish financiers he had met through his wife. The first call was to Knut Tillberg, the Swedish banker who had helped Eyde buy waterfalls and had put 35,000 crowns into Birkeland's Risk Venture in July along with the Swedish consul, Niels Persson. Each had been given a quarter of the company in return, but the money was now spent. Eyde needed Tillberg to use his influence with the Swedish Bank to persuade them to back the company. Tillberg tried and failed, but he did manage to persuade the scion of the Swedish banking family and one of the richest men in the world, Marcus Wallenberg, director of the Swedish Independent Bank, to show interest. Wallenberg promised to look at how the company could be financed, but none of Eyde's Swedish contacts was ready to put more money into the company immediately. Eyde refused to give up just when they had managed to produce saltpeter, albeit in small quantities.

A few weeks later he traveled to Germany with Birkeland to meet Otto Witt, a consultant to BASF, in an effort to persuade Witt to interest BASF in funding the further development of Birkeland's furnace in tandem with Schönherr's design. Witt thought Birkeland's design showed potential, but BASF decided that their Norwegian rivals were nothing to fear and refused to cooperate, assuming that they could buy them out at a later date if it became necessary. Having come to an impasse, the two men returned to Christiania, Eyde to continue searching for backers and Birkeland to his office, finally, to hear the news about the Aurora Polaris Expedition.

Sæland was reinstalled at his desk in Birkeland's office, surrounded by boxes of magnetograms and piles of recording ledgers, trying to put them in some sort of order for the time when Birkeland would be able to start processing the information they contained. The professor was delighted to have him back and for the first time in months he sat down and relaxed, listening to Sæland describe his ten months in Iceland. The experience had clearly been grueling and, at times, dangerous but the expedition appeared to have been a great success. Birkeland looked rapidly through the magnetograms from the four stations. From this evidence, he felt sure he would be able to map the movement of magnetic storms around the polar region for the first time, and judge more accurately not only the way in which electric currents drove these storms but also how they entered the Earth's magnetic field from the sun.

Birkeland explained to Sæland and Dietrichson, who also shared his office, that he intended to use these results in conjunction with laboratory experiments to try to re-create the interaction that he believed was taking place between the sun and the Earth. From his desk he pulled out sheets of diagrams he had made before he was swamped by the fertilizer project and handed them to Dietrichson, asking him to give an opinion on the feasibility of making the instrument depicted. He had christened it the terrella, "little Earth," a term Gilbert had used for the lodestones he used to determine the magnetic nature of the Earth. At a cursory glance, Dietrichson could see that the terrella consisted of a magnetized metal ball (Earth) within a large vacuum tube (space) at one end of which was a cathode to send out electric particles (the sun). He was excited by the notion of the experiment and agreed to make detailed plans. Sæland would start processing the results from the field trips to provide Birkeland with the information he needed along with his machine. It was impossible for Sæland to do more than scratch the surface of the material on his own but for the time being there was no money to hire assistants, to build the machine, or to construct even a basic laboratory. In order to obtain money, Birkeland would have to work on the furnace for at least another six months and they would have to continue alone, following his guidelines.

Sæland and Dietrichson were amazed at Birkeland's stamina and his ability to juggle several projects at once. Now that the saltpeter had been produced, however, Birkeland stopped working on switching mechanisms for the hydroelectric industry—he simply did not have time—but he kept the gun project simmering, writing letters to potentially interested parties and improving its design. In July he had corresponded with a British woman, Lady Sander, in Geneva, proposing to develop the gun full-time if he could be released from the university. He suggested that the British could purchase a world monopoly on the design, at a certain price. He had also received an enthusiastic letter from Major Edward Palliser, who wanted more information about the gun and proposed a meeting with Birkeland. Although nothing developed further from those contacts, Birkeland had come so close to enjoying a huge success with his cannon that he was loath to abandon it entirely.

Birkeland's brief respite from the furnace came to an abrupt end at the beginning of September when Eyde returned to Christiania having made a new deal without consulting him. Eyde had created a new company, which did not use Birkeland's name but was called the Norwegian Nitrogen Company, in which Tillberg and Persson had invested 400,000 crowns each. They had then issued shares to the value of 100,000 crowns, which Wallenberg had bought. Birkeland still owned one-fifth of the shares, as stated in his previous contract with Birkeland's Risk Venture, but he had less control in this larger company. He questioned the wisdom of having such a strong Swedish interest in the project given the tense situation between the two countries, but Eyde ignored him.

The Frogner Bay factory was too cramped for Birkeland to produce an industrial-size furnace and so they moved to a transformer station at Ankerløkken in the northwest district of Christiania. Eyde put tremendous pressure on Birkeland to make a prototype to secure investment and recoup expenses before the German competition entered the fray. Birkeland, Næss, and Dr. Birger Halvorsen, a chemist engaged to work on the gases produced by the furnace, worked every day, including Sundays, inspired by the dedication Birkeland showed for the task. Throughout the autumn and winter the men stopped only for two days at Christmas. Birkeland had been invited to spend the holiday with his brother and nine nieces and nephews, but had to decline. The Mohns asked him to have Christmas dinner with them and Birkeland went, but if he had hoped Ida would be there he was disappointed, as she had returned to Raade to be with her family.

The new year was spent in making further tests and improvements. The strain on the men was beginning to show. Næss, in his methodological manner, followed a prearranged testing program even if the results obtained were disappointing. Birkeland would jettison carefully laid plans in an instant if a better idea occurred to him. The contrast in styles led to tension and disagreement. Birkeland came to see Næss as Eyde's "spy," who questioned his decisions and kept his paymaster informed of progress. The furnace was limiting his imagination and depressing his spirits: he was forbidden by Eyde to discuss it outside the workshop for fear of aiding competitors, although he was usually so drained by the heat and noise at work that going out in the evenings was impossible anyway. Birkeland was beginning to suffer from the pressure he was under. He had worked every weekend and not taken a holiday, even the two weeks he usually escaped abroad from the freezing, dark January. In less than one year he had made more progress than BASF had done in six and yet Eyde was still barking for faster results. Birkeland hated the twilight of the Norwegian winter, the intense cold and the difficulties of getting around in the snow, and since the autumn, his insomnia had returned and headaches and restlessness plagued him. Now, incessantly harried and criticized by Eyde, he came to feel like a hired hand in the service of Eyde's vision of a commercial megalith. This, combined with his deliberate marginalization by Eyde, made him decide to submit all the patents for the furnace in his own name, despite the fact that he had signed an agreement with Eyde that ownership of the patents would be shared. He was aware that this would cause problems when he was found out, but his ideas were his only currency.

Eyde noticed Birkeland's pallor and agitation on his regular inspections and, making discreet inquiries about the professor's health to acquaintances at the university, was informed that Birkeland had been prone to "nervous freezing fits" since his student days. Eyde took this to mean that Birkeland's mental health was fragile and he became worried that progress on the furnace might be slowed if he broke under the strain. He began to plan how he could edge the unpredictable professor out of the company now that most of the theoretical work was accomplished. He quietly wrote to his contacts in Sweden to find an engineer who could replace Birkeland should the need arise and took every opportunity to cement his position as head of the saltpeter enterprise with the shareholders. He told Wallenberg that Næss found Birkeland exasperating; Eyde made references to Birkeland's fragile state of health and raised questions about his reliability now that the project had progressed to a more serious level. Wallenberg agreed to help Eyde look for a replacement engineer.

While Birkeland sweated over the furnace's performance, Eyde sought larger investors to risk capital on developing industrial-scale furnaces and to build a hydroelectric plant on one of his waterfalls to power it. Wallenberg, Tillberg, and Persson were bankrolling the expensive experiments for the time being but their resources were not limitless. It was a difficult balancing act, asking for money for a process that was not yet proven to work on an industrial scale but that needed investment to make it happen. Most financiers were excited by the possibility of a compound that every farmer needed but doubted that the Birkeland furnace would work any better than other methods that had been tried and failed. Eyde needed to speed up the development of the furnace even more. At the beginning of February he wrote to Wallenberg to request that an engineer be sent from Sweden. He wanted more control over the technical aspects of the company and could not achieve that while Birkeland was in charge of the workshop.

The following week, engineer Lindström arrived with Wallenberg and, in a move calculated to tie Birkeland's hands, Eyde took them to inspect the Ankerløkken site. The professor could not object to Lindström's presence in front of Wallenberg but he was clearly shocked that a new engineer had been engaged without his approval. Birkeland showed Lindström the furnace and the absorption system and answered his many questions, but when they left he simply nodded goodbye. Eyde knew that Birkeland would be incensed by this betrayal and further annoyed that he was introducing so many Swedish elements into the company. While Birkeland was not prejudiced against individual Swedes, he would have preferred finance to come from sources other than their oppressor in the Union. He had once written to Bjerkenes, "We will show the Swedes who is boss" after Bjerkenes had delivered a particularly good lecture in Stockholm; Eyde's familiarity with Swedish bankers was undermining this sentiment.

Two days after Lindström's visit, Birkeland collapsed. His housekeeper called his brother, Tønnes, who arrived the following day to find Birkeland in bed, shivering and incomprehensible. Empty bottles of whisky had been pushed under the bedside table and a half-full one stood on top. Tønnes realized his brother was suffering from nervous exhaustion brought on by unrelenting work and that his depression had returned. He went to the local pharmacy and asked for a gentle sleeping powder and a tonic. The pharmacist advised him of a new product that had just been launched, veronal, considered safe enough to buy without prescription. It was produced by Bayer, a reputable German pharmaceutical company. Tønnes read the label carefully:

Veronal—Recommended to be given in hot tea or water. The compound has a soporific action indicated in nervous restlessness, insomnia and depression, for maniacs and in cardiac troubles. Does not affect temperature or respiration. May cause erythema [superficial reddening of the skin in patches]. Produces sleep without subsequent depression.

The pharmacist explained that veronal was diethyl barbituric acid, measured in grains of white crystalline powder and that five to ten grains would promote sleep. As if to assure Tønnes that it would help Professor Birkeland's insomnia, he explained that the strange name resulted from the fact that a pharmacist from Bayer, who was testing the substance on a train journey to Italy, had slept for eight hours and not woken up until the guard shouted the name of his stop, "Verona." Tønnes bought a small bag of veronal. Back home he made a pot of black tea for his brother, warning him that the grains tasted very bitter and needed to be dissolved in warm liquid. Birkeland slept well for the first time in months, but his condition remained unstable and Tønnes advised him to stay in bed for the next two weeks at least. Before returning to Porsgrund, he asked Sem Sæland and the Mohns to call on his brother occasionally.

When Eyde was informed of Birkeland's illness, he was relieved that the professor would be out of the way of the new engineer. Næss was occasionally sent to Birkeland's house to consult with him over insignificant design problems but Birkeland realized that this was to keep him away from the workshop. Næss would not even write a note of his replies. Birkeland was aware that some days Næss found him incoherent, distracted, or so intense it was hard for him to leave. These occasions followed bad nights when Birkeland was driven to distraction by restlessness and unfocused but intense dissatisfaction and frustration. The only release he could find was to take more veronal than his brother had recommended and wash the bitter grains down with whisky rather than tea.

The halfhearted visits by Næss served only to convince Birkeland that Eyde was trying to remove him from the project. He was correct in his suspicions. In a letter to Marcus Wallenberg's brother, Knut, Eyde made it clear that Birkeland's presence was superfluous.

Christiania
14 March 1904

Dear Bank Manager Knut Wallenberg,
The stay here of Engineer Lindström, for which I am very grateful, has been very useful to us. It has been useful not only because Professor Birkeland has been ill in bed all the time since the arrival of the gentleman, but also because I believe his quiet and thorough investigations of various elec-

trical problems will shed light on several problems where we so far have been in doubt. He has made several suggestions during his stay that I am convinced will be advantageous to the project, and I dare to request of you, if possible, to arrange that Lindström come back to Christiania to conclude his investigations. The time is now favourable since Professor Birkeland still has to keep indoors and, accordingly, can do nothing personally at the test plant.

> With kind regards,
> Yours sincerely,
> S. Eyde

When Henrik Mohn was told by Tønnes of his friend's collapse, he rang Ida and suggested that a visit from her might be welcome. Although she had been upset by Birkeland's dropping their meetings in favor of the furnace, she felt somewhat mollified by the fact that the excuse must have been genuine if he had become ill from overwork. On the first Saturday she had free from school, Ida dressed in the narrow-waisted, dark gray jacket she kept for special occasions (as there were twenty-two tiny buttons to be fastened down the front with a special hook) and took the train for the twenty-five-kilometer journey from Lillestrøm to Lysaker. She found her way to the address Henrik Mohn had given her, Villa Granstua, a large house with a gabled roof, red tiles, and numerous wooden balconies. It was more ornate than most on the street and had six bells at the downstairs door. Birkeland's housekeeper let Ida in and showed her into the large drawing room, which had a bay window shrouded in heavy velvet blinds. There were books and papers piled on the desk at the window but otherwise it was an anonymous place, devoid of photographs or personal effects. Even in her small room at the school Ida had photographs and her own drawings on the walls.

Birkeland walked quietly into the room after a long interval. Despite his surprise at seeing Ida, he was pleased that she had come and the visit went well. She returned the following day and on sub-sequent weekends while he was confined to his apartment. She would bring him the journals he asked for, eat with him, discuss politics or her school and family, and inquire closely into his state of health. Birkeland was grateful for the attention as the muffled silence of the house bore into him like toothache after the noise and activity of his life before the illness. His old friends, Amund Helland, Henrik Mohn, and Sem Sæland, and his cousin Richard, also came regularly, bringing news of the university, small items of gossip or controversy that might stir the old Birkeland, the engaged and passionate professor, to rise from the listless invalid who had replaced him.

With the ministrations of his friends, rest, and regular sleep, Birkeland's health slowly improved. The first time he left the house after his collapse was on 12 March for Sem Sæland's wedding to Gudrun Schøning. Birkeland was determined to be there but he knew he was not fit enough to attend alone, so he asked Ida to accompany him. Although nothing was said, their appearance together at the wedding moved their relationship to a different level, from friendship to courtship, and the unusual couple enjoyed the flurry of looks and questions they received, since neither was used to turning heads.

Despite his collapse, Birkeland returned to work at his usual pace, making time only for Ida, who persuaded him to join in the Norwegian obsession of walking in the forests on weekends. Throughout the late spring and summer he worked in his office with Sæland and Dietrichson, devoting some days to the furnace, others to planning a new laboratory, yet others to studying the results of the last expedition. During his convalescence, Birkeland accepted the fact that he would have to cooperate with Eyde's appointees and that the politics of big business reached as far as the factory floor. The reward for relinquishing complete control of the furnace would be more time to work on the Aurora Polaris Expedition.

At the beginning of April the Wallenberg brothers agreed to use their bank as guarantor to create a new company, Electrochemical Industry (ELKEM), with capital of five million crowns, almost four million of which would be controlled by the Wallenbergs. ELKEM took over the majority of the shares in the Norwegian Nitrogen Company and the rights to Eyde's waterfalls. A new test factory was to be built at Notodden, a village in the heart of the Telemark district, southwest of Christiania. Birkeland, already so busy, was put in charge of approving the plans. Rather than cancel meetings with Ida, Birkeland began working through the night again to finish the designs for the factory by the autumn.

Matters between Birkeland and Eyde deteriorated further when Næss, who checked the patent drawings for the furnace that had been returned by Bryn, informed Eyde that Birkeland had been submitting them in his name alone. Eyde was furious. He believed that nothing would have happened with Birkeland's idea without the financing he had put in place, but if Birkeland's name alone was on the patents, he might one day seek to regain control of his invention. For Birkeland, his ownership of the patents was the last shred of influence he retained in the rapidly changing company, and he did not want to relinquish it. The disagreement rumbled on, poisoning an already strained collaboration.

As the short Norwegian autumn was followed by winter, Birkeland's considerable workload was made heavier when he had to travel to Notodden to supervise the installation of the furnaces in the factory. The journey involved four hours on a train to Kongsberg and then another three hours by horse carriage over the hills between the railway station and Heddalsvann Lake, on the north shore of which lay Notodden. The village consisted of about fifty houses, a hotel for the few tourists who ventured that way, a handful of small farms in the clearings, and small fields reclaimed from the pine forest that came down to the water's edge. It was a peaceful, beautiful place although Birkeland had no time to appreciate it. As always, Eyde was pressuring the engineers, construction workers, and Birkeland to finish the factory in record time. Wallenberg had persuaded the French bank Paribas to consider becoming a major shareholder in the enterprise but they would invest only if a committee of experts declared Birkeland's invention capable of producing saltpeter in sufficient quantities to turn a profit. An added incentive to hurry was that Otto Witt had informed Eyde that the BASF furnace was also close to being tested. If it proved more efficient than Birkeland's, no one would put money into the Norwegian company and the whole venture would collapse in a morass of bankruptcy and wasted effort. Eyde set a June date for the experts to inspect the furnace, just a few months ahead.

Although Eyde did not admit it, Birkeland knew there was a further problem, potentially more serious than the others. Relations between Norway and Sweden were worsening; the Union was at breaking point and both nations were preparing for armed conflict in the face of Sweden's refusal to acknowledge Norway's grievances. The investors in the new company were Swedish, but it would become impossible to transfer money from one country to the other if war broke out. There would be a backlash against allowing Swedes so much interest in a Norwegian company using national assets and the Swedish engineers would be forced to return home. In short, the entire enterprise would founder within hours if war were declared.

10

Ida

Monday, 15 May 1905
Pension Parkveien 25, Christiania

To the finder of nitrogen in air, we salute you on this happy day.

Telegram sent to Birkeland by the Norwegian Parliament,
15 May 1905

IRKELAND did not keep a diary. Important information, equations, expense details, phone numbers and social engagements were written on scraps of paper and used as bookmarks, or filed under seat cushions and in his pockets. His housekeeper would collect any notes she found and leave them in a neat pile on the hall table under a piece of rock Birkeland had brought back from Haldde summit. Without a diary, he was prone to forget appointments, which was why he arranged to give a lecture about the aurora to a large group of dignitaries on Monday, 15 May. Only later, once it was too late to cancel, did Birkeland realize that the lecture would clash with an important prior commitment: his wedding.

On the morning of 15 May, Birkeland stood in front of his audience in full formal dress, white shirt and cravat, shiny black patent leather shoes, trying to avoid getting chalk dust on his new suit and talking as fast as he could. Amund Helland, due to act as Birkeland's witness (with some reluctance because he did not approve of marriage), was waiting outside the Festival Hall with a carriage to rush them to Frogner Church, where the ceremony was due to begin just half an hour after the lecture finished. Helland looked only slightly less scruffy than usual in a deep russet, wide-brimmed hat and a cape pushed back over his shoulders to reveal a creased suit onto which ash was dropping from his pipe. Helland was well aware of his sartorial laxness. He had been walking along the harbor by the old railway station a few weeks before when a young dandy offered him a crown to carry a heavy case. Helland had replied, "It is a good wage, sir, but first I have to go to the university to give a lecture!" This incident had shamed him into buying a new suit, although he rarely wore it.

Giving the briefest of bows at the end of his talk, Birkeland hurried out of the hall, brushing the chalk dust from his hands and collecting the leather-bound prayer book Ida had given him as an engagement present. The carriage trotted briskly along the southern boundary of the Royal Palace grounds, then right into Frognerveien. Birkeland and Helland managed to arrive before the bride and were greeted by the priest, who directed them to the front pew. There were no guests waiting and the flowers were those left over from the Sunday service. After Birkeland proposed to Ida, they had visited the local parish church because a church ceremony was the only legal way to marry in Norway, but Birkeland, who had not attended a service since graduating from university, had persuaded the priest to allow them the simplest ceremony, with just two witnesses, no guests, hymns, or sermon. Although Ida was deeply religious, she was well aware that Birkeland was not and she felt too old to indulge in the fuss of a traditional wedding.

Once the few arrangements for the wedding had been made, Ida traveled to Raade to tell her parents. They were shocked that their forty-two-year-old daughter was to marry a man they had not met and who not only was four years her junior and irreligious but also had invented a cannon, of which they thoroughly disapproved. Ida asked her family to attend the wedding and her father to give her a blessing at the ceremony, but her mother and five sisters declined the invitation, and on the morning of her wedding she received a telegram with her father's response:

UNABLE TO DO THE CEREMONY. GOD'S MERCY FOR YOUR DEEDS IS WISHED BY EVERYONE HERE. GOD BLESS YOU.

Ten minutes after Birkeland and Helland took their seats, Ida and her witness, Solveig, arrived. Ida was wearing a long white skirt, pulled in tight around her small waist by a belt with an ornate silver buckle. Her white blouse had puffed sleeves that came to the elbow and were trimmed with lace that fell onto her forearms. The neck was high and a silver brooch, matching the buckle and studded with tiny marcasites, glittered at her throat while a wide panel of lace descended from her shoulders to the buckle of her belt. Ida and Solveig walked down the aisle together as Birkeland and Helland stood, Solveig taking her solitary place on the bride's side of the church and Helland on the groom's. The ceremony lasted less than twenty minutes, and once they had signed the church book, Kristian and Ida were husband and wife. Emerging into the sunshine of the May morning, the small group climbed into the waiting carriage and went to lunch at the Grand. Helland livened up the occasion by walking with his hands in his pockets, kicking the door to the Grand open with his foot and letting it swing back on the unfortunate Solveig behind. Birkeland knew of several occasions when Helland's guests had come to serious grief on the return of this door, including him. This time Helland repaired his lack of decorum by spending the meal lightly flirting with Solveig and trying to find out where she lived so that he could send her some potatoes.

After lunch, Birkeland took his new wife to a smart pension on Parkveien, just behind the palace, where they spent the first night of their married lives. A large pile of telegrams was waiting for them there, from Knudsen, Eyde, Ida's cousins, Birkeland's mother, brother, and sister-in-law, Sigrid, and the Norwegian Parliament, wishing them a happy life together.

There was no time for a honeymoon after the wedding, so Birkeland took Ida to Notodden with him. They traveled by train to Porsgrund where Ida met Tønnes and Sigrid, Birkeland's mother Ingeborg, and the nine children—five girls and four boys and another baby expected. From there, a short train journey took them to Skien, where they boarded a narrow steamer for the trip up the Løveid canal, through four locks, until they reached Norsjø Lake, the length of which the boat traveled to reach a canal connecting with Heddalsvann Lake and Notodden. It was a long journey but it passed through some of the most beautiful landscapes in Norway. As the boat emerged from the narrow canals to the broad, upland lakes, the grandeur of the scene on this beautiful summer's day was breathtaking. In the distance the mountains of Telemark, made famous by the first downhill skiers in the 1880s, soared into the bright blue sky. The snow on the best-known peak, Gausta, ran in streaks down its steep sides and gave the view a Japanese air.

Telemark was a romantic place, the heartland of national pride and culture that differentiated Norway from her Scandinavian neighbors. From here came the fiddlers who toured European capitals to great acclaim and the finest "rose-painters," whose characteristic flower painting decorated furniture, pottery, cornices, and church interiors, including those of the Norwegian stave churches, the finest examples of which were in this region. The farmers were wealthy and famously spoke to all as equals, including the king. Here, Sondre Nordheim had pioneered downhill skiing, starting the skiing craze that spread across Norway and then, through the popular articles and adventures of the explorer Fridtjof Nansen, throughout Europe. There was no better place for the country's first major industrial enterprise. Beyond its symbolic resonance, Telemark also contained the Møsvann mountain reservoir, a natural lake at high altitude from which many of Europe's most powerful waterfalls issued. It was a sparsely populated region and there were few to object when Eyde bought the Rjukan and Svælg waterfalls to power hydroelectric plants, despite their beauty and fame as tourist destinations for European travelers. Those who did object—including the Norwegian Tourist Association, whose first hut for walkers was situated beside the Rjukan Falls—were simply told by Eyde:

> You are misinformed. We have not put an end to the Rjukan Falls, but have only lifted it one hundred metres up the mountain and led it into steel pipes that it can do useful work for us.

When Birkeland and Ida arrived in Notodden, they checked into the hotel Viktoria on the lakeside. The following morning Birkeland went to the factory, leaving Ida to wander the hills and fir forests or stroll through the few streets of the town. At the nitrogen plant, the engineers were frantic; the output of the three furnaces, measured by how much fertilizer was produced for every kilowatt of energy used over a year (a kilowatt-year), was only 450 kilos. At that level of production, one furnace running for a whole year would produce enough fertilizer for only a few hundred small Norwegian farms. Eyde had made extravagant promises to the directors of Paribas that they could produce 600 kilos of saltpeter per kilowatt-year, rising eventually to 900 kilos, double the present capacity. An international committee of experts was expected in only six weeks to scrutinize productivity and report back to the bank.

During the first few evenings, Birkeland made light of his work and his worries, trying to amuse Ida with stories of disasters they had encountered during the day, but he soon abandoned his attempts to put on a brave face and sat silently, sipping whisky. Ida was not much interested in the furnace and was appalled when Birkeland returned in the evenings, grimy and smelling like a stoker, but she tried to understand his situation. She did not complain about the long, solitary hours spent walking or reading, or about the way the furnace had completely overshadowed their enjoyment of being newly married. Birkeland was aware of how little time he spent with Ida and arranged a dinner at the hotel for her to meet his colleagues and their wives, hoping that the women would take pity on Ida's situation and invite her to spend time with them.

The work was hard and frustrating and the tensions between Birkeland and Eivind Næss re-emerged. Næss seemed more punctilious than before, trying one solution after another to increase productivity in a systematic manner that was poisonous to Birkeland. The two men chafed and sweated under their mutual dislike while the other engineers, sensing the discord, sided with Næss due to his connection with Eyde, who paid their wages. To make matters worse, news was filtering into the factory of the crisis looming with Sweden. The engineers became distracted, worried that war would break their links with the continent, from which they received equipment and technical support. The Swedish engineers were nervous of how their hosts would react if war was declared, and everyone was aware that war between such close neighbors was the worst sort of conflict. The Norwegian government had submitted a resolution to set up a Norwegian Consular Service, a compromise until Sweden granted them a foreign office, a minister, and ambassadors. The debate between the two countries grew fierce following this apparently reasonable proposal, and became a focus for the grievances that had built up over the ninety years of the Union. In Notodden, the engineers' wives worried for their husbands, sons, and brothers who might soon be called up to fight. Norway's army was small and ill-equipped despite efforts to rearm over the previous five years, but any war between the two countries would undoubtedly be drawn out and cost many lives.

After a fortnight, Ida decided to return to Birkeland's apartment at the Villa Granstua in Lysaker, which was now her home. She had had little time to arrange her possessions before leaving for Notodden and thought she could be more usefully employed there than at the Viktoria. At Notodden Birkeland was kept busy round the clock, trying to finish work on the furnaces before war erupted. Eyde and Wallenberg were frequently on the phone from Christiania and Stockholm, making contingency plans and organizing alternative methods of communication should war be declared. At the beginning of June, against the advice of his cabinet, King Oscar of Sweden vetoed Norway's resolution to form its own consular service, and the Norwegian government declared this an unconstitutional act because the king could only veto a proposition in agreement with his cabinet. On 7 June Norway unilaterally ruptured the Union and waited anxiously to see if Sweden would declare war.

Birkeland and his engineers were pushed ever harder in Notodden while Norway sent envoys to foreign governments to elicit support for independence and to demonstrate to Sweden the futility of trying to impose the Union by force. Norway had no ambassadors as Sweden had restricted membership in that class to her own aristocracy, but her explorer-heroes and shipowners were sent out instead. Just as the Swedish engineers at the factory were preparing to return home, Sweden was persuaded to postpone war in favor of burdensome stipulations such as the dismantling of Norway's newly erected frontier defenses, before independence could be considered. A referendum was demanded to prove that a majority of people, not only the Parliament, wanted an end to the Union. Everyone, from board members to apprentices, involved in the fertilizer furnace rejoiced at the country's temporary deliverance from war, and returned to work.

Birkeland's health was again suffering from the long hours spent in a chemical-laden atmosphere; he lacked fresh air, sunlight, sleep, and appetite. He worried too that Ida was already unhappy with married life. He was relieved when, on 20 July, a steamer pulled up to the jetty in Notodden with the committee of experts. He wanted their approval not for professional pride but so that Paribas would invest and he could earn enough money to return to his wife and the university, to continue his auroral research.

Although Birkeland had spent much of the past few months in Notodden since construction started the previous autumn, it was Eyde who behaved as if the place was his home away from home, settling the expert committee into the Viktoria Hotel as if it were his own house. The group consisted of Marcus Wallenberg, the director of the foreign loans department of Paribas, and three outstanding scientists, one each from Britain, France, and Germany. The British scientist, Professor Silvanus Thompson, chaired the committee and already knew Birkeland since they worked in related fields. He had once said to Birkeland, "Make an invention to earn you a million, and then you can think of science." Birkeland hoped he would decide the furnace possessed such earning capacity. The German expert was Otto Witt, already a confidant, and from France, Alphonse Théophile Schloesing. Eyde talked to them all like old friends, despite his difficulty with languages. The Swedes could understand his Norwegian; his German was good, but his English was poor and the French expert had difficulty containing his mirth as Eyde mangled the language. Eyde was oblivious to his shortcomings, particularly here in Telemark, where he had bought the rights to the waterfalls that would propel Norway into the modern era and him into wealth and power.

The following day, Birkeland explained the principal characteristics of his furnace and demonstrated it in action. Electric arcs were created by two electrodes, less than a centimeter apart, cooled with water to prevent their fusing together. These arcs were swept into a fifteen-centimeter disc by strong electromagnets around the electrodes. The hot gas created by passing air over the disc was fed into a series of four granite towers, where it was absorbed into water to create nitric acid. Limestone was then dissolved into the acid in a fifth tower to make saltpeter. The process demanded a huge amount of power, however, with 520-kilowatt furnaces, electromagnets, pumps, and other equipment using expensive electricity provided by the privately owned hydroelectric plant nearby. It was important to convince the experts that sufficient saltpeter could be produced to offset the large cost of electricity. At the end of the demonstration Birkeland showed the committee six wooden planters containing irises, each labeled with the amount of fertilizer it had been given, if any. The two plants with no fertilizer grew short, thin stems with few and small blooms. The two fed with a small amount of saltpeter were taller with better blooms, but the two well-fertilized planters displayed a profusion of tall, luxurious stems and glorious flowers. The experts were amused by the directness of the demonstration but were sensitive to the point being made: fertilizer would feed the world.

Although the committee would not give an opinion immediately, both Birkeland and Eyde felt its members were impressed by what they saw. Production was still 100 kilos short of the promised target but Eyde was able to tell the committee that the trial factory could already make a profit if they sold the saltpeter they made. After the experts left, Birkeland remained in Notodden for another few weeks, during which the referendum for independence was held. It was a day of great excitement and Birkeland encouraged all the engineers at the test plant to vote, making them aware that he himself was choosing independence. Only men could vote officially, having been granted suffrage only seven years before. The result was 368,208 votes to end the Union and 184 to retain it. A women's private poll, in which Ida enthusiastically enlisted her friends, added another quarter of a million votes to the "Yes, End the Union" vote. So insistent was Birkeland's enthusiasm for independence that Kloumann, one engineer working with him, wrote a letter to the professor to dispel rumors that he had been among the 184 voting against it.

Dear Professor Birkeland,
Whoever told you that I voted "No" in yesterday's referendum is not telling the truth. I did not vote "No," of course.
Yours sincerely, Eng. Kloumann

After the nearly unanimous vote, the country waited for the Great Powers to recognize their independence and force Sweden to do the same, but they reacted instead with disapproval or indifference. Britain, France, and Germany all had subject states clamoring for independence and so were not keen to express approval for Norway's rejection of Sweden's hegemony. A second referendum was held by the Norwegian Parliament to decide whether the country should become a republic or a monarchy in order to reassure their nervous neighbors that anarchy would not follow a declaration of independence. Monarchism was heavily promoted in the hope that adopting a crowned head would provide links to other European royal families, giving Norway's bid for independence respectability and resolving the crisis more quickly.

Birkeland wanted the country to become a republic but he, along with many other prominent citizens, saw the benefits that a monarchy might confer. He went as far as to put his name to a declaration made by members of the political party Venstre in the newspaper *Dagbladet* on 2 November 1905, signed also by friends and colleagues, including Alfred Bryn at the patent office; Johan Bredal, Birkeland's lawyer; and three professors at the university, the most influential being Waldemar Brøgger.

> The undersigned members of Venstre urge all followers of Venstre to support the resolution made by Parliament on 31 October by voting "Yes" to the Kingdom on the referendum of the 12 and 13 November. Under the present circumstances, we believe this is in the best interests of the country.

In the absence of trained ambassadors, Fridtjof Nansen was sent to invite a Danish prince, Carl, to become king. Carl was married to Princess Maud, the daughter of King Edward VII of England, a connection welcomed by those seeking the most acceptable monarch available. Prince Carl agreed to become king of Norway after the positive referendum results were known; he adopted the Norse royal name of Haakon and rechristened his son with the name Olav. In the autumn the Swedish king acknowledged that proceedings had gone too far to salvage the Union and an agreement was drawn up between the two countries granting Norway independence. Birkeland's dream of living in an independent state was at last a reality. Now he hoped his scientific dreams would also come to fruition. The furnace was sapping his energy and occupying all his time and he was becoming desperate to return to the Northern Lights.

AFTER NEARLY three years of intense work, mostly carried out in secret, Birkeland and Eyde could reveal to the world what they had achieved. Friday, 5 December 1905, was decided upon to launch the company publicly and announcements were put in the newspapers. The expert committee report had been generous in its praise for the science behind the invention of the furnace and agreed that 500 kilos of saltpeter per kilowatt-year was a reasonable expectation. Paribas backed the venture and work began on a new hydroelectric power station at the Svælg waterfall. By December most of the international patents on Birkeland's process had been secured; the name of the company, Norsk Hydro, was finalized; and even the logo for the barrels of saltpeter was ready. Paribas owned nearly half the shares in the new company and the Swedish Independent Bank the other half. Norwegians owned only 8 percent, a fact that sparked off an intense debate in the Norwegian Parliament about the selling of the country's natural resources to foreign interests. Although controversial, Norsk Hydro was Norway's first multinational company, with a value of 7.5 million crowns.

The argument between Eyde and Birkeland over the ownership of the furnace patents was resolved with a compromise before Norsk Hydro was officially constituted. Neither man was entirely happy but Birkeland came off better, owning twelve patents, including the main one for the furnace. Eyde leveled the score when the board was appointed and Birkeland was mentioned only as a "technical director." Eyde was managing director with fellow board members Marcus and Knut Wallenberg, the director of Paribas, Admiral Børresen of Norway, Tillberg, and Persson. Birkeland was furious when he first heard about the appointments but after a while decided it was for the best. He did not want to be in such close cooperation with Eyde, and, most importantly, he could at last start work on the data from his second auroral expedition. He made fewer trips to Notodden and attempted to settle into married life with Ida. The apartment in Lysaker now contained her modest possessions as well as his. She had given up her job as a teacher as the post was open to single women only and took care of running the household instead. Birkeland did not slip naturally into the role of husband, resenting the limitations it placed on his time, but he tried to adjust.

On the launch day of Norsk Hydro, phones in Eyde's office began ringing with journalists from as far afield as Japan wanting details about the process of making fertilizer from air. The newspapers were full of cartoons of Birkeland wringing dung from the skies. It had been decided that two talks should be given on the same night, one by Birkeland to the Academy of Science in the university's Festival Hall, and one by Eyde to a general audience at the Polytechnic Society. This was the only way of avoiding the problem of who should speak first. Both men gave speeches to audiences of curious people, delighted at the prospect of Norway taking a leading role in saving the globe from agricultural crisis.

After the public launch, Wallenberg suggested to Eyde that they propose the furnace to the Nobel Committee. Although it was a new prize, founded only three years earlier as part of the will of the reclusive Swedish explosives magnate Alfred Nobel, it had already become a unique accolade in the burgeoning arena of science and technology. To be awarded the Nobel Prize, even jointly with Birkeland, would put an end to the insecurity Eyde felt over his lack of education. He was painfully aware that many of the people he mixed with, including most of his business colleagues, his wife, and her family and friends, were better educated than he was. He had been taken out of school at fourteen to work on a naval ship as he was a slow learner and his parents thought a spell at sea might cure him of being work-shy. He returned to school after a year and eventually finished an engineering course, but he was not gifted academically and made up for the deficiency with his business acumen and a habit of mentioning at every opportunity the famous, well-connected people he knew.

Birkeland also wanted to be nominated for a Nobel Prize, particularly in recognition of his auroral theory, although he realized the furnace was a more likely recipient. When the Nobel Prize was first announced in *Aftenposten* on 26 June 1900, he had cut out the article and kept it carefully among his papers. As the English did not award the prize, he felt a Scandinavian had more chance of winning it, and he hoped to be asked more details about his furnace by members of the Nobel Committee. He did not know that Eyde, meanwhile, had already furnished the committee with detailed drawings and test results.

Wallenberg informed Eyde within a few weeks that the Nobel Committee wanted to nominate Birkeland alone for the prize in chemistry in recognition of his invention. Eyde was furious, as it was his money that had enabled Birkeland to develop the furnace in the first place, but the committee was only interested in the science behind it, not in its commercial success. Eyde was not a man easily dissuaded from pursuit of a cherished goal and he launched an underground campaign to be jointly nominated for the prize, using all the contacts he had made through his aristocratic Swedish wife. The situation was very delicate for the committee, who balked at awarding the prize jointly but did not want to create a diplomatic incident by angering one of Norway's most prominent businessmen. Relations between the two countries were still strained after the rupture of the Union and a prize as prestigious and symbolic as the Nobel was a fertile subject for discord. Eyde's machinations rendered Birkeland's nomination potentially controversial and it was quietly dropped without Birkeland ever knowing that he had been considered.

Ignorant of Eyde's sabotage, Birkeland rejoiced in his first financial returns for the years of exhausting work. He sold his patents and shares in the Norwegian Nitrogen Company to ELKEM for 75,000 crowns and received a guaranteed consultancy fee from Norsk Hydro of 5,000 crowns a year for the rest of his life. He retained his position as a director of the NNC and his shares in ELKEM. In one day Birkeland had fifteen times his annual salary deposited in his bank account and the promise that the equivalent of his salary would be paid to him annually for what he hoped would be a few weeks' work a year. He would have the financial freedom to build his own laboratory, pay a team of assistants, and operate well beyond the scope of the university's pitiful resources.

II

Looking Back from Space

1906–8
Christiania

The value of his hypotheses I cannot measure and nor can anyone else in the present audience. It is too brave not to be unlikely at some points but even if he has made some mistakes he has also uncovered many remarkable facts and with his extraordinary intuition he had a feeling for the huge electrical importance of the universe. Future research may show that such messages from the sun are equally important to us as Galileo's understanding of messages from the stars when he took his telescope and studied space for the first time.

SEM SÆLAND, memorial address, 22 September 1919

Dear Professor Wille,
Thank you for your Christmas greeting and I send you best wishes for a Happy New Year. I have in mind acquiring a cat and some advice from you would be very valuable.
Best wishes from Kristian and Ida Birkeland

Professor Wille, cat lover, wrote a long and detailed letter to Birkeland on the characters of different breeds, particularly emphasizing those known for keeping mice at bay. Birkeland enjoyed Wille's poetic descriptions of feline hunting skills but thought a more affectionate cat was called for as he and Ida had decided to buy one to keep her company when he was away. The cat was only one factor in the changes Birkeland had agreed to in the hope of making Ida happy; the most significant was Ida's desire to find somewhere new to live, a home of their own that she could decorate and to which she could invite people. Birkeland's apartment in Lysaker was shabby and masculine despite Ida's efforts to improve it and she launched into house hunting in the smart area of Christiania behind the palace. The professor felt released to go back to his work, where he lost all notion of time; frequently Ida had to ring his office to remind him to come home and occasionally she even went to the university to collect him. Their relationship had settled into a pattern that suited them both for the time being.

During the years Birkeland had worked on the nitrogen furnace, he had not had time to analyze the results of his Aurora Polaris Expedition or to publish scientific papers. He decided that it was time to plan a major scientific treatise, based on these new data, in which to present his ideas to a wider audience and convince those who still doubted the correctness of his vision. He now had the money to hire assistants and to build a laboratory in which to do experimental research. Although most professors bemoaned the impossibility of hiring and keeping good assistants, Birkeland was able to poach the best young men with promises of exciting research and a generous salary. Ole Andreas Krogness and Lars Vegard, both graduates of Birkeland's physics course, were employed to help Sæland process measurements and observations from the Aurora Polaris Expedition.

Birkeland wanted his treatise to be a monument in the vast landscape of scientific publications and decided to make it a three-volume work to be published in stages. The first was to be written immediately and would cover the Northern Lights research and his theories about magnetic storms and currents. His assistants set to work writing descriptions of the Arctic stations, the instruments used, the weather conditions, and the results obtained. Records were collated and processed, maps drawn, and notation systems established. Since the end of the expedition three years earlier, magnetograms had also arrived from twenty-three observatories across the globe: Honolulu, Bombay, Dehra Dun at the foot of the Himalayas, Baldwin in Kansas, Sitka in Alaska, Cheltenham near Washington, D.C., Christchurch, Toronto, Kew, Stonyhurst, Greenwich, San Fernando in Spain, Wilhelmshaven, Munich, Potsdam, Pola on the Istrian Peninsula, Pavlovsk, Tiflis, Ekaterinburg, Irkutsk, Batavia on Java, Zi-ka-wei in China, and Val Joyeux near Paris. As Birkeland wrote in the resulting book, "Our observational material of magnetic storms was, I may safely say, the largest that has ever been dealt with at one time."

While the professor's office filled with enthusiastic assistants, the new king and queen were crowned in Norway's ancient Nidaros Cathedral in Trondheim on 22 June 1906, the first rulers of an independent Norway for over 600 years. Birkeland was not in Christiania to enjoy the coronation celebrations because Eyde had asked him to go to Berlin to present a lecture about the fertilizer furnace, arranged by Otto Witt. It was part of Eyde's plan to secure the cooperation of BASF and Birkeland had little choice but to interrupt his laboratory preparations. His scientific rival, Schönherr, was in the audience, and Witt introduced them after the talk. Schönherr, now a director of BASF, saw that collaboration with Norsk Hydro might be favorable due to the latter's access to cheap hydroelectricity. Germany had only expensive coal-fired plants, and it was no longer an option to buy Norwegian waterfalls since the Norwegian Parliament had introduced the Concession Laws to protect the country's natural resources from foreign interests. Schönherr promised to look into the possibility of building a new factory in Norway and combining BASF's technical developments with those of Norsk Hydro. The two men enjoyed each other's company so much that Schönherr confided in Birkeland that his wife was suffering from depression and sleeplessness. Birkeland wrote to him upon his return to Norway recommending the use of veronal and enclosing the label from one of his own packets of the drug. He had used it only rarely since his collapse two years before, but he kept it on his bedside table in case of a relapse.

Now that Birkeland had the financing for his scientific work, the furnace was a distraction. On 15 August 1906 he resigned the directorship of the Norwegian Nitrogen Company that he had retained when he had sold his shares and patents the previous year. He no longer felt the need to be involved in a company that was simply a subsidiary of Norsk Hydro and ELKEM. He also wanted to sell his shares in ELKEM. To put these decisions into effect, Eyde asked Birkeland to meet him at his office to sign a new contract. An uneasy truce had developed between the two men. They were like opposite ends of a bar magnet, inexorably tied together through the company they had forged but unable to connect.

On the closely typed pages of the new contract it was stated that the professor, co-inventor of the Birkeland-Eyde Fertilizer Process, would receive a one-time payment of 60,000 crowns for his shares in ELKEM, plus an annual salary of 5,000 crowns to act as technical consultant to the company. Combined with his 5,000-crown consultancy salary from Norsk Hydro and previous one-time payment for the sale of his Norwegian Nitrogen Company shares, Birkeland had earned 135,000 crowns from shares and would receive 10,000 crowns a year as a consultant plus his 5,000-crown professor's salary. In return, he was bound not to set up a competing company and to be available to give technical advice if needed. Birkeland felt sure he would not be needed, as he was certainly not wanted. Næss in particular had made it clear that he could get on better without the professor. Watching Norsk Hydro turn into an international corporation had confirmed to Birkeland that power came from wealth and ownership. Intelligence was necessary but was always outmaneuvered by the influence that money conferred. Eyde's entrepreneurial skills had given him the biggest weapon in the battle for ownership of the nitrogen process.

As Birkeland read the contract, he realized that to sign it meant bowing out of a project that had absorbed his every waking moment for three years and wrecked his nerves. But he could see that he was not suited to big business; he could not be economical with the truth, hide his opinions, or care enough about money to pursue it as a goal in itself. He signed the contract. As he left the building a sense of freedom and optimism rose in his chest. He strode down Carl Johan Gate to the university and his own domain.

14 November 1906

Professor Birkeland,
Dr. Isaakson will take over your teaching duties at the university in order that you may continue to process your data from the 1902–3 Aurora Borealis Expedition. You are responsible for paying him to teach your lectures.
University Administration

Birkeland decided to return to his plan to re-create the Northern Lights in a laboratory, but at the university he had none of the facilities he required. The university had never needed to build and equip a modern research laboratory since so few students chose to study physics. Of the 250 students admitted each year, only fourteen majored in sciences and those were divided among geology, botany, mathematics, zoology, astronomy, mineralogy, chemistry, and physics. With his usual lack of regard for convention, he wrote to the administration of the university, informing them that he would need to convert the basement below his room to hold a generator. He also notified them that

I have taken half of the lecture hall for a new laboratory. By putting the students closer together, there is enough space in the reduced hall.

A testy reply granted him permission to use the room but stressed that all alterations and equipment must be provided at his own expense. Telegrams were dispatched to the best scientific equipment manufacturers in Europe and Russia with requests for catalogues and prices, technical performances, and speed of delivery.

Within weeks, the first of Birkeland's purchases began to arrive in the university courtyard, including a 15,000-watt Swiss-built generator that delivered a voltage as high as 20,000 volts and provided a loud background hum to the law lectures given nearby. Boxes marked "fragile" and "heavy" appeared in his office, and, like a child at Christmas, Birkeland rushed to discover their contents. Over the course of a few weeks the bare concrete shell of the basement was festooned with wires, fuse boxes, tool racks, wooden plinths, camera tripods, buzzing and sparking machines, vacuum flasks, electric cables, plugs, batteries, buckets of pitch, and brushes. It soon became apparent that the room was too small for Birkeland's extraordinary plans and the lecture hall too distant to be practical. The only solution was to put some of the equipment in his office, linking it with the basement below by boring small holes in the floor through which to pass electric cables. Birkeland asked the administration for yet another room to use as an office. Meanwhile, a third science graduate, Olaf Devik, was hired to help Birkeland and Dietrichson with the experiments.

To the casual visitor, the laboratory appeared to be the work of medieval visionaries with futuristic dreams. The noises, flashes, smells, and heat were overwhelming and lurking within were a number of very real dangers. The vacuum pumps released poisonous mercury fumes; the small amount of radium salt that had been given to Birkeland by Marie Curie was left on a shelf beside a box of new lightbulbs, leaking lethal radiation; explosions and implosions from the vacuum flasks were an ever-present risk; the generator had moving parts that could slice off fingers. Everyone working there suffered frequent electric shocks of varying severity caused by experimental, hurried wiring and the occasionally capricious behavior of electric currents and equipment. Birkeland and his assistants adopted the practice of working with one hand in their pockets so that, if they sustained a large electric shock, it would travel down their bodies rather than across their hearts. Birkeland's own safety precautions caused some comment among his assistants and colleagues. On arriving in the morning, he would replace his hat with an Egyptian fez and put on a pair of red leather Egyptian slippers with long, pointed tips. To those who asked the reason for his fanciful attire, he explained that he suffered from frequent headaches due to the harmful rays emitted by his experiments and that the fez protected his head. Although it was true that he suffered from headaches, he was perfectly aware that a small felt hat would not stop radiation and he told the tale merely to see who was gullible enough to believe it. As for the slippers, it was simply to avoid wearing wet boots in the laboratory.

Birkeland's Egyptian accessories were more than just a joke, though. Egyptology had been fashionable throughout the West in his youth due to the enthralling excavations in the pyramids and Valley of the Kings. His isolated boyhood had been punctuated by Professor Lieblein's Sunday lectures about ancient Egypt. Lieblein's son, Johan, was one year older than Birkeland and the two were friends. Birkeland used to go to the professor's house, where he listened to stories about the excavations in Luxor and at the pyramids at Giza, heard about the glories of the pharaohs and the worship of Ra, the sun god. Lieblein, together with Ibsen, had represented Norway at the opening of the Suez Canal in 1869 and he had described how they had sailed up the Nile to the cataracts, as the guests of Khedive Ismail, Egypt's ruler.

The sun was the celestial body that held the greatest fascination for Birkeland. When his interest in physics developed, he realized that Egypt was also the land of a strange phenomenon as mysterious as the aurora borealis. The Zodiacal Light appeared in equatorial skies after sunset and was sometimes considered the natural explanation behind Moses' "Pillar of Fire" because it was shaped like an elongated pyramid of glowing light stretching from the horizon into space. It was another of Earth's mysteries that taunted the scientists who traveled to study it, and Birkeland hoped that one day he would experience for himself this mystical phenomenon. Until then, his fez and his slippers were a reminder that the sun's influence stretched around the globe, from the flickering lights of the Arctic to the glowing columns in the night skies of Arabia.

The instruments for re-creating the Northern Lights did not exist beyond Birkeland's dreams and drawings, so he and Dietrichson set about constructing them themselves. Initially they used Crookes tubes, glass cylinders first made in the 1850s for experiments where a vacuum was needed. At one end of the tube was a cathode, a negatively charged electrode that emitted a beam of high-velocity electrons or "cathode rays" when heated; at the other was an anode to receive the rays. In Birkeland's experiments the anode was given the form of a small, magnetized metal globe, representing the Earth. He called it a terrella, after Gilbert. Birkeland found it immensely satisfying to be performing his experiments almost exactly three hundred years after Gilbert first published his thesis on the Earth's magnetism. The terrellas Gilbert used were naturally magnetic lodestones whereas Birkeland was able to magnetize his globes artificially by fitting them with an electromagnet consisting of an iron core wound round with copper wire insulated with silk. The ball itself was made from a thin sheet of brass covered with a coat of barium platinocide that was phosphorescent and would glow when hit by flying electrons. The magnet within was mounted slightly off vertical to imitate the tilt of the Earth's poles. When Birkeland turned on the cathode, the electrons would stream into the vacuum in all directions until he turned on the magnet in the globe. Once in a magnetic field, the electrons were guided to the poles of the Earth in spiraling streams, creating glowing ovals around them, just as Birkeland suspected auroral ovals formed around the poles of the planet.

When Birkeland tried to perform these experiments on a larger scale, the tubes either shattered at the crucial moment or the curved glass of the cylinder distorted the view of the phenomena occurring inside. He searched in vain for a vacuum chamber that would avoid these problems until, after several months of inquiries, a tube arrived that satisfied most of his requirements. It was almost the size of a man's torso, oblong with curved corners and sides as straight as it was possible to make. On the morning of the first test of this large terrella, Birkeland arrived at his office early. Standing outside, he could hear the regular breathing of the vacuum pump and the distant grind of the generator. He had slept little the night before, not because of nerves but because of excitement. Birkeland donned his Egyptian fez and slippers and then sat down to do some calculations before his assistants arrived. By ten o'clock the laboratory was buzzing with excited conversation: Birkeland and his assistants had been joined by professors and students who had heard via the grapevine that Birkeland was to make his own Northern Lights that day, in his own miniature universe. Amund Helland was there, laughing loudly at Karl's retelling of Birkeland's practical joke of shutting him into the vacuum chamber one day while he was cleaning it. Birkeland loved playing jokes on his assistants. He had once strongly magnetized a metal bar and then casually asked Devik to move it. It was impossible to budge. After a while the other assistants joined Devik and struggled to move it a few centimeters. Just as they were all heaving on the bar as hard as they could, Birkeland switched off the power to the magnet and the bar went flying off the metal table and his assistants flew with it. On this day, however, Birkeland was too preoccupied to think of playing games.

With his usual flair, Birkeland explained to his impromptu audience—which by now also included the director of the Christiania observatory as well as several professors of math, geology, and law, the latter wanting to see the fruits of the process that had been disturbing their lectures for months—the principles behind the vacuum chamber, how it represented the Earth and would show, for the first time ever, how our world reacts to unknown forces in space. The room was crackling with anticipation as Birkeland closed the shutters of the three large windows, orchestrating his own sun-down. The noise of the generator increased and the audience had to shout their questions and observations. After a little while the tip of the cathode, "the sun," began to glow hot. Still "the Earth" lay in darkness. Once Birkeland was satisfied that electrons were stream-ing from the cathode, he flicked the switch beside the chamber and powered the electromagnet in the terrella. Within seconds, a purple glow could be seen encircling the Earth at the equator. As Birkeland increased the strength of the magnetic field around the Earth, the circle divided, and two circles began to move toward the poles. The audience fell silent as the two spiral rings of glowing, phosphores-cent light hovered around the poles of the Earth, eerie and magical. The miniature auroras were the most supernatural phenomenon the men in that room had ever seen, and yet it was a scientific exper-iment, aiming to provide explanations and boundaries to an occur-rence that had always defied definition. Even the least fanciful of those gathered around Birkeland's terrella had a fleeting moment of awe, looking at the Earth as if from space. Only Birkeland had any idea of how auroras could be conjured out of nothing, could glow with such lively intensity, could find their way to the poles of the Earth, could be so beautiful. After a few minutes Birkeland turned off the magnet and the cathode in the terrella; the glow disap-peared, and the audience took a collective breath. He opened the shutters and laughed at the stunned faces of his visitors. He could not have hoped for more. With this experiment, he was going to make his doubting detractors sit up and acknowledge the value of his theories. Beyond that, he had realized during this first test how much more he had to say about the world. He no longer wanted to concentrate on the Lights alone because here was the canvas he needed to look beyond the Earth to the universe itself.

As Birkeland immersed himself in the excellent results achieved by his second expedition and continued to pursue his terrella exper-iments, Eyde entrenched his position as director of a multinational industry. He bought one of the first cars to be imported into Norway, a Mercedes with license number plate 50, using large sums of company money. Other board members were furious with him for his profligacy but Eyde explained that he needed to impress visiting dignitaries—the king of Siam was to tour the factory the following year, as was the new king of Norway. For these occasions Eyde actually used different cars and kept the Mercedes to drive around Christiania, where he soon founded the Royal Norwegian Automobile Club, a new forum in which to display his wealth. Eyde was also spending a huge sum building a grandiose "administration" house at Notodden, in conjunction with the new factory. It was an extravagant statement of national and personal pride. There was a central room capable of holding over a hundred people, where he could entertain his guests and impress upon them the glory of the Norwegian landscape with a magnificent view that stretched for many kilometers over Heddalsvann Lake to the Telemark mountains in the distance. The finest wood-carvers in Norway had transformed Old Norse and Viking tales into decorative friezes and reliefs around the fireplace, columns, grand stairway, and gallery. A huge office for Eyde adjoined the main room, and the principal bedroom suite was also for his use. A guest suite, more modest than Eyde's, was available for important visitors. He was relieved not to have to stay at the old Viktoria Hotel, which was pleasant but could no longer contain his ambitions.

In December 1906 Eyde made an agreement with BASF to utilize the power potential of the Rjukan waterfall, eighty kilometers north of Notodden. They would collaborate in building a power station and factory there, for which they formed a new company, Saltpetreworks. Birkeland renounced his present consultant position with ELKEM (the company owned mainly by the Swedish Independent Bank), for which he was paid 5,000 crowns, and entered into a consultancy contract with Saltpetreworks that paid 12,000 crowns per year. The position was for life. Surprisingly, Eyde seemed keen to keep Birkeland in the employ of Norsk Hydro, perhaps fearing that he would be outnumbered by the directors and engineers from Germany who now descended on Notodden and Rjukan to plan the latest factory. The permanent factory at Notodden was now finished but still producing under 500 kilos per kilowatt-year. Birkeland tried not to get too involved in the problems and the politics.

WHEN THE FIRST volume of Birkeland's book was published in early 1908, it was a triumph of completeness, handsome in its gold-embossed calfskin binding. Published in English and distributed by Scandinavian, German, British, and French presses, *The Norwegian Aurora Polaris Expedition 1902–1903* assumed landmark status. This monumental achievement, made more remarkable by the fact that Birkeland had needed to earn most of the money to make it possible, cemented Norway's position in the international scientific arena and encouraged those who were trying to progress beyond the limited vision of the previous generation of Norwegian academics.

The book opened with personal accounts of Birkeland's adventures in Finnmark, his battles with the weather, descriptions of the local Sami, Hætta the postman, and assorted curiosities to intrigue the reader. He then described the Arctic stations from his second expedition, again emphasizing the tremendous obstacles faced by the pioneering researchers because of the weather and the remoteness of the locations. Encounters with whalers, hunting trips, meetings with Samoyed families, and photographs of the fur-clad explorer-scientists were included to give the work the aura and mystique of polar pioneering. The magnetic recordings from the field studies and from stations around the world were analyzed and compared with the experiments Birkeland had been making with the large Crookes vacuum tubes and terrellas. A few photographs of the small globes with artificial auroral ovals around the poles were included to great effect. Long tables of equations, magnetic recordings, hundreds of maps of the world bristling with arrows showing the direction of the magnetic storms across the surface of the planet, diagrams of current systems and copies of actual magnetograms were also included. It was a paradigm of scientific craftsmanship and research.

The book's conclusions were no less extraordinary. From the recordings around the globe, Birkeland divided all known storm patterns into three categories, one of which, the "polar elementary storm," was his own discovery. Birkeland had suspected this form of magnetic disturbance was responsible for creating the auroras during his first trip to Haldde, but did not mention it in the resulting book because he lacked proof. His single Arctic station was too limited to reveal magnetic changes across the region, and most other magnetic observatories were in the midlatitudes and did not pick up evidence of polar perturbations. Establishing four stations during the second expedition had provided the evidence he needed to describe this new category of magnetic disturbance and its relationship to the auroras. Through his study of these well-defined and quite local storms, Birkeland was able to deduce, from his knowledge of electromagnetism, that the energy powering these storms and the Northern Lights had to originate outside the Earth, in space, ultimately from the sun.

This was the most controversial element in his book, as many scientists refused to believe that the sun could be the origin of cathode rays that reached as far as the Earth. Their main objection was that if only electrons, negatively charged rays, were emitted, the sun would eventually become positively charged and also that the repulsive electric forces between electrons would quickly disperse the beams. Birkeland, however, knew that corpuscles of both charges escaped from the sun but deduced, accurately, that mainly negatively charged electrons caused magnetic storms and auroras.

From a physical point of view it is most probable that solar rays are neither exclusively negative nor positive rays, but of both kinds ... if any positive rays do penetrate into the Earth's atmosphere, they have hardly any perceptible magnetic effect.

In this way, by using the terrellas in conjunction with magnetic results, Birkeland had surmised the existence of a continuous outpouring of equal numbers of positively and negatively charged particles from the sun. He knew that the sun must continuously emit charged particles and suggested that the cathode rays that caused auroras were forced into space from the areas around sunspots, and that some were responsible for magnetic storms around the Earth. This conclusion had far-reaching consequences, as Birkeland wrote in his book:

> Besides making clear the origin of important terrestrial phenomena, the investigations give promise of the possibility of drawing, from the energy of the corpuscular precipitation on the Earth, well-founded conclusions regarding the conditions on the sun ... Further researches may lead to a solution of the most attractive scientific problems of our age—the origin of terrestrial magnetism and the origin of the sun's heat.

Birkeland believed that the electromagnetic influence of the sun on near and distant space was as important as that of gravity. He took the laws of electric and magnetic forces, first written in Maxwell's equations, and applied them to space. It was a major advance in the understanding of the forces at work in the solar system. Before Newton, it was believed that terrestrial mechanics and celestial mechanics obeyed different laws, but Newton showed that a falling apple on the Earth moved according to the same laws as it does the moon—a great breakthrough in physics and particularly in mechanics. Although later scientists revealed limitations in

Newtonian law, Birkeland was the first to stress the importance of electromagnetic effects in cosmic physics. As he realized, cosmic matter is usually conducting and magnetized and these effects are often as great as—if not greater than—mechanical forces in near and distant space. From trying to understand the origins of the aurora borealis, he now wanted to test the boundaries of his theoretical electromagnetic universe.

Copies of Birkeland's 300-page book were sent to the great scientists of Europe, to crowned heads of state, to Wallenberg and Eyde. He received acknowledgments from King Edward, King Haakon, King Oscar, and Kaiser Wilhelm, as well as from Henri Poincaré, Sir William Crookes, and many other scientists. In France his work was read with interest but elsewhere, particularly in Britain, it was largely ignored, and the few reviews it received were negative. Birkeland was furious that the British refused to even consider the possibility that he might be correct and was disappointed that he was now unlikely to be proposed as a Fellow of the Royal Society. It would have been a great achievement to convert his detractors to his ideas, as he knew that British science was increasingly predominant in the world and that it was necessary for the British scientific establishment to accept his theories if they were ever to become widely disseminated. There seemed no chance of that now. As Arthur Schuster, Fellow of the Royal Society and a prominent scientist in the field of terrestrial magnetism, said about Birkeland's work, "The limits of allowable heterodoxy in science are soon reached" and Birkeland had stepped too far out of line. Schuster condemned Birkeland's theories for assuming that only negative rays were emitted by the sun. Had he read more carefully, or with a more open mind, Schuster would have realized that Birkeland knew that both positive and negative particles were thrown out, but had deduced that only negative ones caused auroras. However, Schuster dismissed Birkeland's huge volume with a terse comment in the Society's *Proceedings*:

Even originally well-defined pencils of cathode rays from the sun cannot reach the Earth. For Birkeland's theories to be correct, the existence of such cathode rays is clearly presupposed to be necessary . . . and this assumption is untenable.

12

The Divine Option

March 1910
Christiania and Notodden

The Years like great black oxen tread the world,
And God the herdsman goads them on behind,
And I am broken by their passing feet.

W. B. YEATS (1865–1939), *The Countess Cathleen,* 1892

OR TWO YEARS after the publication of his book Birkeland enjoyed a period of relative peace. Ida, keen to leave Lysaker, found an apartment in Drammensveien, at number 45, midway between the palace park and the waters of Christianiafjord, into which they moved temporarily. A year later the perfect house came on the market and they moved again. Ida occasionally persuaded Birkeland to spend time with her in the evenings and the postcards they sent at Christmas and New Year were signed "Kr. and Ida," but these were rare shows of unity. Her success at enticing Birkeland away from his laboratory was limited; his fascination with the relationship between the sun and the Earth far outweighed interest in his own marriage.

While Birkeland was pursuing his terrella experiments, he began to hear rumors that all was not well at the new factory site of Rjukan. Relationships between BASF and Norsk Hydro were strained to the breaking point. BASF was unhappy about the original agreement it had made in 1906; they wanted more control over the planning and execution of the new sites. It was not only a managerial problem. The international band of workers in the Rjukan valley, where a power plant and the new factory were being built, were close to coming to blows. As Admiral Børresen, a Norwegian shareholder in Norsk Hydro, wrote to a friend, "The Scandinavians and French on one side and the German interests are opposing each other like hostile forces." Birkeland tried to ignore the gossip he heard, mainly at Helland's salon, but soon he had no choice but to listen.

In the early spring of 1910, he was working in the laboratory when the door opened and Sam Eyde stood blinking into the darkness, outlined against the light in the corridor. Birkeland was in the process of taking a photograph of the terrella and shouted to Eyde over the din of the machinery to shut the door. Eyde entered but did not move from the door lest he touch one of the electrified surfaces or fall over the instruments scattered across the floor. After a few minutes of clicks and shuffling about, Birkeland shut down the generator and turned on the light. He was intrigued by the sudden appearance of Eyde, whom he had not seen for many months, and knew it must be related to the rumors.

Eyde did not hide the urgency of his visit. He told Birkeland directly that his furnace was going to be scrapped in favor of the German version unless he could prove by the end of June that it was a superior design. It was March already and Birkeland's mind was not on saltpeter but on space. Eyde explained that BASF had been complaining to the shareholders of the Saltpetreworks Company that the Birkeland-Eyde furnace was inefficient compared to the German design. The shareholders, mostly non-Norwegians, had no loyalty to either furnace and simply wanted the best return on their investment, so it had been decided that a competition should be held over a twenty-four-hour period and the most efficient furnace would be chosen for the new factory at Rjukan. Birkeland would have his consultancy fees canceled if the furnace was abandoned and Eyde would lose the entire value of his half of the patents as well as the influence that using "his" furnace gave him on the shop floor. Moreover, if the German furnaces were adopted, Norsk Hydro would be Norwegian in name only. For Eyde, whose business interests operated on an international level, this would be a deep blow to his reputation, his prospects, and his finances. Birkeland, meanwhile, saw the luxury of having his own laboratory crumbling before his eyes. Without the annual salary from Norsk Hydro and the Saltpetreworks he could not afford to hire assistants and would have to scale down his experiments dramatically.

The alternative to this bleak scenario also had its costs. To save his furnace from extinction he would have to live in Notodden for the next three months, working night and day, abandoning his laboratory and leaving his assistants rudderless among complicated and dangerous equipment. Ida would be upset that work, as always, took precedence over their life together. Birkeland was curious about why Eyde had come to him to ask for help rather than relying on Næss and the other young engineers, but he knew that Eyde would not give him an honest reply. He told Eyde he needed time to think about it and would give him an answer by the end of the week.

By the time Birkeland arrived home, his mind was made up. He told Ida that he needed to spend the next three months in Notodden. She was very upset, but Birkeland felt unable to put their marriage before his work; he simply did not think it was as important. Ida had already come to suspect that it never would be. He had wanted their marriage to be comfortable, companionable, and convenient for them both. Ida would look after him, and, in return, he would provide financial security, a pleasant house, and company whenever possible. Helland had warned him that Ida would not be happy with that arrangement. The silences that had grown between them over the past eighteen months were so frosty that when Birkeland left for Notodden, Ida did not come downstairs to say goodbye.

Ida found her husband's obsession with work the largest obstacle to her own happiness. From the first month of marriage, when

Birkeland had taken her to Notodden, loneliness had gnawed at her. She had tried to amuse herself by looking around Christiania's properties for a new house and was pleased with the villa she had found on the corner of Incognitogaten, in sight of the palace and within ten minutes' walk of the university. It had an Italian feel, with white walls, arched windows, and a central tower one story higher than the rest, with two wings on either side. The house had four large bedrooms, a sitting room looking over the garden toward the palace, an elegant dining room, a study for Birkeland, servants' quarters, and a carriage house and was approached by a gravel drive sheltered from the street by a low wall, a sturdy hedge, and trees. Ida spent much of her time decorating it as she wished with furniture, crystal, and carpets. The only things Birkeland showed an interest in were paintings and unusual objects that his art dealer, Mr. Wang, occasionally procured from the Far East. Whenever Wang left his card, Birkeland became excited and took Ida to the gallery immediately. He was building up a small collection of paintings by contemporary Norwegian artists, Torolf Holmboe and Eilif Peterssen in particular, who specialized in Norwegian subjects. Holmboe took Nordland in Northern Norway as a theme and Birkeland liked to have reminders on his walls of his time spent watching the aurora. He also bought several large vases and pots from Japan and China painted with exotic birds and plants, but Ida was not fond of these and persuaded Birkeland to keep them in his study.

Just as Ida was beginning to doubt the wisdom of her marriage, her family were coming to accept it—now that Birkeland's name was connected to the fertilizer process and he was able to look after her well. Her favorite sister, Camilla, had been writing to her from Raade and hoped to visit before the winter set in, while Helga, her youngest sister, who worked as a nurse and was an amateur pianist in Christiania, came round occasionally. Ida had received a telegram from her parents on her birthday and another on Birkeland's but had not yet visited them. Her father's refusal to perform the wedding ceremony had hurt her deeply.

Ida was lonelier than she had ever been. Although she volunteered to help with the Tuberculosis Society, through which she met a few other wives, and occasionally managed to entice Birkeland to the theater, she spent much of her time alone. When Birkeland had scientists visiting from abroad, his wife enjoyed having company in the house, even though the conversation always turned to science. Her understanding of Birkeland's work remained very sketchy; his scientific explanations contradicted her notions of Divine Will and confused her.

BIRKELAND traveled by train to Kongsberg, then took the usual carriage route across the hills to Notodden. Norsk Hydro was building a railway connection from the factory to the south coast, but it was still unfinished. Notodden had developed from a tiny hamlet to a bustling town of at least 5,000 people since the arrival of the Norsk Hydro factory. Further up the valley by the Rjukan Falls, or where the falls had been, the old settlement of a few farming crofts had been supplanted by a population of 10,000 in less than five years. Once a major beauty spot, the falls were now contained in steel pipes at the head of a valley full of rapidly built houses with the smell of saltpeter hanging in the air. The steep sides of the Rjukan valley blocked sunlight from the settlement for six months of the year and the workers and their families were as pale as new shoots.

One hundred million crowns had been poured into the Saltpetreworks. The factory was almost finished; the hydroelectric plant was already providing electricity although work was continuing on the dam that controlled the flow of water to the plant, despite Parliament's attempts to limit its size. Eyde was not popular with the Norwegian Parliament; it was largely due to his actions that strict Concession Laws regarding foreign ownership of natural resources were being implemented. But Eyde's contacts in the government kept him informed of attempts to curb his freedom, and he was often closeted with lawyers until past midnight, thinking up ways to circumvent the legislation before it came into effect. Eyde's informants warned him at ten o'clock one night that a parliamentary debate on tax was actually a cover for new measures to limit the size of dams for hydroelectric plants and for their reversion to state ownership after sixty years. The law was to come into effect at midnight. At eleven o'clock Eyde rang the Rjukan night manager, ordering him to wake up his workers and tell them to start increasing the height of the dam wall immediately. As long as he could prove that work had started before midnight, he could not be stopped.

Arriving in Notodden, Birkeland was relieved that Næss was away working at the Rjukan factory. Birkeland left his bags at the administration building and went straight to the factory. He realized immediately that the problems could not be solved quickly as the engineers had tried everything to fine-tune the furnace and it was still producing only three-quarters of the projected capacity. Birkeland enjoyed the company of his team of young engineers and admired their dedication so he felt comfortable inviting his new colleagues back to the administration house for good food and laughter after frustrating days at work. One of the engineers, Carl Holmboe, wrote home to describe these gatherings.

We have many pleasant evenings in front of the fireplace, together with Birkeland. He unfolds his brilliant knowledge, his view of the universe, his theories of the Northern Lights and, not least, his opinion of life and mankind.

He predicts the possibility of splitting atoms. The existence of ions, he said, demonstrates that atoms have the ability to limit and absorb electric charges, and thus they must be divisible. I asked if the great harmony observed in the living as well as dead nature might not point to some kind of guiding conscious will in the universe, that theologians might call God. This he does not believe in, but said that such questions are in the borderland between knowledge and faith, and you must be an ignorant fool to consider impossible the divine option.

Six weeks before the furnace competition date, Birkeland was sitting in front of the fire in the administration building, feet almost on the burning logs. It was a rainy April evening and, although the house was well insulated in the manner of Norwegian buildings, the exhausted Birkeland was shivery. For over a month he and the engineers had attempted to improve the furnace, to little effect. For the past two days he had not gone to the factory but had lain in bed or sat staring into space, thinking only of the furnace. When the fire burned low, he expected the maid to build it up again but it was Sunday, her day off. He grudgingly heaved a large log onto the embers, and then another. In that instant, he found the answer. The furnace needed to be much larger—perhaps two or three times the size. He scribbled equations through the night, shuffling his papers together at dawn to walk to the factory through the sharp-scented pinewoods. When his small team of engineers arrived, he explained to them that the furnace was inefficient because it was too small. Instead of 1,000 kilowatts, it should be 3,000. The engineers were appalled. They had only six weeks to completely change the furnace. And there was no guarantee that he was right. They all knew of Eivind Næss's distrust of Birkeland's seemingly eccentric suggestions. Perhaps Næss was right. Birkeland sensed the mood and quickly set about explaining his thinking. Few men could have persuaded these discouraged engineers that a complete overhaul of the furnace was a wise decision, but Birkeland's infectious enthusiasm and obvious brilliance tipped the balance in his favor. Eyde had been right to return to the original inventor: only Birkeland could have seen the flaws in his own thinking and taken such dramatic mea-

sures to overcome them. However, it would take only one component to be miscalculated, miscalibrated, or misaligned for the entire
furnace to malfunction and make them all look ridiculous.

Back in Christiania, a few days after Birkeland's departure for
Notodden, Kaya Geelmuyden called on Ida, knowing he was away
and his wife might be at loose ends. Kaya was the sister of Hans
Geelmuyden, director of the Christiania observatory and professor
of astronomy at the university, and of Marie, who had been a student of mathematics and physics at the same time as Birkeland and
was married to his great friend Wilhelm Bjerkenes. Birkeland knew
the Geelmuyden siblings well and had invited them to dinner on a
few occasions since his marriage. Kaya had an interest in spiritualism and was hoping to start a Norwegian Society for Psychical Science with her friend Ella Anker and an Englishwoman, Hermione
Ramsden, granddaughter of the Duke of Somerset, who was living
in Norway. The society would investigate the possibility of communication with spirits, taking as its model the Society for Psychical
Science in London, which boasted many eminent scientists among
its members, including Sir William Crookes. It had been established
in 1882, with the objective of seeking scientific explanations for psychical phenomena, spiritualism included. Many mediums used
quasi-scientific ideas to bolster their credibility, following the success of Madame Blavatsky, who established the Theosophical Society with the aim of reconciling ancient spiritualistic traditions with
modern science. She attracted followers with dazzling psychic tricks
and attempted to convince them that all matter was an expression
of immaterial force that scientists called "energy" but she knew was
"spirit," a "*conscious* guiding" influence, "Angel or God, Spirit or
Demon." As she related in *The Secret Doctrine*, which appeared in
1888, only a few individuals were blessed with the gift to see the spirits that gave life to physical phenomena:

Standing on an open plain, on a mountain summit especially,
gazing into the vast above and the spatial infinities around,

the whole atmosphere seems ablaze with them, the air soaked through with these dazzling coruscations. At times, the intensity of their motion produces flashes like the Northern Lights.

Blavatsky's philosophy had been popular in Paris when Birkeland was working there, although he had never paid any heed to it. She was eventually exposed as a fraud by the Society for Psychical Research but it did not dent her appeal. Although she died in 1891, Blavatsky's theosophical quest to unite the spiritual and the scientific realms continued among her large following.

Kaya invited Ida to attend a séance conducted by "The Extraordinary Madame Wriedt," whose specialities included levitation, materialization of spirits, and, most important, summoning spirits—"channeling"—who spoke to her through a metal tube like a trumpet, often in foreign tongues, even though she herself spoke only English. Kaya showed Ida an advertisement for the event in the newspaper *Morgenbladet*, dominated by a picture of the medium sheathed in glowing light. As a Christian, Ida did not believe in fortune-tellers but she decided to attend the séance for amusement and to take her mind off her failing marriage. When she had been in London and New York, ten years before, spiritualism was all the rage and queues often stretched around the block for séances with the best mediums. In Norway too, over the past three or four years, séances had become a popular form of entertainment and Ida would not be flouting social convention by attending.

Mrs. Wriedt was an American medium employed by "Julia's Bureau" in London, performing in Norway for one week only at the Saint Olav's Hotel near the state hospital. Arriving at the dingy hotel with Kaya, Ida saw row upon row of women, occasionally accompanied by sad or embarrassed men, all waiting for news, relief from mental anguish, or something to talk about to their friends. After a few minutes of whispering, the audience fell silent as the lights were turned off and Mrs. Wriedt appeared behind a glowing, phosphorescent screen. As she began to speak, in English, her face changed as rapidly as the sky on a windy March day. One moment laughing, the next sobbing and crying out, she would throw her body around and then stand as if frozen, with a strange glow hovering around her like greenish-gray steam. After twenty minutes of these calisthenics, Mrs. Wriedt abruptly stopped "channeling" and placed a metal tube in the center of the floor, explaining that the spirits would send a message through the "trumpet." She bade the spirits to enter it and, after several tense moments, a small bang was heard and the metal tube flew into the air and landed in the lap of an elderly lady. The medium rushed to grasp the surprised woman's hands and stared into her eyes with utmost concentration. After several minutes of general observations to the woman about the spirits wanting her happiness, Mrs. Wriedt was overcome by exhaustion and left the séance.

It was still light when Ida took her leave of Kaya to walk back to Incognitogaten, deep in thought about the séance. As she walked up her drive she saw a gentleman at the door, ringing the bell insistently. He turned as she approached, an Asian man with an extremely thin mustache that fell from the corners of his mouth to the lapel of his cape. On his left cheek was a dark mole from which grew two or three black hairs that exceeded the droop of his mustache. His face was round and soft, the color of pale honey, but his presence, so soon after the séance, seemed sinister. The stranger executed a quick bow and introduced himself, in English, as Professor Terada from Tokyo University. He had come to visit Professor Birkeland, whose famous work on the Earth's magnetism and the Northern Lights had reached Japan. Ida explained that her husband was working away from the capital and was not expected to return for some weeks, and gave him the number of the administration building in Notodden. She invited Professor Terada to stay for tea but he seemed embarrassed to be alone with a woman, handed her his business card, thanked her, and left. The card was printed on both sides, one giving his name in English, the other in Japanese.

The episode disturbed her and she put the card on Birkeland's desk in his study, where she would not have to pass it every time she went out.

Her trip to Mrs. Wriedt gave Ida a taste for séances. It was not so much the "messages" from the spirits that she enjoyed as watching the audience's reaction to them. She rarely told Kaya when she was attending a séance because she did not want Birkeland to find out about her new interest, sure that he would disapprove. She scoured the papers and was usually able to attend at least one séance a week. She loved to watch the different techniques of the women with their props. Mrs. Wriedt's "trumpet" was not exceptional; there were jumping tables, flashing lights, books that opened by themselves, and all manner of voices, dances, and contortions performed as the spirits moved the "vessel." People from all backgrounds were drawn to the events, which allowed them to reveal and indulge their emotions, to think about what might bring them contentment. Few left disappointed. In Ida they awoke a powerful desire to seek happiness.

THE TEST DAY at Notodden was a tense affair. The German engineers kept to themselves, even at mealtimes, and the competition had a gladiatorial air. The furnaces were started at four o'clock in the afternoon and left to run for twenty-four hours. The engineers could make adjustments and repairs to the machines if necessary, and neither furnace was left unattended at any moment for fear of sabotage. The following morning Eyde, a number of shareholders, board members, and two independent overseers arrived to begin their inspection. The overseers spoke only to ask technical questions and sat by themselves at lunch, despite Eyde's attempts to draw them into conversation. The furnaces were switched off at four o'clock, the precious white powder carefully sifted and weighed, and power consumption recorded to produce the final figures that would show which machine was the most efficient at saltpeter production. For two hours Birkeland and his team of engineers speculated about the result. They were delighted that the new furnace, three times more powerful, had functioned perfectly but they were still not sure that production was as efficient as they hoped. The absorption system had always been the weak point, and a third of the gases were escaping before they combined with the water in the cooling towers.

At seven Eyde called Birkeland, the leader of the German engineers, and their senior assistants to his office in the administration building. He explained that, technically, the result was a draw. While the Norwegian furnace was slightly more efficient, the BASF design had better absorption ratios. Birkeland was briefly elated; developing this larger furnace would improve its efficiency and was the best solution for the new factory, perhaps combining it with the German absorption system. BASF, however, wanted the Norwegian furnace disqualified. The German engineers were furious that the Norwegians had changed the size of their furnace at the last moment and complained that this contravened the rules of the competition. Birkeland protested that there was no regulation to say that such changes could not be made and that their furnace had proved the equal of BASF's, and in some respects its superior. Eyde had been aware of Birkeland's plan and had not made any objection to it so the professor expected him to back up his argument. Eyde, however, said little. Tempers were high as the engineers had been working for thirty-six hours without sleep and some of Birkeland's team had been working at this pace for the past two weeks.

The draw had turned a simple decision into a sensitive situation in which politics played the leading role. Eyde explained the decision had been made that four-fifths of the furnaces in the new factory were to be of German design and one-fifth Norwegian. Birkeland was dumbstruck. It made no sense and would cause deep divisions among the workers unless a satisfactory explanation for this seemingly arbitrary act was forthcoming. Eyde explained that Birkeland, although not technically wrong in making such large changes to his design, was ethically wrong. In practice, the German machine had been competing against a different furnace and this was not in the spirit of the competition. Birkeland realized that Eyde had expected the Norwegian furnace to lose all along and had asked him to spearhead their entry into the competition, rather than his favorite engineer, Næss, so that Birkeland could bear the responsibility and shame of losing to the Germans. If Næss had been in charge, Eyde would have had to accept ultimate responsibility, as Næss was clearly his employee. As Birkeland was the inventor, Eyde could hide behind him. Birkeland felt tricked into abandoning his wife, his laboratory, his work, and his assistants in order to be the scapegoat for Eyde. He went to the factory, explained the situation as he saw it to his disappointed engineers, and took a carriage to Kongsberg.

As soon as he returned to Christiania, Birkeland wrote a letter to Eyde and the board of Norsk Hydro:

> 7 July 1910
> It is evident that when such a cowardly deal becomes known to the public, then it will be clear to all that it is without honour for the people from Baden, and possibly also for Norsk Hydro, because they have given in to the brutality of the Badeners.

As he picked up the blotter to dry the ink, he noticed a folded piece of paper underneath it. It was a short note from Ida informing him that she was leaving him and had gone to stay with a friend.

13

Vast, Infinite Space

1911–13
Christiania

"So what do you say, Captain?" I asked at last. "I can really do
anything, whatever you wish. What am I saying? I would have to be a
poor fellow if I didn't do more than just what I was set to do. I can take
two watches in a row if necessary. It'll do me the world of good, and I
believe I can take it." Then he put me to work. Once out in the fjord I
straightened up, wet with fever and fatigue, looked in towards the
shore and said goodbye for now to the city, to Christiania,
where the windows shone so brightly in every home.

KNUT HAMSUN (1859–1952), winner of the Nobel Prize for
Literature; *Hunger,* 1890

FTER IDA'S DEPARTURE, Birkeland rarely left his laboratory. His house felt like a museum, full of strangers,
lawyers, friends of Ida, and appraisers poking into every
corner to draw up inventories and assess the worth of the contents.
He was concerned for Ida, as she must have felt desperate to take
the drastic step of leaving. For the daughter of a vicar, divorce was
only slightly less shameful than suicide, and the unsteady relationship with her family must now be in tatters. Birkeland instructed his
lawyer, Johan Bredal, to provide generously for his wife, so generously that the lawyer demurred and asked him to reconsider, bearing in mind there were no dependent children. Birkeland insisted,

demanding that a clause be inserted into the divorce papers to the effect that Ida was blameless and any fault lay entirely with him. Bredal warned Birkeland that the divorce would not be granted until he and Ida had lived apart for two years and that drawing up a settlement would take time due to the extent of Birkeland's assets.

J. Bredal & Sons, Solicitors
Langes Gate 23, Christiania   26 February 1911

Draft: Divorce settlement for Mrs. Birkeland; itinerary of household items to form part of her settlement. NB: silver, glass and cellar contents not yet listed. J.B.

If I, Kristian Olaf Bernard Birkeland, die before Mrs. Ida Charlotte Birkeland, from my estate 50,000 crowns will be put into an account the interest on which will go to Mrs. Birkeland and after her death to Tønnes Birkeland or his children if he so decides.

chaise longue	family photographs
dining room table and	silk-covered chairs
12 chairs	green damask stools
watercolor by Holmboe	candelabra
double bed	portrait of Napoleon
gilt mirror	writing desk
several carpets	4 sets curtains
portrait of Kaiser Wilhelm	washstand
15 bottles red wine Haute	brass vase
Lafitte 1905	sewing machine
rosewood table	oil lamp
brass lamp	footstool

As his personal life disintegrated, Birkeland threw himself into work with dedication. Back in the laboratory, the presence of his young, enthusiastic assistants and the extraordinary beauty of the terrella experiments helped block out the pain and difficulties of life outside. Birkeland frequently fell asleep on the old fold-up bed at night or, if he did go home, slept in the chair he had inherited from his father, nursing a large whisky into which several grains of veronal had been dissolved.

He hired several more graduates to help process further results from the 1902–1903 expedition in order to publish the second volume of the Aurora Polaris book and to assist with the large number of experiments he was performing. Two of his favorite assistants were moving to higher positions: Sem Sæland had been appointed to the Trondheim Technical High School and Krogness was preparing to live on the summit of Haldde with his family. Money had been granted by the Norwegian Parliament to make Haldde a permanent observatory and to build a more comfortable house, linked to the observatory by a tunnel. Birkeland hoped that it would operate for at least two solar cycles, or twenty-two years, to provide valuable continuous information about the solar-terrestrial relationship. Magnetic readings would be taken, and the permanent station could provide weather forecasting details, give early warnings of storms and eventually provide evidence for the effect on the weather of the auroras and the changes in the magnetic field. Meanwhile, Dietrichson, Birkeland's old friend, had fallen seriously ill and could no longer work in the laboratory. Birkeland felt his loss keenly but Olaf Devik was available to help with the new experiments he was planning.

Birkeland's main preoccupation was to build a much larger terrella machine in which to re-create many phenomena of the solar system beyond the Earth. He drew up plans for a new machine unlike anything that had been made before. The simplicity of the design reflected the brilliance of the idea. Instead of using a Crookes tube, he would make a large glass box, like a spacious aquarium, which would provide a window into space. The box would be pumped out to create a vacuum and he would use larger globes and a more powerful cathode to produce charged particles. With so much more room he would be able to see effects, obscured in the smaller tubes, that could take his Northern Lights theory one step further—into a complete cosmogony, a theory of the origins of the universe.

No one had ever attempted to create a vacuum chamber on this scale before and the task was fraught with difficulties and dangers. The four sides were of flat plate glass, 20 millimeters thick, made specifically to Birkeland's calculations to withstand a high vacuum. It took many hours and much sweat to make the glass plates because even the slightest fault could cause the chamber to implode under pressure. With the strength of vacuum Birkeland required, an implosion would fling shards of glass at great force around the small office, certainly proving fatal to those nearby. Once the specially made plates arrived, they were cemented together and fitted with a bronze roof and floor. These conducted electricity when the machine was on and touching them would cause a severe, possibly lethal, electric shock. The glass box was placed on a sturdy wooden frame with a rail extending beyond the metal to keep people away from the electrified parts.

Then the laborious work of sealing the joints began. To keep the vacuum chamber airtight, layer upon layer of foul-smelling black "picein," a tarlike sealing agent, was painted over all the joints. For this, Birkeland hired Olaf Devik's younger brother, Karl, who showed tremendous patience with the task and was also slim enough to fit inside the box to clean it. Once the joints were airtight, a circular globe and a cathode were fitted.

The size and flat sides of the terrella made visibility much better than had been the case in the Crookes tubes, and Birkeland realized quickly that with such a machine, he could change the globe from simulating the Earth to simulating the sun. The terrella, without its phosphorescent coating, became the cathode emitting charged particles—like the sun. All sorts of beautiful solar phenomena could be re-created this way, such as the sun's corona, the shining layers of the sun's outer atmosphere, usually visible only during a total eclipse. He could reproduce sunspots that moved across the surface of the terrella and down toward the equator as he increased the globe's magnetism. By examining the terrella under a microscope afterwards, Birkeland found small pits and craters where the sunspots had been, providing more evidence for his theory that the sun throws out material during solar flares. Birkeland knew that sunspots could not be the sole cause of magnetic disturbances, however, as their appearance did not always coincide with maximum disruption to the Earth's magnetic field. "The results suggest that sunspots and magnetic storms are both manifestations of the same primary cause." He deduced that there must be regions on the sun that emitted huge disruptive electric discharges into space, the source of magnetic storms, the aurora borealis and the Zodiacal Light. These areas remained active during several complete rotations of the sun, causing similar auroral displays at periods of twenty-seven to twenty-nine days. Similar processes could also explain planet formation, according to Birkeland, as "atomic dust" thrown up by the sun slowly clumped together into large masses under the influence of magnetism. He considered the asteroid belt to be solar dust halfway through the process of transforming into planets.

With this extraordinary machine Birkeland was able to simulate Saturn's rings, comet tails, and the Zodiacal Light. He even experimented with space propulsion using cathode rays. Sophisticated photographs were taken of each simulation, to be included in the next volume of Birkeland's great work, which would discuss the electromagnetic nature of the universe and his theories about the formation of the solar system.

As the experiments yielded increasingly spellbinding phenomena and startling results, Birkeland decided that even bigger terrellas were needed. Over the next two years, yet larger vacuum chambers were built, until they reached the huge size of 1,000 liters, with glass walls 5 centimeters thick. The resulting phenomena were remarkably beautiful, as Birkeland acknowledged in his written accounts of the terrella experiments.

> It will be easily understood that in addition to the purely scientific reasons for doing this, I have also a secondary object, which is to give myself the pleasure of seeing all these important experiments in the most brilliant form that is possible for me to give.

Birkeland's immersion into the universe of his vacuum chamber was so complete he had little time for any other activities other than, as always, keeping abreast of theoretical and technological advances in physics and other fields that interested him, such as astronomy, weather prediction, engineering, and mineralogy. He was fascinated by experiments of the Nobel Prize–winning physicist Ernest Rutherford, reported in 1911, that proved that the atom consisted not only of electrons, as J. J. Thomson had shown in 1897 (in a paper in which he cited Birkeland's work), but also of a nucleus. Until that time, it was known that atoms must have negative and positive charges in order to be electrically neutral, but the model used was Thomson's "plum pudding," in which electrons were embedded in a positively charged material that constituted most of the mass and volume of the atom. Rutherford devised an ingenious experiment in which tiny alpha particles, emitted from a radioactive substance at high speed, were shot at a strip of gold foil. The particles passed through the foil almost as if it were empty space but a few were strongly repelled as if they had hit something very hard. If atoms were compact spheres, as Thomson had suggested, most of the alpha particles would have been scattered by the foil. Rutherford deduced that the few alpha particles that were deflected had hit the nuclei of the gold atoms, a concentrated area of positive charge. From this, Rutherford was able to conclude that the atom is mainly empty space, roughly one-hundred-millionth of an inch in diameter but made up of a positively charged nucleus

10,000 times smaller than that and negatively charged electrons, minute in comparison to the nucleus. Rutherford did not know the exact structure of the atom but discovering the nucleus was an important stepping stone toward learning it. Reading Rutherford's paper, Birkeland regretted not pursuing his own idea of splitting the atom to create energy. He had written to Wallenberg in 1906 for funding to explore this but Wallenberg had politely declined, accepting Birkeland's idea as "titanic" but explaining that he needed the nitrogen furnace to be working efficiently before he had money to spare for further speculation.

The laboratory became a beehive of productivity with Birkeland throwing out ideas like confetti. His assistants described how he would go out for walks and return a few hours later, refreshed, hat pushed back on his head, with an idea for rocket propulsion or a hearing aid or a new telephone. In tandem with his terrella work, he began experiments with hydrogenating vegetable oil to make margarine. The law professors soon complained of the terrible stink of burning fat disturbing their lectures. They also complained that he had taken over half the lecture hall for other experiments; nor did they care for the large antenna that he requested be fixed to the roof so that modern communications technology could be installed.

Birkeland was aware that his work was unpopular with many of his colleagues, and assumed that they were resentful that he had effectively given up teaching and was free to pursue his ideas without the financial constraints they labored under. The fact that he employed the cream of the university's graduates only added to their jealousy. When Birkeland complained about the ill-feeling to Helland, the latter agreed that there was a certain Norwegian temperament that did not like one person doing better than others. To add to his colleagues' chagrin, the newspapers were full of the triumph of Birkeland's furnace being officially adopted for the newest factory, Rjukan II, in the Rjukan valley, eighty kilometers north of Notodden. The decision, however, had been motivated by politics rather than design following a crisis in Morocco. An uprising in

Agadir had been suppressed by the French military in July. In order to protect their own interests in the face of the unrest and French military activity, the Germans sent a gunboat to Agadir as a warning that they would not tolerate increased French influence in the region. An agreement was eventually reached but the French government put pressure on Paribas to push the Germans out of Norsk Hydro to hinder their access to saltpeter, a key component in explosives. Aware of the reason behind the decision, Birkeland could take little personal pride in the choice of his furnace, but he was pleased that his consultancy fee had been almost doubled to 22,000 crowns a year, averting the funding crisis he had envisaged had only German technology been used at Rjukan II. Birkeland was also delighted that this triumph of Norwegian technology added to the glory of the emerging nation, still only seven years old. On 14 December 1911 Roald Amundsen planted the Norwegian flag at the South Pole—first in the race to reach it. The country's fight for recognition, in which Birkeland played a prominent part, was being won.

IN THE NEW YEAR of 1912 Birkeland was invited to lunch by his lawyer, Johan Bredal, to sign a number of papers concerning the divorce agreement. Although it would not take effect for another year, the details were now largely decided. Once the legal matters were dispensed with at Bredal's office, the two men went for lunch at the Grand, during the course of which Bredal asked for Birkeland's help. It emerged that Bredal had allowed himself to be elected to a committee at the suggestion of two women, Ella Anker and Hermione Ramsden. He explained that they wanted to arrange a séance with a famous medium, to be performed under the supervision of a scientific committee that would give unbiased evaluation of her abilities. He explained that Oskar Jæger had been the only professor at the university to show any interest in spiritualism but would unfortunately be away at the time of the proposed séance. Kaya Geelmuyden had suggested Birkeland as a replacement.

Bredal himself had agreed to join because the number of his friends and acquaintances espousing the virtues of spiritualism with vague and spurious evidence distressed him. He worried that in this era of tremendous scientific and technological advancement, people wanted to switch off their new electric lighting and return to the mysticism of the Dark Ages.

Birkeland agreed to join the committee, hoping to repeat the success of the Society of Psychical Research in unveiling Madame Blavatsky. He knew of her notion that the Northern Lights were manifestations of spiritual energy, as Silvanus Thompson had sent him a copy of Blavatsky's *The Secret Doctrine* to amuse him. Bredal told Birkeland that a medium had been chosen, a Mrs. Wriedt, who had been popular during a previous visit to the capital. She had been expected in April, but due to the sinking of the *Titanic* had had to postpone her visit. The owner of Julia's Bureau, for which she worked, was a Mr. Stead, who had perished in the disaster. Mrs. Wriedt claimed to be able to contact him, and her services were in great demand by relatives who hoped to have messages from their loved ones, directly or through Mr. Stead's spirit. Birkeland was relieved that the ordeal would be delayed and returned happily to his laboratory.

Mrs. Wriedt eventually arrived in Christiania on 12 August and retired with her retinue to Saint Olav's Hotel. The following day, Birkeland, leader of the committee, met his colleagues in the foyer of the hotel. They were Johan Bredal, Mr. Damman, a wholesaler, and the editor of *Elektroteknisk Tiddsskrift* magazine, Hans Berg-Jæger. They attended three of Mrs. Wriedt's famous gatherings, after which Birkeland reported the findings of the committee to Ella Anker and Hermione Ramsden and wrote a long article, printed in *Aftenposten* on 25 August, exposing Mrs. Wriedt as a fraud:

> I have been present at three séances with Mrs. Wriedt, to see and hear her spirits in action, and I shall give an account of her best performance—the thin aluminum tube through

which the spirits "speak" by suddenly jumping a meter or so off the ground and hitting one of those present. I wanted to blow into the tube before the séance began but Mrs. Wriedt refused, explaining that the spirits would not speak through it. At the séance, nothing noteworthy happened until we heard a little bang followed by "noises from the spirits" as the tube jumped and hit the head of Miss G. When the light was switched on again I felt inside the tube where water had condensed and I could smell explosive gas. This was substantiated by three of those present. I had briefly examined the tube before the séance, until it was wrested from my hand by the medium, and it had been dry.

I must admit that I am thankful to the Madam that she stopped me in my examination of the tube for if I had gone any further I would have blown my fingers off.

Jesus, what a woman! We could easily enter the darkest Middle Ages if we give in to monsters such as Mrs. Wriedt. I am giving my scientific name and reputation as a guarantee that the medium, Mrs. Wriedt, is a cunning swindler.

In principle, I am against burning witches, but a teeny weeny fire in honor of Mrs. Wriedt would not be out of place.

His article stirred up a heated debate in the capital that led to the condemnation of the growth of spiritualism and religious cults in Norway and to the idea of setting up a Psychical Society, whether scientific or not. Birkeland thoroughly disapproved of the séances and was pleased to have exposed the fraudulent antics of the medium, but the episode had made him acutely aware that the collapse of his marriage had been his fault. He had been very disturbed by Kaya's admission that Ida had been attending séances secretly during the year before she left him. That he did not know his wife had enjoyed the performances of a duplicitous American spiritualist revealed to him how little interest he had shown in her. He wished he had declined the invitation to lead the committee—it had been a sad distraction—and retreated to his laboratory.

IN JANUARY 1913 Birkeland arranged a public lecture to demonstrate his terrella machine and to announce the theories emerging from his work on the Northern Lights. He was planning to publish the second volume of his treatise later in the year and wished to rekindle interest in his work. He would simulate sunspots, the solar corona, the Zodiacal Light, Saturn's rings, comet tails, and other cosmic phenomena that no one in the audience would ever have seen before. He would draw the solar system into his glass box and explain how all these cosmic events could be understood as aspects of the same phenomenon that created the Northern Lights: the electromagnetic power of the sun, the very source of the solar system. He announced the event in *Aftenposten* and within a few days had news that the king of Norway wished to attend. King Haakon had followed Birkeland's progress since his first visit to Norsk Hydro in 1908, when the professor had explained aspects of the furnace design to him, clearly and absorbingly. The title of the lecture was announced as "The Creation of Our Solar System and Other Worlds in the Universe" accompanied by the world's first "terrella demonstration," to be given in the Festival Hall of the university where Birkeland had infamously demonstrated his cannon.

On the day of the lecture, 31 January, the king walked from the palace along Carl Johan Gate, attended by a small retinue of friends, family, and retainers, all intrigued by the professor's latest invention. As usual, the king was wearing a naval uniform, since he had trained as an officer and served as Supreme Admiral of the Fleet. He rarely wore anything else in public as his great height made suits look ungainly on him. Once in the hall, he was ushered to the front row.

Birkeland knew that his lecture involved such advanced physics that no one in the audience would truly comprehend his overall theory. He was possibly the only man in the world who had the breadth of knowledge to create his own cosmogony based on the laws of electromagnetism. In this gathering of the capital's elite, no other person could know whether what he said was true. At the last moment he decided to abandon his sophisticated talk and instead to take the audience on a journey around the solar system in the terrella, accompanied by simplified explanations of his theories. The hall lights dimmed and the box started to spin with miniature suns, planets, and comets. Birkeland began:

> To understand the distances that I have captured in this vessel, imagine that our sun is a grain of sand a millimeter in diameter. In that case, the Earth would be an invisible speck of dust ten centimeters away. And the next nearest star, Alpha Centauri, would be twenty kilometers away. It is in this vast, infinite space that the genesis of all celestial bodies is to be found. All matter that we see, be it our own bodies, our Earth, other planets, the sun, our solar system, and other solar systems, all matter is composed of flying atoms that are continuously ejected from our sun and other suns by electrical forces and that condense to form particles. And these in turn condense to form large spheres, ultimately planets and all thereupon. It follows from this that everything that is matter, all living beings in the universe, is linked, one to the other.

Sitting inches from the sun, Saturn's rings, and a comet, the audience was spellbound by Birkeland's words and the dazzling worlds that were unfolding before them. Few had any previous inkling of the grandeur and mystery of space, the teeming activity within it and the forces that ruled beyond the boundaries of Earth.

> It seems to me to be true, from what I have already said, that new worlds emerge in space more frequently than human beings are born on the Earth. Each world has its *éclair de nuit,*

its flash of lightning in the dark, the struggle of intelligent beings with their thoughts and their discoveries to banish ignorance. Such moments of illumination disappear without trace, and it also follows that such worlds must die more frequently than human beings die upon the Earth or, more accurately, they are born and die in such a number that surpasses our imagination.

Although he received positive reviews in Norway for this lecture, the printed versions that appeared in science journals elsewhere received little comment. In France, where his work was usually well received in the Academy, it was largely overshadowed by the tragic news that his scientific mentor, friend, and supporter, Henri Poincaré, had died, aged only fifty-eight, after a simple operation. Poincaré had been Birkeland's champion on the international stage of science; his loss was a personal and professional blow, soon to be followed by others.

At the end of January Birkeland received a letter from Tønnes, informing him that their mother was ill and unlikely to recover. He boarded a train for the five-hour journey to Porsgrund and found her sitting quietly in a large armchair by the stove, a frail figure wrapped in shawls and blankets. Birkeland had little to talk about; he did not want to burden her with news of his divorce and she would not understand the progress he was making in his scientific research. He held her hand and sat in silence. After she had gone to bed, Tønnes explained that she might last for a few weeks but no more. Birkeland stayed for four days but left after realizing that his presence was tiring her. The day after he returned to the capital, Tønnes called to say that she had died, aged seventy-one.

Birkeland's mood became distracted and depressed and he resorted again to veronal and whisky to help him sleep. His divorce papers arrived in the mail in March at the end of a winter of unmitigated grayness. He occupied himself with the final corrections to his manuscript for the second volume of *The Norwegian Aurora*

Polaris Expedition but as soon as they were finished he fell ill with an ear infection that confined him to bed for several weeks.

When Aschehoug, the oldest publisher in Norway, which had produced the first part of the book, published volume two in the early summer, Birkeland felt a sense of pride in the photographs of the terrella, the breadth of the content, and the originality of his ideas. No other study of the Earth's magnetism had ever been as thorough and complete as this. His work was overshadowed, however, by scientific developments occurring elsewhere. Einstein's special theory of relativity was published in 1905, and only a few months before Birkeland's book appeared Niels Bohr announced his model of the atom in which electrons orbited the nucleus as the planets orbit the sun. Physics was taking scientists into new atomic worlds that seemed more exciting than the grand sweep of the visible solar system. Although Birkeland's ideas were too far ahead of their time to be fully understood, they also seemed curiously old-fashioned. His work, which had once caused intense disagreement, was now met by a wall of indifference.

In the second volume of his book, Birkeland wrote:

> We have arrived at results that seem to us so valuable, that they have rewarded us for the exertions and personal sacrifices that the work has cost.

He still believed this to be true, despite his poor health, broken by overwork to fund his research, his drinking, a failed marriage, his alienation from the industrial giant he had helped to create, his mother's death, the criticism and resentment of his colleagues at the university, and the lack of acceptance or recognition abroad for his theories. He was still sure that what he had discovered justified the path he had chosen, yet he could not face another grinding winter in Christiania, tired and alone. Following Birkeland's most recent illness, Tønnes had advised him to drink less whisky, keep his use of veronal to a minimum, and move to a warmer climate until he had recovered his full strength. Birkeland's thoughts turned again to Egypt. There he might find what he needed, both to gain acceptance for his theories and to recover his health. The terrella experiments led him to believe that the Zodiacal Light was the only phenomenon visible from Earth in which one could directly measure the amount of electrically charged particles thrown out from the sun. It lay beyond the Earth's magnetic field, allowing electron beams, or cathode rays, to be studied before they were affected by the magnetic field of the Earth. The auroras, by contrast, were the light trails of the tiny fraction of electrons not deflected by the magnetic field. The Zodiacal Light was perhaps the faint but visible evidence Birkeland needed to prove that the sun did emit cathode rays that could extend throughout the solar system—the last brick he needed to complete his theoretical house. If he could find a way to measure the cathode rays, even his critics at the Royal Society would be forced to accept his theories.

Birkeland spent the summer making preparations to leave the country, closing up his house, telling friends and colleagues of his plan to travel to Egypt and the Sudan and informing Krogness in Haldde that he would send a telegram upon his arrival so that they could coordinate magnetic observations between Northern Norway and the equatorial zone. The two assistants Birkeland chose to travel to Egypt with him were Karl Devik, who was talented at performing experiments and whose company Birkeland greatly enjoyed, and Thoralf Skolem, a young, gifted mathematician who would help with theoretical calculations concerning the Zodiacal Light. In an act of extreme generosity that also showed Birkeland planned to be away for several years, he wrote to the Senate of the university:

> Professor Kr. Birkeland declares by letter to the Senate that he conveys a gift to the university of all his machines and instruments located at the Department of Physics. The professor does, however, reserve the right to use the equipment.

In the late summer, once preparations were complete, Birkeland went to the Swan Apothecary on Carl Johan Gate. It was an alluring shop, muraled on the ceiling with swan designs in cooling greens and blues. The back wall was entirely given over to narrow drawers in classical columns, their smooth wood punctuated by white enamel labels denoting their contents. Birkeland asked for two bags of veronal, which the pharmacist provided reluctantly, warning the professor that side effects had been reported. Birkeland did not listen. From the pharmacy he walked across the square to Rådhusgata to the offices of the Meridian Shipping Company. He bought a first-class ticket to Alexandria, stopping in London and Marseilles, leaving the following week.

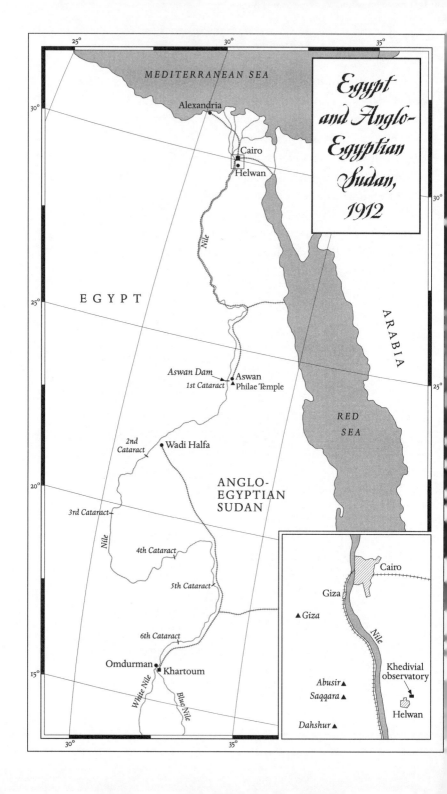

Egypt and Anglo-Egyptian Sudan, 1912

MEDITERRANEAN SEA

Alexandria

Cairo
Helwan

EGYPT

ARABIA

Nile

Aswan Dam
1st Cataract
Aswan
Philae Temple

RED SEA

2nd Cataract
Wadi Halfa

ANGLO-EGYPTIAN SUDAN

3rd Cataract

Nile

4th Cataract

5th Cataract

6th Cataract

Omdurman
Khartoum

White Nile

Blue Nile

Cairo

Giza

▲ Giza

Nile

Abusir ▲
Saqqara ▲

Khedivial observatory

Dahshur ▲

Helwan

PART III

Zodiacal Light

Kristian Birkeland dressed as the Prophet during his stay in Omdurman, Sudan, late 1913. Courtesy of the Norsk Hydro Archives

14

The Dusty Disc

Autumn 1913
Alexandria, Egypt

May you enter favored, and leave beloved.

Ancient Egyptian prayer

IRKELAND, Karl Devik, and Thoralf Skolem arrived in Alexandria at the beginning of October. At the docks, porters in long, loose robes unloaded the crates of scientific instruments. They were being sent directly to an observatory south of Cairo where Birkeland had arranged with the British director for them to be kept until the spring. Egyptian customs officials, overseen by a British observer, stamped their import papers and painted the crates with the delivery address: KHEDIVIAL OBSERVATORY—HELWAN. In the meantime, Birkeland, Skolem, and Devik would travel to Omdurman in the Sudan, where Birkeland had decided they would stand the best chance of observing the elusive Zodiacal Light. The subtle phenomenon was most clearly visible in equatorial regions, where the sky grew dark more quickly after sunset than it did further north. Here, the Zodiacal Light formed a nearly ninety-degree angle with the horizon, making it less likely to be obscured by mountains or buildings, and the weather in Africa afforded many more clear, cloudless nights for observation than in Norway.

They stayed that evening at the Cecil Hotel, having driven there in an open carriage through narrow streets behind the Abu el-Abbas el-Mursi Mosque and the Corniche, the graceful waterfront of the eastern harbor. The hotel had a long mahogany reception desk staffed by Englishmen with hushed voices, several large paintings of the late Queen Victoria, and a pair of the latest electric lifts whose wrought-iron grilles and polished wooden doors were controlled by Egyptian bellboys in full livery. From Birkeland's room a tiny balcony looked over the eastern harbor and the squat fort of Qait Bey, the medieval Mamluk stronghold built on the site of the Pharos Lighthouse, which had been one of the seven wonders of the ancient world. Birkeland recalled Lieblein's lectures about the once great entrance into Egypt; this bay had been the stage for over two thousand years of history. Alexander the Great decided to build the capital of his empire on the site of the tiny village that had stood here and it grew to rival Rome, attracting great scholars like Euclid and Archimedes to its library. Mark Antony arrived here to be with Cleopatra, a relationship that led eventually to their suicides and the sacking of Alexandria. The city was left to decline until a few decades before Birkeland's arrival, at which time it was redeveloped by the rulers of Egypt, the khedives, as Egypt's principal port.

The train to Cairo, from where they would travel to the Sudan, did not depart until morning and so they decided to attend the evening piano recital advertised on the hotel's bulletin board. Birkeland's deafness, caused by radio experiments he had conducted as a student, made concerts rather hard work but the program looked interesting: Bach, Debussy, Brahms, Scarlatti, Rameau-Lechetizky. They found the torchlit passageway between a jeweler's and a coffee shop that led to the theater, a striking building whose architectural features perfectly reflected the history of the city—Greek pillars, a Roman lintel, and papyrus decorative reliefs interspersed with elaborate Egyptian wrought-iron lanterns.

The audience at the concert was primarily European, although there were a few Egyptian men wearing western dress but sporting the deep red fez on their heads. Although Alexandria was now the first port of Egypt and the main gateway to Africa, the city felt more Mediterranean than African, and often more Greek than Egyptian. The khedive of Egypt during the first half of the nineteenth century, Muhammed Ali, had encouraged immigration in the hope of improving trade with Europe. Workers had arrived from Italy, England, and Germany but mainly from Greece. Greek businesses thrived in Egypt, exporting cotton, manufacturing cigarettes, running restaurants, and financing new businesses.

The performers were introduced in Greek and a slender woman in her mid-thirties walked on stage, leaning on the arm of a young man carrying a violin. The woman's name, deciphered by Birkeland from the Greek program notes, was Miss H. Spandonides; the initial was never elaborated into a full Christian name, unlike that of her accompanist, Efstafiou Likouvi. Miss Spandonides had a very pale complexion and wore a dress modeled on an ancient Greek tunic, white with geometric patterns around the neck, hem, and sleeves. She appeared too fragile to play with much gusto, but after a few bars, it was clear that she was a very fine pianist. For two hours the Norwegian scientists sat among Greeks listening to European music in the heat of an Egyptian night. They returned to the hotel bar afterwards and were soon joined by the pianist and her friends, with whom they struck up conversation. Miss Spandonides was not on tour but had given the concert to please some friends who lived in Alexandria. The main purpose of her trip was to take a cure for several months in Helwan, twenty-five kilometers south of Cairo, where she would stay at the Tewfiq Palace Hotel. The three men agreed to call upon her should she still be there when they returned from the Sudan.

The following morning, Birkeland, Devik, and Skolem caught a train to Cairo, the first railway connection in Africa. It had been built with British technology imported when the British invaded Egypt in 1882 under the pretext of protecting her citizens from discontented Egyptian nationalists. In fact, it was primarily an excuse for the British to interfere in the affairs of this strategically important country. The train rattled across the Nile delta, where the landscape had changed little since pharaonic times. It was a picturesque scene of small, fertile fields tended by families of peasants in long robes and dresses of striped cotton, with donkeys and small carts. Despite the fact that they made only a precarious living from the land, on them fell the main burden of Egyptian taxation and the expenses of the British occupation. Although they did not experience any hostility, the visitors soon became aware of the political tensions and social divisions in the country. As the train left the fields behind, the mud shacks of Cairo's outskirts came into view, swiftly followed by houses of several stories with washing strung from window to window.

The men stayed just a few days in the city, long enough to arrange transport to Omdurman, to set up a bank account, and to meet the Norwegian consul, Mr. Hooker. Birkeland sought his advice on buying a property in Egypt but he proved unhelpful and Birkeland left disappointed. However, at Shepheard's Hotel, the unofficial embassy, post office, luggage room, club, and office for European visitors to the city, Birkeland met the Danish consul, Dr. Eriksen. The two men instantly took a liking to each other and Eriksen promised to look into property matters for Birkeland. The consul was fascinated by Birkeland's plans to study the Zodiacal Light and made him promise to visit him in Cairo on his return to relate all that he discovered in the Sudan.

The journey to Omdurman was surprisingly easy. They took a night train from Cairo to Aswan, the most southerly town on the Egyptian Nile, where they were joined by a number of European tourists for the final few kilometers of track, which skirted the Aswan Dam and terminated at the banks of the Nile beyond the First Cataract. From here, small boats carried the tourists to the semisubmerged pillars and courtyards of the Philae Temple, past hieroglyphs and monumental gateways and over the sacred sanctuaries and statues of the gods lying beneath the translucent green waters of the Nile. A short carriage journey took them to the Nile steamer that carried them up the majestic river to the impassable Second Cataract and the bustling village of Wadi Halfa. Here, the railway recommenced and crossed the desert to Khartoum. The incongruous train line, over eight hundred kilometers long between Wadi Halfa and the capital of Anglo-Egyptian Sudan, passed through unbroken, unpopulated desert. It had been constructed by Lord Kitchener about twenty years before in order to capture the Sudan from the Muslim Mahdi, bringing it under the "protection" of the Egyptians and British. During the major battle of the campaign, 11,000 Mahdists were slaughtered by the superior firepower of the Anglo-Egyptian force, who lost only forty-eight troops. Kitchener burned the Mahdi's body in the furnace of a steamship and contemplated using his skull as an inkstand. Birkeland had heard this story: it had been a source of disquiet in Norway. Perhaps this colored his judgment of the British administration of the Sudan and, particularly, of its leader: "The governor of the city of Omdurman is a young noble Englishman. When talking he often seems somewhat embarrassed although he rules the city with a firm hand."

The train arrived in Khartoum, the bustling capital built where the Blue and the White Niles converged. A little to the north, on the east bank of the Nile, was situated the more ancient city, the former capital, Omdurman. Omdurman was at the crossroads of several trade routes across Africa. The large market square teemed with camel sellers, ivory and spice merchants, goldsmiths, horse dealers and slave traders, farmers and tribesmen from southern Sudan and beyond, Nubians and Tuareg. During the mornings, women could be seen haggling at the stalls, some seminaked, others swathed from head to foot in black or white cloth, faces and even eyes often concealed behind metal visors and close-link chain mesh. Despite the variety found at the market, Omdurman itself was suffering from several years of poor harvests, and *durra,* a grain with which bread was made, was selling for ten times the price it had fetched four years earlier. Most inhabitants lived at subsistence level by keeping a few animals. As Birkeland observed in an article he wrote for the newspaper *Aftenposten,* after he had been in Omdurman for a few weeks:

> There are a considerable number of cows, goats, and sheep at Omdurman. Each day thousands of animals are led out in the morning and in the evening they return in a cloud of dust exactly at sunset.

To accompany the article Devik took photographs: of the view from their balcony, a holy man, a water carrier, and other sights that struck him during the first few weeks. Birkeland gave a taste of their living and working conditions for the readers:

> Skolem, Devik, and I are living in a comfortable house with three rooms, a large balcony and an outhouse. I have rented it from a Greek and furnished it in a simple manner. The house is situated on the outskirts of Omdurman close to the desert, a location favorable for our observations. When observing the Zodiacal Light at night, the wind is often so strong that I, in contrast to my assistants, am not able to stay on the roof of our house but instead prefer a site by a wall, somewhat further out in the desert.

The last photograph in the piece was of Birkeland himself, dressed from head to toe in a prophet's costume with a turban and glittering *galabiyya.* As he wrote, "The turban is from Mecca and in Arabic silver letters is written 'the prophet'—in Norwegian, in order not to insult the Arabic silversmith."

Although taking time to explore the city, Birkeland was impatient to begin observations of the Zodiacal Light. First, however, he had to surmount an unexpected obstacle. He had assumed that the ancient city of Omdurman would be barely electrified, but street-lights were widespread and ruined their observations of the Light. In order to see the Zodiacal Light better, Birkeland sent a letter to the assistant governor of Khartoum with a very unusual request:

October 1913

Dear Mr. Sandford,
    I have come especially to the Sudan to study the Zodiacal Light because the origin of this has not yet been discovered.
    We are working from sunset until 9 P.M. and from 3 A.M. to 5 A.M. each night for twelve nights after each new moon. We wish to photograph the Light but the lamps in the streets make this impossible and I should be very much obliged if you would kindly arrange for the lights (as shown in the attached plan) to be extinguished by 3 A.M. each morning.
    Yours very sincerely,
    Kr. Birkeland.

Mr. Sandford obliged, and the three scientists began their observations in earnest. Even without the street lamps, to see the Zodiacal Light they had to keep the lights turned off in the house after sunset to allow their eyes to grow accustomed to the dark before venturing into the desert. The subtle phenomenon appeared about one hour after dusk above the western horizon and one hour before sunrise above the eastern horizon, so the scientists lived a nocturnal existence. It appeared softly as their eyes adjusted to its ethereal presence, an elongated pyramid of pale light that reached from the horizon far up into the night sky. There had been reports of the Light making a complete arch over the sky to the opposite horizon, although Birkeland did not observe this. The pyramid of light was not exactly at right angles to the horizon but tilted about ten or fifteen degrees and appeared to glow with a constant intensity until it faded after an hour or so as the Earth turned. The opposite occurred before dawn. The darkness was gradually illuminated by the column of light about an hour before dawn until the Earth turned sufficiently for it to be swamped by the bright dawn light.

The first person to write about the Zodiacal Light, observed on 18 March 1683, was the eminent Italian astronomer Giovanni Domenico Cassini. He saw a cone of brighter sky that stretched up from the horizon along the ecliptic of the celestial sphere, on which were also situated the constellations of the Zodiac—hence the name he gave to the phenomenon. Cassini's explanation, that the Light was caused by sunlight scattered off small particles orbiting the sun, was still considered valid when Birkeland set out to study it further. He agreed with Cassini that a substantial constituent of the Zodiacal Light was created when light illuminated the disc of dust particles that spread out from the sun. The effect seen from Earth was similar to a beam of sunlight illuminating a dark room through a narrow gap in the curtains. Specks of dust could be seen dancing in the beam but not beyond it, although dust was there. If the beam fell directly on the viewer, no dust would be seen either for the eye would not perceive it against the intensity of the sunlight. Similarly, the Zodiacal Light was seen only from the night side of the Earth, without the interference of direct sunlight. The dusty disc was thought to be lens-shaped, or like a fried egg, as if the sun were the yolk and the dust the white. It rotated around the star along with the planets embedded in it.

Unlike Cassini and most other observers of the Zodiacal Light, however, Birkeland also believed that a small but significant constituent of the Zodiacal Light was not caused by light bouncing off dust, but by light being deflected by electrons emitted from the sun's surface—the same electrons that caused the Northern Lights. He had read in earlier reports about the Zodiacal Light, particularly that of the American Reverend George Jones, published in 1856, that it pulsated or was not entirely constant. Birkeland surmised that light particles, or photons, traveling from the sun would hit the electrons and be deflected. A number of them would reach Earth and, Birkeland hoped, could be measured. However, photons deflected by the dust particles would also be measured. The only way to distinguish between them was to observe whether there was any variation in the number of photons detected. The light emitted by the sun was constant, a fact established by two scientists, Langley and Abbot, in America, in 1881, and confirmed many times subsequently. They used a spectrobolometer, which measured the relative intensity of the spectrum, and a pyrheliometer that calibrated the results, to show that the number of photons emitted by the sun varied by less than 1 percent, if at all. If there were rapid variations in the Zodiacal Light, this would be caused by irregular emissions of charged particles from the sun that would scatter the photons. The same particles would also cause magnetic storms, which Birkeland hoped to record with the magnetometers he had brought with him. If he could find a way to accurately record variations in the Zodiacal Light, he would have the indisputable evidence he needed that cathode rays were emitted from the sun.

To begin this process, it was important to know more about the dusty disc and the Zodiacal Light. Birkeland and Devik made many drawings of the Light pyramid in relation to the horizon and the stars. They could gain an impression of variations in the Zodiacal Light by comparing it to the stars. The intensity of starlight was first categorized by the ancient Greek astronomer Hipparchus in the second century B.C. He made a catalogue of about a thousand stars in six categories designated by numbers, with 1 being the brightest and 6 those just visible. In 1856 a British astronomer, Norman Pogson, proposed the numbers to be "stellar magnitudes" described mathematically. He calculated that each number represented a two and a half times increase in brightness; thus a star of 1 was 2.512 times brighter than one of 2 and the difference between 1 and 6 was a 100 times brightness. His mathematics made it possible to have subtle fractions of magnitudes and to extend the scale into negative numbers, as with the sun at −26. Birkeland and his assistants used Pogson's scale to note the overall intensity of the Zodiacal Light and any variations they perceived. In February, for example, the

Zodiacal Light stretched from the constellation of Aquarius to Pisces, and the stars of Pegasus were visible through the Light to the upper right, whose intensities varied from 2.5 (Markab) to 2.8 (Algerib).

Birkeland also hoped to map the distribution of the Zodiacal Light in space with hand-drawn sketches. For the drawings to be useful, the observers' impressions of the outer limits of the Light needed to conform to the same standards. To practice this, Devik and Birkeland would draw the phenomenon at the same time but from different places, in order to compare the similarity of their drawings. After the first few weeks it was hard to tell them apart. Birkeland was planning to send Devik to Rhodesia or South Africa the following year in order to make simultaneous observations of the Light from a distant location.

As well as making drawings, Birkeland attempted to photograph the subtle phenomenon to see whether the variations in light intensity would register across a series of plates. Unfortunately, the exposure time needed to register an image was so long that any hope of seeing variations was abandoned. Birkeland set his mind to finding an alternative method, meanwhile setting up the magnetometers to trace any correlation between variations in the Light and movements in the magnetic field. He kept the equipment in a sturdy canvas tent outside, as it was too difficult to remove all iron objects, which would affect the readings, from their house. Skolem and Devik guarded the tent all night from the curious locals who would come and sit near them, saying nothing but watching every movement. Theft was common in Omdurman and Birkeland became the target of a number of attempted burglaries. His house servants—he paid seven as an act of charity, although only two actually worked—tried their best to keep the house secure but in the end Birkeland was advised by Mr. Sandford to buy a gun. He bought a 7.6-bore revolver in February and kept it under his pillow at night, an act that brought the subject of defense back into his mind.

Two days after receiving a license for his new gun Birkeland wrote two letters about his electromagnetic cannon. The first was addressed to the Right Honorable Lord Rayleigh, fellow and former president of the Royal Society, winner of the Nobel Prize for Physics in 1904 and president of the Commission for the Examination of Inventions of War. The second, similar in content to the first, was sent to Dr. Glazebrook, who was also on the commission and whom Birkeland had met during a trip he had made to London in July 1906 to explain the principles of his fertilizer furnace at the invitation of the Faraday Society. During his brief sojourn in England, Birkeland had attended a lecture at the Royal Society.

Omdurman (Sudan), 7 February 1914 Confidential
To Dr. R. T. Glazebrook, CB, FRS

Dear Dr. Glazebrook,
I have seen from the newspapers that there was a meeting in Mansion House on Saturday 5th, discussing how to protect England from airships. Do you remember that I made allusion to an invention for such a purpose some years ago after a meeting at the Royal Society? The same invention may also be used in the navy as it is easily installed in battleships.

If you think my invention would interest military authorities in England, I will give further explanations. Perhaps the best would be to explain the invention to Lord Kitchener in Cairo. He would certainly be one of the best judges in the world. There are three conditions:

1st Absolute discretion. My name must never be used in connection with the invention.

2nd When the model is ready and adopted, it shall be given to the Norwegian state without costs.

3rd The arms must never be used against the Scandinavian peoples.

I am here in Omdurman studying the Zodiacal Light.
Please send your answer to Professor Birkeland, Aswan.
Yours sincerely,
Kr. Birkeland

Birkeland asked for complete discretion because he had begun to fear that his invention of the gun could lead him into danger. Frequent military skirmishes between the major European powers, particularly between the French and the Germans, had caused him to worry that he would be seen as a threat as long as he was free to offer his invention to any government he chose. To solve this situation, he decided to offer first refusal to develop the cannon to the British, who were now linked to Norway through Norway's Queen Maud, who was the daughter of King Edward VII. Birkeland hoped, therefore, that the British would be the least likely of any European power to use the cannon against his own people. Glazebrook was requested to reply to Aswan as Birkeland planned to return along the Nile to Helwan in the early spring, stopping in Aswan to make observations.

Birkeland worked hard and productively during his time in the Sudan; he wrote papers for *The Cairo Scientific Journal* and the French Academy's publication *Comptes Rendus*, about his preliminary research into the Zodiacal Light, and his relationships with Devik and Skolem were close and fruitful. With Skolem, Birkeland made theoretical calculations and mathematical models of the density of the Zodiacal Light, pioneering work necessary to deduce the shape and structure of the dusty disc. Comparisons of the model with their observations confirmed that it was indeed disc-shaped and extended at least beyond the Earth. There was no way to measure exact numbers of dust particles in any particular area of the disc; as a result their model resembled a map without a scale, showing the size of features and contours relative to each other rather than in absolute terms. They estimated, however, that the dust particles were microscopic and the density very low, about twelve grains per cubic kilometer of space. The sparsity of the dust grains in the disc made it invisible except in the ecliptic plane, right across the white of the egg, where the tiny numbers of particles added up to millions because the distances involved were so great. Even in perfect viewing conditions, the Zodiacal Light was one million million times less bright than the sun, one million times less strong than the moon, and around 10,000 times weaker than a strong aurora.

As for the oscillations that Birkeland was keen to measure, these were elusive to record although he was sure he saw them with the naked eye. On some nights the variations might have been due to atmospheric smoke and dust from the desert that intermittently obscured the Light. Bright starlight also interfered with the observations, and their recording efforts were frequently impeded by high winds and buffeting sand. Even though Birkeland tried using different varieties of plate and lens to shorten the exposure time for photographing the Light, the improvements were minimal. It was frustrating to be unable to record what he was convinced he saw with the naked eye.

Despite the warm weather and enjoyable challenge of the work, Birkeland's health had not greatly improved since his arrival in Africa. The lack of sleep from night-time observations was making him nervous and edgy, but on the nights when the full moon obliterated the Zodiacal Light and he could have caught up on his sleep, he still suffered from insomnia. His drinking also increased.

Omdurman, Sudan, PO Box 50   31.1.1914
INVOICE TO: *Professor Birkeland*

THE GALANIDES BROTHERS,
WINE AND SPIRITS, MINERAL WATER FACTORY AND
GENERAL PROVISIONS MERCHANTS

JANVIER IST	2 DOZ SODA	10
2ND	I DOZ SODA	5

3RD	I DOZ SODA, I BOTTLE WHISKY	5, 14
4TH	I DOZ SODA	5
IITH	I BOTTLE WHISKY, 4 DOZ SODA	14, 20
13TH	I BOTTLE WHISKY, 2 DOZ SODA	14, 10
16TH	I BOTTLE WHISKY, 2 DOZ SODA	14, 10
19TH	I BOTTLE WHISKY, 2 DOZ SODA	14, 10
21ST	I BOTTLE WHISKY, 2 DOZ SODA	14, 10
24TH	I BOTTLE WHISKY, 2 DOZ SODA	14, 10
26TH	I BOTTLE WHISKY, I BRANDY V.S.O.P., 2 DOZ SODA	14, 35, 10
28TH	I BOTTLE WHISKY, 2 DOZ SODA	14, 10
31ST	I BOTTLE WHISKY, 2 DOZ SODA	14, 10

The amount of soda Birkeland drank might have been explained by his suspicion of the drinking water in Omdurman:

I learned recently to my horror that Omdurman has a lot of leprosy. Among the 45,000 inhabitants of the town, there are around 100 leprosy patients who are not kept isolated, but live among other people and eat from the same pans. Several of the sick are allowed to serve as water porters in the town. Close to our house is a public water tank, filled several times a day by a leprous woman. I have seen her cleaning the tank with her diseased arm and adults as well as children drink that water!

The whisky, however, was drunk in too great a measure to be medicinal. Birkeland's writing, never neat, became a near illegible scrawl and his observational notes barely comprehensible.

By the beginning of March temperatures in Omdurman started to soar. Birkeland decided that it was time to travel north, away from the intense desert heat to the more temperate climes of Helwan and the resources of the Khedivial Observatory. The idea that Miss Spandonides might also be there was an added incentive, for

Birkeland, although he enjoyed the presence of his assistants, missed female company.

The three men packed up their house in Omdurman, gave the furniture and kitchen supplies to their servants, and took the train and boat back to Aswan. There they booked into the Cataract Hotel, where polite replies to Birkeland's letters about the cannon awaited him. The recipients promised to bear his invention in mind but did not make any immediate commitment to it. There had not been a major European war for more than a hundred years, and although weaponry had been developing during that time, Birkeland's idea for an electromagnetic cannon was still considered too advanced, experimental, and potentially expensive to develop.

Birkeland, Devik, and Skolem discovered, with delight, that the Cataract Hotel, established in 1899 and run by the Upper Egypt Hotels Company, was a very superior establishment. Its luxurious bedrooms, fine dining room, and cool marble halls worked like a balm on the men who had spent the previous six months in dusty, near-monastic surroundings. Sun- and sand-bathing (the practice of immersing the body in hot sand to ease pain and stiffness in joints and muscles), a golf course, boat trips, donkey rides into the desert, billiards, a library, and exquisitely planted gardens were just a few of the amusements provided for the hotel's guests. The most entrancing feature of the place, however, was the terrace with its stunning views of the Nile at the First Cataract, busy with sailboats and a few steamers carrying tourists to ancient sites and to view the engineering feat of the Aswan Dam, constructed in 1902. To the strains of a discreetly placed orchestra, the three men enjoyed tea there every day, Birkeland chasing his with whisky and water. As the sun sank lower over the hills in the west, they would take a carriage into the desert with a magnetometer and drawing boards, to study the Zodiacal Light until dawn.

After eight days of delicious teas, the full moon made observation of the Light impossible and Birkeland decided it was time to leave for Helwan. He could send Devik back to Aswan later in the year to make simultaneous observations there before he traveled on to Rhodesia to do the same from a more distant location. The three left the paradisical terrace with some regret and took the sleeper train to Cairo, arriving at Ramses station early the following morning. There they changed to the local Helwan train, a luxurious affair. Painted on the side of the locomotive, amid an intricate pattern of green and gold papyrus flowers, was a roundel bearing the legend EGYPTIAN STATE RAILWAYS flanked by the Egyptian flag of three gold stars above a sickle moon and the royal turban. The carriages were plush, with leather seats and polished wooden tables, a suitably ornate mode of transport for the wealthiest of Cairo's citizens, who had villas and mansions in Helwan to which they escaped from the heat and dirt of the capital. The khedive and his family came to Helwan to take a cure in the naturally occurring sulphur springs of the town, and since the 1850s it had become a small but fashionable spa. An hour from Cairo, the train pulled into Helwan station, an impressive concoction of ornate plaster and pink paint, from which broad, tree-lined avenues radiated in several directions. On their way to the hotel, they passed small palaces behind elaborate wrought-iron railings, as well as a sign for the golf course.

The Tewfiq Palace Hotel was a grand building, set in well-ordered grounds, with a wide gravel path leading from the street to a broad terrace and the cool marble reception area. They were given large rooms overlooking the gardens and planned to stay there until Birkeland could find a suitable house in which to build his own observatory and laboratory. He left a polite note for Miss Spandonides, who was still resident at the hotel, and the following morning took a carriage, with Devik and Skolem, to the observatory.

From the hotel, in the northeast of the town, the road rapidly became a narrow street, running between disheveled houses where the servants of the rich lived. As if a line had been drawn at the edge of the last house, the desert began. The carriage emerged into the intense light and parched air of the Sahara, which lapped at the edges of the settlement. The horses climbed a steep track to the top of an escarpment from where they could see the town laid out below in ordered streets. In the distance, the great pyramids loomed out of the shimmering horizon on the opposite bank of the Nile, an extraordinary image that Birkeland had first pictured as a boy when listening to Lieblein.

The carriage continued down a dip between two hills and climbed again, around the escarpment. Looking into the valley below they could see the golf course, made entirely of sand: hard-rolled for the putting greens, raked for the fairways, and loose for the bunkers. They could see a few Europeans playing, accompanied by Egyptian caddies wearing red sweaters over their *galabiyyas*. As they rounded the bend, the crest of a shallow hill came into view, on top of which two buildings stood on either side of the track. A bungalow to the left was substantial, built of rough stone, consisting of two wings connected by a central hall, set back to allow for a deep, shady veranda. On the right a tall tower built of the same rough stone bristled with weather instruments and around its base was a simple quad of offices. There was nothing green as far as the eye could see and the buildings appeared to float on the sea of sand that stretched to the horizon.

The Khedivial Observatory was Egyptian-owned but run by the British Survey Department, which used it to study the geography and the weather of the region as well as the night skies. The new director, appointed the previous year, was Harold Knox-Shaw, a young graduate of Cambridge University who was not yet thirty years old. His dark hair was cut short, parted down the middle and smoothed away from his forehead with wax. He wore a sober tweed suit and tie and small round spectacles and walked with a pronounced limp due to an attack of childhood polio. When he greeted the visiting scientists, his manner was shy and quiet but friendly. He explained the functions of the buildings they passed as he walked toward the observation dome, situated further along the track, over the brow of the hill. In the main house was the dining hall, where everyone ate together, and the dormitories where they slept. If these were full, tents were pitched behind the house on the rock. The quadrangle of offices was the center for fieldwork of geodetic, seismic, and magnetic surveys, precise leveling and other geographical activities performed by mathematics graduates from Cambridge for the British Survey Department under the direction of a Captain Lyons. In one of these rooms, Birkeland's boxes were awaiting him. Further on was a building containing the automatic magnetometers, whose recordings Birkeland was invited to use, and nearby was a workshop where several English technicians were repairing instruments. Five hundred meters further into the desert, perched on an incline, was the observatory. It was an elegant, circular building of pale stone with a tapering stairway ascending to double doors. Inside, the desert sand collected in small heaps against the walls and eddied across the smooth flagstones when the men entered the dark lower floor. They climbed a steep wooden ladder and emerged into the dome, where Knox-Shaw wound the mechanism of cogs, wires, and pulleys that revolved the dome to open the shutter, allowing a bright shaft of sunlight to light up the room.

Knox-Shaw's main interest was studying star nebulae such as supernovas, stellar nurseries, or clusters of stars, the usual object of the telescope's gaze, but he was interested to see whether the telescope could be used to help Birkeland with his research. It was the largest in Africa and the gift of a Birmingham industrialist, John Reynolds, a keen amateur astronomer. The weather around Birmingham severely hampered his observations and he decided to place a telescope in a better climate as an act of benevolence to other astronomers. He built a thirty-inch reflector and asked the Royal Astronomical Society where it should be situated. They suggested Helwan and Reynolds promptly donated it to the Egyptian government. Knox-Shaw explained that he had come to Egypt immediately after graduating in 1908 to supervise the installation of the telescope. He thought it could be used to help Birkeland measure variations in the intensity of the Zodiacal Light. Birkeland wanted to connect the telescope to a piece of new technology, a photocell, which had been introduced for astronomical use only a few months earlier. Just as he had been able to procure radium from Marie Curie only one year after she had first isolated it, Birkeland now planned to pioneer a revolutionary technique for observing astronomical phenomena.

The photocell was 100 times more sensitive than a photographic plate and worked by pointing a lens at a small area of the sky. A light particle, or photon, passed through the lens into a lightproof box in which was a cathode coated with an alkaline metal. When the photon hit the cathode, an electron was released that traveled across to an anode. The moving electron set up an electric current that could be measured using an electrometer: the stronger the current, the greater the density of light. The German scientist Wilhelm Hallwachs had discovered this photoelectric effect in 1888. He realized that certain metals released electrons when exposed to light, although the theory behind the reaction was not established until 1905 by Einstein; it was for this that he received the Nobel Prize, not for his theory of special relativity, announced the same year. The instrument Birkeland had brought with him to Egypt was made by Elster and Geitel, pioneers in the field and the foremost constructors of photocell equipment in the world. Birkeland was the first to point it at the Zodiacal Light.

He explained that he wanted evidence of electron radiation from the sun to prove his theory that electrons caused magnetic storms, the Northern Lights, and the pulsating Zodiacal Light. Knox-Shaw agreed to begin the observations as soon as Birkeland brought him the photocell equipment, but he seemed dubious that electrons from the sun could reach the Earth, citing the work of Schuster. Birkeland was dismayed that even in Egypt, so far from the Royal Society and other institutions of British science, he still could not escape from these prejudices. Fortunately, Knox-Shaw's study of star nebulae furnished him with knowledge of the forces of magnetism and some interest in the influence of electromagnetism and he kept an open mind.

After an introductory tour of the observatory, Birkeland arranged to return the following day to search through his boxes for the photoelectric equipment. The three Norwegians retreated to the Tewfiq Palace Hotel, pleased to be able to work with Knox-Shaw but thankful not to be living in an English enclave on a barren escarpment. Miss Spandonides was sitting on the terrace when the three men arrived back at the hotel, and the acquaintance formed briefly in Alexandria was renewed over dinner.

15

War

Helwan, Egypt
Spring 1914

And so I beg the darkness:
Where are you my loving man?
Why gone from her whose love
Can pace you, systematically, to your desire?

Song, Egypt, 1300 B.C.

URING THE SPRING of 1914 Birkeland settled into life in Helwan. He spent many days at the observatory with Harold Knox-Shaw, working on the photocell equipment and trying different telescopes to achieve better results. Using the large telescope had initially proved disappointing, as the Zodiacal Light appeared very distant and faint in the huge, thirty-inch silver reflector. They changed to a smaller, refractor telescope using lenses to focus the image of the Light onto the photocell, but this was not very effective either. Birkeland realized that perhaps he needed to use much thinner lenses with a shorter focal length. As he noted in an article in *The Cairo Scientific Journal* later in 1914, he should have learned from his experiences of photographing the aurora:

> I had a similar misfortune before in photography; it was in
> 1899 when photographing the polar aurora from the then

newly erected Haldde observatory. We used great heavy Zeiss lenses, constructed solely for that purpose, and got nothing of value. Some years later, Professor Störmer succeeded very well using a little thin cinematographic lens.

As always, Birkeland was well informed about scientific developments occurring elsewhere. He chanced upon a small article in a German scientific journal in which he read that two scientists had examined the power of various metals to reflect light and noticed that each metal had different reflective properties, absorbing or reflecting different wavelengths. Birkeland noted that silver did not reflect ultraviolet light well, which was a problem, as he believed the Zodiacal Light consisted in large part of ultraviolet and blue light, near the end of the spectrum visible to the human eye. The silver reflector of the Reynolds telescope was absorbing light at these wavelengths and thereby obliterating Birkeland's evidence of variation. He needed to find the substance that would reflect it powerfully onto his recording equipment. Another article, this time in French, about the light wavelengths allowed through different types of lenses, confirmed Birkeland's suspicion that the ordinary glass lenses he had been using were not ideal as they also absorbed ultraviolet.

It is obvious that the most effective rays in the Zodiacal Light must have a wavelength of about 0.32μ and thereunder. If we want to construct a good lens for photographing the Zodiacal Light, we therefore have to choose from the materials: fluorspar, quartz, and Jena glass. If we want to produce a mirror to reflect the rays of the Zodiacal Light it is best to choose Mach's mirror metal which reflects ultraviolet light very much better than all other known metal or nickel.

Birkeland sent off to Europe for new, thinner lenses and a mirror made of Mach's metal and set about creating his own photocell equipment, which appeared to work far more efficiently. He was able to record small variations in the intensity of the Zodiacal Light and worked with Knox-Shaw to check his results. They decided to focus the photocell equipment on stars to verify that they did not register variations, light emitted from stars being constant with only a few exceptions. They saw almost no variations, which reassured Birkeland that his new device was working well.

These happy and productive months in Birkeland's life were marred only by news from home, in a letter from his cousin, Richard Birkeland, at the end of March:

> Eyde is working hard to get the Nobel Prize and it is said that he is doing it so that you don't get it but I'm not sure about that. It will be an enormous scandal if he gets it and you don't. He is going to make a speech at the Swedish Technology Association in Stockholm and has been making speeches everywhere it seems, in universities and schools, to give himself a "scientific image."

Eyde's scandalous rewriting of the history of the furnace did not surprise Birkeland. Eyde was attempting to impress influential people—be they scientists, politicians, newspaper owners, aristocrats—using Norsk Hydro's leverage, and often money, to render favors that could help him win the prize. It seemed that his tactics were bearing fruit, but there was little Birkeland could do from Egypt and he tried to ignore the news.

Birkeland, Devik, and Skolem spent many days absorbed in the complexities of the Zodiacal Light, sometimes with the help of Knox-Shaw, sometimes in their own small team either at the hotel or in the desert at night. After a few weeks, however, it became clear that the hotel was not a suitable home for the three men as their nocturnal hours were causing some complaints. Birkeland asked Miss Spandonides whether she knew of a villa they could rent through one of her Greek friends. Within days, a suitable house had been found not far from the hotel but nearer the desert and the road to the observatory.

> Mister K. Birkeland, professor of the University of Christiania (Norway), hires the house of Mme. Salech Pascha, Helwan, near Cairo for a price of 85 Egyptian pounds a year. He has the right to erect a wooden wall on the roof, to put two stoves in one of the rooms and to use one of the two kitchens as a laboratory.
> Helwan, 1 May 1914
> Kr. Birkeland
> Mme. Salech Pascha

The wooden rail was to keep the scientists safe while making observations from the roof at night, the laboratory was primarily for developing photographs of the Zodiacal Light, and the stoves were to keep Birkeland warm. Despite the balmy days of April and May in Egypt, Birkeland often suffered from shivering attacks and cold feet and hands. His drinking remained steady, and his consumption of veronal was more frequent than his brother had advised, although he tried not to take too much because it produced unpleasant side effects, including drowsiness and shaking hands. He considered the other symptoms from which he suffered to be due to the deleterious effect of working so intensely on the fertilizer furnace and his inability to tolerate extremes of temperature, cold or hot. It was primarily through his ailments, and his need to find accommodation, that a relationship developed between Birkeland and Miss Spandonides. Birkeland learned that the initial 'H' on the concert program from Alexandria stood for the highly unusual name of Hellas, the Greek word for "Greece," although she usually shortened it to the more European-sounding Hella when abroad. She had been named after her country by parents proud of their heritage, an attitude Hella had adopted wholeheartedly. She not only wore ancient Greek designs onstage but also played and promoted the music of contemporary Greek composers throughout Europe.

During April and May Hella helped Birkeland find linen, items of furniture, and even a bath and lavatory for his new villa, recommending merchants Birkeland should visit. On several occasions she accompanied him to Cairo on shopping trips. She learned of his delicate health and he of hers: Hella was in Helwan to be treated for tuberculosis. The small town was home to a renowned medical center devoted to the treatment of the disease, located in a palace donated by the sister of the khedive.

Within weeks, Birkeland was doing Hella's shopping for her when she felt ill and was visiting her in the evenings. On the days they could not meet because she was singing, playing the piano, or feeling unwell, they would write short notes to each other.

Tewfiq Palace Hotel   Telegraphic address: Palace Helwan
Helwan (EGYPT)   9 April 1914

Dear Friend,
From the Fleurent Delicatessen please buy:
Colonial Ware marmalade, unsalted butter from Europe, milk—very important, it comes from a Hygienic dairy in Hungary, cream, slow-cooked chicken, biscuits. There are many things that you will need to buy for the house, I shall tell you where to find them. I have been looking for a servant for you and have written to Bertha Ryman, who is a maid at the Hotel Continental. She is efficient and not too pretty, therefore not too much of a temptation for three Don Juans! You can buy a bath at Gastin's, 11 Ville Nationale. For your kind and friendly letter I thank you with all my heart. You cannot believe how glad I am to be with you. Come briefly at 7 p.m. to see me. I am not very well but will try to get better soon.

    With my heart's friendship,
    Hella Spandonides

In early May Hella and Birkeland made their first excursion out of Helwan together, to the Khan el-Khalili market in Cairo to buy furniture for the house. Hella took Birkeland to the famous El Mahal el Kadeem, "the Old Shop," that had been a caravanserai built, legend had it, by Saladin as a place for traders to meet and rest. In its lofty halls and balconies men could sit and smoke *shisha,* do business or play cards, eat, sleep, wash, and pray. There they would water their horses and camels before the long treks between oases, across the deserts of Africa to distant trading centers—Omdurman, Marrakesh, St. Catherine and Medina. Now the grand old building was home to Hazem Moustafa Nono & Brothers who bought any object, modern or antique, that had once been desired in the hope that it would be wanted again one day. Narrow walkways ran through towering piles of wardrobes, washstands, lamp bases, chairs, bathtubs, hatstands, umbrella stands, sheaves of walking-sticks, picture frames, screens, chaise longues, vases, dinner sets, small statues, inkstands, clocks of every dimension (though none working), and much else that was hidden behind bedsteads or under the thick layer of dust that coated every object, rather dimming the riot of color that would otherwise have startled the eye.

Birkeland bought several pieces of furniture, as he had decided to stay in Helwan for at least two more years. The location was good for observing the Zodiacal Light and he was becoming attached to Hella. They shared many characteristics. She, like him, was driven by her work and, despite her illness, had conducted grueling tours across Europe, was a respected teacher at Athens' first music school, and was retraining her voice to professional level. She had not married or had children in order to concentrate on the career that, she claimed, kept her sane and distracted her from her illness. Although she knew little about science, she had shown a passionate interest in Birkeland's researches, accompanying him onto the roof of his house to learn the names of the constellations and to hear his theories about the Northern Lights, the Zodiacal Light, and the formation of the solar system. She had started to learn basic mathematics in order to understand Birkeland's work better and began to turn down requests to perform at concerts that she received from her agent in Athens—on grounds of health and out of a desire to stay with her new friend.

Birkeland wrote to Amund Helland:

I am experiencing my life's greatest adventure here although its character is still a hundred times more diffuse than the Zodiacal Light. But what I have experienced is incredible.

On the evenings when bright moonlight ruined the possibility of observing the Zodiacal Light, Birkeland would take long walks with Hella to the edge of the desert or through the town, to drink coffee and talk. On clear days Birkeland and Karl would leave Skolem to work on his mathematical models with the new photocell results, to venture alone into the desert. They would set off soon after lunch, traveling as far south as they could by dusk, which fell at around 5 p.m., to escape the soft light that could be seen above Cairo, thirty kilometers to the north. Although it was only April, the desert around Helwan reached 30 degrees Celsius at noon and both men suffered badly with their fair Nordic skins. After several of these excursions, they found a good location opposite the four pyramids at Dahshur. They would drive beside the Nile until the massive shapes of the Bent and the Red pyramids, built by Pharaoh Sneferu nearly four thousand years before, were behind them. A track up to their left led to a small area of ancient tombs that had been partially excavated. Their entrances served as shelter from the wind and dust for the magnetic recording equipment. During these nights, Devik and Birkeland grew yet closer, the professor always referring to Karl in his articles as "Devik, my indefatigable assistant and friend."

They also found evidence using the magnetometers that there were very slight variations in the magnetic field during appearances of the Zodiacal Light. To confirm his hypothesis that electron radiation caused at least some of these variations, Birkeland continued his work at the observatory with Knox-Shaw, using the new photo-cell equipment. Despite registering subtle variations, Birkeland could not convince Knox-Shaw that they were emissions from the sun rather than changes in the atmosphere of the Earth. The two men were working on the same experiments for different ends—Knox-Shaw to pursue his interest in the penetration of ultraviolet light through the Earth's atmosphere from star nebulae and Birkeland to gather evidence for his cosmogony. In June, Birkeland decided to send Devik to Salisbury, in Rhodesia, to make simultaneous observations of the Zodiacal Light from a location as far south of the equator as Helwan was north. By observing the Light from two locations too far distant to share the same weather or atmospheric conditions, he hoped to record similar variations in the Light and thereby prove that atmospheric effects could not cause them.

Devik had been gone only a fortnight when news was received in Egypt that the Archduke Franz Ferdinand of Austro-Hungary and his wife had been assassinated on 28 June in Sarajevo. Birkeland immediately recalled how the assassination of the Empress of Austria in 1898 had been preceded by the dramatic displays of red Northern Lights across Europe. Few political ramifications had followed that grisly event, and Birkeland assumed the consequences of these murders, too, would be resolved diplomatically between the countries involved. Hella was more distressed by the news, understanding better than her new friend the unsettled situation in the Balkans. She decided she could not delay her departure any longer and told Birkeland that she planned to leave Helwan to travel to a sanatorium in Germany, as Egypt was too hot for her in the summer. In Europe she would take singing lessons and give concerts, then take a cure in the beautiful mountains of Thessaly in Greece, and return to Helwan in late September for the winter. They arranged a meeting in Berlin in late summer and, three weeks after hearing of the assassination, Hella took the train to Alexandria to board a steamship for Europe. Before leaving, she wrote a note to

Birkeland, explaining her desire to buy a house upon her return where she wanted him to have a room as she looked forward to the day that they could live together.

Birkeland and Skolem pored over the news reports that arrived in Egypt after Hella had left. Nearly a month after the assassination of Archduke Ferdinand, it seemed a political crisis was indeed brewing in its wake. Isolated from Norway, both men prayed that there would not be a major conflict, but on 2 August the German ambassador delivered a declaration of war on Russia. Two days later Great Britain declared war on Germany. The following day Austria declared war on Russia, and Great Britain and France declared war on Austria on 12 August. The Serbians, perpetrators of the original crime, had seemingly been forgotten. Birkeland and Skolem were left horrified that such a conflagration could have arisen from a single act of violence they had all but dismissed.

Skolem left immediately for Norway before it became too difficult to travel but Birkeland chose to stay. He had little to return to and in Egypt his work was progressing; he also had the hope that Hella would manage to return in the autumn. After Skolem's departure, Birkeland was alone. He and Devik sent messages by telegram concerning observation times, but otherwise Birkeland had only his work for company. The declaration of war was the start of his own, inexorable slide into tragedy.

AFTER WAR was declared, Egypt was pronounced a British protectorate. The tranquil town of Helwan filled with British and Egyptian soldiers and Cairo, already a teeming city, was swollen with the personnel and paraphernalia of war. Birkeland made regular trips to the city to visit his friends at the Danish consulate, the Eriksens, and their physician, Dr. Louis Roeder, whom they recommended to Birkeland when he complained of kidney pains and other ailments. The doctor's surgery was in an impressive block of apartments on the Sharia el Dine, built by the khedive for those of his relatives who could no longer afford to live in palaces, or chose not to. Glamorous residents walked through the courtyard of the building, traveling in gilded lifts to their apartments or passing into the street to their waiting chauffeurs. Roeder, doctor to many of them, as well as to the Scandinavians in Egypt, was a competent and discreet professional, but perhaps too accommodating of his patients' neuroses. He gave Birkeland prescriptions for veronal and other medications to alleviate his symptoms, without making any attempt to understand the underlying cause of his frequent maladies. Consequently, Birkeland spent a great deal on medication but his health improved very little. In Cairo, he stayed at Shepheard's Hotel, where the famous terrace was now crammed with officers from the British HQ, including T. E. Lawrence, later known as Lawrence of Arabia. Drunken soldiers wove through the prostitute district. Thousands of posters, signed by General Allenby, whose name in Arabic was Allah-Naby, "Prophet of God," called upon the fellahin to volunteer. The posters, thus authorized, would have been a persuasive invitation had the fellahin not been asked to fight for the British Protectorate of Egypt, "protectorate" in Arabic being translated as *himaya* or "degradation."

The war was beginning to affect Birkeland's research, as he noted in *The Cairo Scientific Journal:*

> We have at different times tried to make simultaneous registrations of the Zodiacal Light from two distant stations. My friend and indefatigable assistant, Mr. Devik, has gone three times to Aswan and Salisbury while I was working in Helwan. But owing to celestial, terrestrial, and even military difficulties, we have not succeeded so well as we want to do, so have to continue.

Without Hella and Skolem and with Devik away in Aswan or Salisbury, Birkeland was lonely but the Eriksens became good friends, and he relied on work to fill his long days. He wrote regularly to Hella and received replies every fortnight or so.

16 July 1914

Dear Friend,

I have the pleasure of answering your lovely letter, that everything goes well and smoothly. My health is almost better here than in Egypt, I sing every day and the voice is returning. The mathematics keeps less pace, but I still have hope there as well! My work is my all; it compensates me for everything that I have ever sacrificed. I have been to the opera only once, to see "Elektra," but it made up for everything that you and I missed during the first performance.

I miss our long, open-air walks, full of harmony. I await with anticipation the results of your work and look forward to the time that I will be able to live with you. My plan is to come to Egypt in September.

Good work. Always in faithful friendship,
Your H. S.

The war, however, prevented their planned meeting in Berlin.

Devik, meanwhile, visited Helwan every three or four months throughout 1914 and 1915 and the tireless efforts to record the elusive phenomenon of the Zodiacal Light continued. Birkeland's theoretical models of the density of the Zodiacal Light had been well received on their publication in *The Cairo Scientific Journal,* earning praise even from Schuster and the Royal Society:

The Council of the Royal Society at its meeting held this afternoon passed a resolution expressing their sense of the importance of the experiments, which Professor Kr. Birkeland of Christiania has undertaken to investigate the nature of the Zodiacal Light. At the same time, they express the hope that all facilities will be given to Professor Birkeland in order to enable him to carry his experiments to a successful conclusion.

Arthur Schuster
Secretary of the Royal Society, Burlington House,
London W.
15 October 1914

Birkeland kept the letter carefully, aware that he might need it should the British army commandeer the Helwan observatory for military operations. He was gratified to receive an endorsement from the Royal Society, after a lifetime of repudiation, hoping this might be a turning point in his relations with the British scientific establishment. If he could prove his ideas about the Zodiacal Light, perhaps at last they would acknowledge his wider theories about the influence of electromagnetic forces in the solar system, or at least his solution to the mystery of the Northern Lights.

Hella wrote to Birkeland that she would have to delay her arrival in Egypt as she was needed to perform charity concerts for refugees in the Athens Royal Theatre and possibly in Paris as well. She sent him a program of the music she was to play and wished that he could be there to hear it. Birkeland also wanted to see her and asked her to find out whether the coast between Sparta and Navarino would be suitable for observations. She replied that there was nowhere to stay there and in a tent they would freeze. He should remain in Egypt, as she would soon return.

By the end of the year Birkeland was becoming increasingly homesick and ill. He wrote to his colleague and friend at the University of Christiania, Ellen Gleditsch:

12 November 1914

I have been ill for seven days with "sandfly fever." I thought I was going to die several times and although I am now much better, I am still not back on my feet. Apparently, a small mosquito is blown in from the desert but it particularly attacks people with sensitive nerves, as you know I have. In Egypt, people lie in the sun to cure themselves and I was thinking of inventing a "solar blanket" impregnated with "phosphorer liquende," a radioactive material that will imitate the effect of the sun for those living in colder climes. What do you think?

Norway is the most beautiful country in the world if you don't have to spend winter there. Summer here is even worse for my health than winter there . . .

Despite his ailments, Birkeland was constantly having new ideas for inventions. At Christmas 1915 he sent a warm letter to Amund Helland, accompanied by a box of Turkish caviar, having cajoled the recipe out of an Egyptian acquaintance, and suggested the idea of making caviar out of cod roe in Norway. Helland's response, received several weeks later due to the disrupted postal services, was positive. He promised to give the caviar and the recipe to a friend in the fisheries industry. In the meantime, Birkeland and Ellen Gleditsch had taken out a patent for the "solar blanket," and Birkeland also had plans for new telephone designs. His insomniac nights were always productive, even if his ideas were becoming increasingly unusual.

Sometimes disturbing news from home caused Birkeland to regret that he was not there to defend his interests. After his efforts to gain the Nobel Prize, Eyde was now trying to write Birkeland out of the history of Norsk Hydro and the development of the furnace. A pair of books were published in Norway and Denmark in early 1915 called *Lives of the Inventors* in which the biographies of inventors of the past few hundred years were summarized. Richard Birkeland sent the entry on Birkeland and Eyde to his cousin, who was incensed by its contents.

[. . .] In 1905, Eyde established "The Norwegian Hydro-Electric Nitrogen Company." As director, he was responsible not only for the technical development of the method, but also the administration and economical management of the company as well as the others based on this industry.

Eyde was quoted as saying that the project was a success because he used young engineers with no experience, thus ignoring Birkeland's role and dramatically undervaluing his expertise. The author, Per Wendelbo, had given the text to Eyde to make any corrections required, but had not sent it to Birkeland. Eyde had a free hand to present his own version of events and he made full use of it. Birkeland decided not to let the matter stand and wrote an open letter to *Aftenposten,* which was published on 28 June 1915.

[...] The author's exposition is so incomplete that it becomes entirely misleading and I thus, regrettably, have to make objections.

The core of our invention was created through tedious and persistent experimental work over several years under my leadership. Eyde was mainly occupied with administration work: we were both directors of the Nitrogen Company. This is not mentioned with one single line. On the contrary, it is said the invention was due to the lack of experience! The fact is, very few inventions have been made with more experimental experience than the Norwegian method for nitrogen production . . . Despite the fact our field was partly new, we managed to proceed at the high speed Eyde required.

For a long time I fought, without noticeable support, for my opinion that larger ovens were the way to defeat the new Baden oven. Had I given up, only German nitrogen ovens would be burning in Norway today and Eyde, at best, would be sitting as director of a German industry in our country.

I hope you understand that my remarks are necessary when having the future in mind.

Yours sincerely, Kr. Birkeland

The author promised to make changes to the account should the book be republished, but it never was.

Toward the end of 1915 Birkeland realized that Hella was not going to return to Egypt that winter, so he decided to purchase a house himself. When Devik returned from Rhodesia, they divided their time between comparing their drawings and photocell recordings of the Zodiacal Light and looking for a villa on the edge of the desert that they could make a permanent home containing a well-equipped laboratory, an observatory, and a purpose-built darkroom.

If they stayed up at night to observe the sky, Devik would sleep until lunchtime, waking to an impatient Birkeland, who wanted him to work at the same hectic pace as he himself did. Birkeland had become more short-tempered and suspicious since Devik had last seen him, sleeping even less than before and drinking large quantities of coffee and whisky. In his worst moods, he would accuse his favorite assistant of being deliberately unhelpful and difficult. Devik saw that the professor's nerves were frayed by the war and its effect on his work and personal life.

After a few weeks they found a rundown house in the perfect position; it belonged to a Greek merchant who sold it for 8,000 Egyptian pounds. Birkeland christened it "Villa Mea" and was proud to be founding his own research institute in Egypt. Although working at the observatory had been useful, Birkeland needed the freedom to study rather different phenomena from those that interested Knox-Shaw. He also wanted the intellectual freedom to work uninhibited by the doubts and disagreements that hampered his research at the Khedivial Observatory.

The alterations necessary to transform the villa into an observatory commenced slowly and with many problems for Birkeland, who had only Devik and the Eriksens to help him manage the Egyptian employees and ensure he was not paying too much for wages and building materials. Birkeland had asked the Norwegian consul, Hooker, for advice, but once again he found the man unhelpful and even deceitful. Despite these difficulties though, Birkeland was delighted to have his own house in such a beautiful spot.

1 December 1915   PASSED CENSOR

Dear Helland,
I have just moved to a house on the edge of the desert. You couldn't find a better place to observe the Zodiacal Light. One and a half kilometers away the Nile flows majestically fringed by a border of palm trees. On the other bank, I can count twelve pyramids, among them the five biggest in existence. Are you well? Please send me a few lines now and then. I have just finished a major treatise that I think will interest you.
    Best regards, Kr. Birkeland

Birkeland did not give further details about the treatise he had written in this or other letters, nor did Devik know what it contained. In February 1916 Devik was recalled to Norway for military service and the professor was left entirely alone in Egypt. Devik did not see Birkeland alive again.

16

Letters from Home

Helwan, Egypt

1916

And on the pedestal these words appear:
"My name is Ozymandias, king of kings:
Look on my works, ye Mighty, and despair!"
Nothing beside remains. Round the decay
Of that colossal wreck, boundless and bare
The lone and level sands stretch far away.

PERCY BYSSHE SHELLEY (1792–1822), *"Ozymandias,"* 1818

IRKELAND had a postcard made at the beginning of 1916, showing him sitting on the steps of his new villa, in a white linen jacket and pith helmet, looking tenderly at a small menagerie of newly acquired pets. He sent the card to Holland for New Year and wrote on the back:

It's me, with my newly born pig, my little kitten—very lively, the monkey—very serious and thinking about things, and my large tortoise.

Birkeland appeared to find comfort in his animals in the same way he had hoped Ida would when he had bought her a cat. He missed home and wrote frequent letters and telegrams to his friends, asking for news. To Devik he sent regular missives requesting information on how the laboratory was faring in the war, suggesting experiments he could carry out with the terrella concerning the Zodiacal Light, inquiring after both his health and the state of the capital. He also had some ambitious ideas about what he would do once he returned to Norway.

22 July, Hotel Nelson, Aboukir

Dear Helland,

Be sure, I am very glad to have letters from home. I am glad Miss Gleditsch got the assistant professor position. Thanks for the photograph, it is very good. I can see you before me as if you were alive. I have just arrived in Aboukir, I feel like I have come from hell to heaven in just five hours by train. In winter there is no place more lovely than Helwan but you can't imagine how terrible it is for my health in summer. It's worse than Christiania in winter. One gets stones in the kidneys and the liver and even in the heart maybe and rheumatism everywhere, because one cannot protect oneself from such heat. But here in Aboukir, everything vanishes in a couple of days and one feels more energetic. Today I have written five letters and in Helwan I haven't written one in two weeks. Since Devik left I have been busy, going to Cairo ten times in fourteen days to find everything I will need for my new observatory.

And finally, I am going to tell you about a great idea I have had; it's a bit premature but I think it will be realized. I am going to get some money from the state and from friends, to build a museum for the discovery of *the Earth's magnetism, magnetic storms, the nature of sunspots, of planets—their nature and creation.* On a little hill I will build a dome of granite, the walls will be a meter thick, the floor will be formed of the mountain itself and the top of the dome, fourteen meters in diameter, will be a gilded copper sphere. Can you guess what the dome will cover? When I'm boasting I say to my friends here "next to God, I have the greatest vacuum chamber in the world." I will make a vacuum chamber of 1,000 cubic meters and, every Sunday, people will have the opportunity to see a ring of Saturn ten meters in diameter, sunspots like no one else can do better, Zodiacal Light as evocative as the natural one and, finally, auroras around the poles of a terrella four meters in diameter. The same sphere will serve as Saturn, the sun, and Earth, and will be driven round by a motor. We could build the whole thing of steel, but then my phenomena would not be so beautiful.

Because of my health, I might go home for a while. There are all possible reasons to end this war.

Best wishes, Kr. Birkeland

Letters from home were a lifeline, but they were becoming less frequent and his replies often included complaints about the paucity of news he received. Birkeland did not realize that many letters were withheld by the censor or were lost with the ships that carried them in the North Sea and the Atlantic. A few did escape the torpedoes and the censor's red crayon, including some from Hella.

Athens, Friday 4 April 1916

My dear friend,

I will throw such a party when I return home, because home is Helwan, but only when *you* are there. You cannot imagine how much I miss the communication of ideas and the daily meetings with a friend so sensitive and sincere as you. I go every week to the legation to see when I can travel back to Egypt. Now you have bought the Villa Mea I am firmly decided to buy my house too.

I am beginning to like physics more and more. Now I am occupying myself with Roentgen X-rays and I go nearly every day to a doctor who uses them. It's truly a shame that I have become interested in such things so late, I would definitely have done something with it otherwise . . .

With fondest wishes,

Your Hella S.

As 1916 progressed, more and more mail was lost and Birkeland rarely received replies to his letters to Hella. He became convinced that she had forgotten him and sent her bitter letters of recrimination, some of which reached their target.

Dear Professor Birkeland,

I am really amazed by your telegram. I don't understand why you reacted that way. I am unwell, even very unwell. Hopefully a letter from you will arrive soon and clear up the misunderstandings.

Yours, Hella S.

Birkeland became increasingly paranoiac and suspicious, not only concerning the lack of correspondence from his friends and from Hella but also regarding his own staff and the people around him. In particular, he became convinced that the plans for his cannon were vulnerable to espionage and that his own safety was compromised. During the course of the year he received occasional telephone calls and correspondence from both the French and British authorities inquiring further about his invention. Despite these hints of interest, no plans were discussed to purchase or develop the cannon and Birkeland worried that the British were trying to take his gun design without informing or paying him. He installed a safe in his bedroom, carefully locking away the copies of his patents, and bought two guard dogs and two more guns. Egypt's strategic geographical position made it fertile ground for spies—British, French, and German—and Birkeland was determined not to let his invention be stolen from him. In the autumn of 1916 Birkeland decided he could no longer trust his servants and dismissed them all except the housekeeper. Nor did he feel comfortable with the builders altering the villa and they, too, were sent away.

In October the death of his old mathematics teacher, Elling Holst, depressed Birkeland further.

11 October 1916

Dear Mrs. Holst,

I have just read in the paper that Elling Holst is dead. The war prevented me hearing about it earlier. No other man ever touched me as deeply as Elling when I was young and I am thankful to have known him. He was such a special person, his loss will be felt by many. I send you my very deepest sympathies.

Kr. Birkeland

The month following the news of Holst's death, Birkeland was cheered by a written request to demonstrate his gun:

General Headquarters   Egyptian Expeditionary Force
TOP SECRET   Savoy Hotel, Cairo
                                        10 November 1916

Dear Sir,

I understand that you have drawings, specifications etc. of an invention which some time past you offered to both the British and French governments. I also understand that you are quite ready to explain the principle and the details of your invention to an officer with mechanical knowledge who may be delegated by General Headquarters.

If this is correct, will you kindly inform me what day and what time would be convenient to you for such an officer to call on you.

I am, Sir, Your obedient servant,

Francis Dalrymple, Secretary, Inventions Board

Birkeland was delighted that after thirteen years of trying to develop his cannon for widespread use, it might finally come to pass. He worked hard during the day, preparing the drawings for the inventions board and finding craftsmen who would be able to make a small prototype if necessary. At night, meanwhile, he worked on improving his photocell equipment, trying to isolate a range of rapid variations in the Zodiacal Light. He spent all his time in the silent, half-finished house, speaking to no one except the housekeeper and eating little. He increased his consumption of whisky, coffee, and veronal to compensate for his lack of nourishment, physical and emotional. On his birthday, 13 December 1916, no one called to see him, there were no letters or telegrams and no one in Egypt knew that Birkeland was forty-nine that day. He sent a telegram to Devik in the morning: 'Birkeland desires Karl come to Tokyo.' No further explanation was given, even though a rendezvous in the Far East had never been discussed before. If Birkeland had already decided to leave Egypt and travel to Japan, he had not asked the Norwegian consul for an exit visa, or informed anybody else of his plan.

Birkeland did not receive a reply from Devik, but far from forgetting his beloved professor, Karl had written numerous letters on returning home. Few survived the journey. Some arrived too late.

Christiania   13 March 1917

Dear Professor Birkeland,
I have received a letter from your bank manager in Cairo, Mr. Mustakki, where he mentions that you have heard nothing from me for a long time. The long letter I sent in December must have disappeared somehow. In this letter I told how the work at the laboratory was proceeding. My service with the King's Guard has been so hard that it has been difficult to work at the same time. In these critical times all leave has been canceled, the military exercises have been very tiring

and the new officer in charge is too strict in my opinion and does not understand that soldiers are human beings. We have been on watch for four days continuously without being allowed to take off our uniform for sleep. We often sleep in tents in temperatures of −32° Celsius, it's the coldest January for eighty years and we have very little for heating.

When I have evening leave I have been working hard to restore the vacuum in the terrella, it is very hard because cracks appear due to the huge variations in temperature when the laboratory is not used. I shall have to strip the entire machine and start again—time-consuming and laborious but the only way to achieve a proper vacuum. The gas is shut off from 7 p.m. and so I have made an electrically heated lamp to seal the cracks—this device will be useful in Helwan too where there is no good gas. When I have finished my Guard Service I shall use my full power to restore the terrella and get results to you very soon.

Best wishes, yours sincerely, Karl Devik

Birkeland never received this letter. By the end of the year, he had become too ill to live alone and was taken to recuperate in Cairo by the Eriksens. Mrs. Eriksen later wrote to Karl Devik and related to him what had happened to the professor during his final months in Egypt.

Mrs. Eriksen
Danish Embassy
Cairo, Egypt   25 January 1918

Dear Devik,

So, eventually a letter has arrived in Egypt from you, it has been underway for a long time but now it is here. You asked my husband for news about Professor Birkeland but he has been terribly busy and has asked me to reply.

Last autumn I was several times out at the professor's, he was very busy with some instruments for measuring light and with letters he had received from the British Admiralty. He was somewhat excited and told me he was drinking a great deal of coffee to work without feeling tired. He replied to our warnings about his health that his work was very interesting—this was the end of October 1916.

Around New Year Doctor Roeder, the physician for Scandinavians in Egypt, came here one evening and said he had been to Helwan to see a patient and had called in at the professor's. He came to us very worried and asked whether we could go and visit the professor occasionally as he was in a very poor condition. Three people whom the professor trusted went to visit him the next day. They could tell that Birkeland was terribly thin and worn out, very paranoid and his eyes were flickering everywhere. He was convinced that the English were after him, he claimed that they were walking around the house, day and night, spying. He thought they had persuaded his housekeeper to spy as well and so he had sacked her at Christmas. He was not sleeping and the only remedy he had was half a beer glass of whisky and two grams of veronal. He had bought two dogs, a revolver and a shotgun, all ready in his bedroom. The trains move slowly around here and although Dr. Roeder went regularly to treat Birkeland he remained deeply paranoid and grew paler and paler. Birkeland said that his own consul, Mr. Hooker, and his associates were among the worst spies. He started to work again but he was like a child and could not be left alone and kept insisting that he could not stand another summer in Egypt.

Oh poor professor! He had a terrible time down there and I have blamed myself many times for not taking the trip out to see him. The reason he was so depressed, I think, was the abuse of coffee, too much work, whisky, and veronal. Other circumstances too—he was convinced people were watching him and we can't say for sure that they weren't, although his life was probably not in danger. He had been in touch with the British Military HQ who were helpful but he felt it was to give him a false sense of security.

What mattered most to the professor was that he didn't get an answer from you, Karl, despite him and my husband sending lots of telegrams. He fabricated all sorts of explanations for your silence although the only correct one was the censorship.

The consul persuaded Birkeland to leave his house and found a good room in a pension close to the consulate. There Birkeland received medical treatment and proper food and began to recover so well that he thought whisky was disgusting and went for long walks with the consul. By February, Birkeland could amuse himself and laugh again like the old days. His feelings of being spied upon and followed were receding and he was thinking he should go back to Norway for his fiftieth birthday celebrations. To stay in Egypt was out of the question but to return via England was too dangerous and he could not travel alone and so the consul suggested that he return via Asia with him. Birkeland was delighted and he returned entirely to his old self. He amused all the people in the pension; they loved him and called him Monsieur Le Professeur!

They left on 10 March and Birkeland was radiating with happiness and promised to drown all English spies in the Red Sea. My husband said he kept his word and after Colombo said there was no sign of Birkeland's paranoia and it was a lovely journey. They arrived in Japan on 3 April where they planned to stay for ten days but Birkeland suddenly changed his mind as he met some colleagues at the University of Tokyo and wanted to work with them for some months. My husband got in touch with the Norwegian General Consul,

Mr. Anker, in Japan, who invited Birkeland to a Japanese resort. Mr. Eriksen informed Mr. Anker about Birkeland's illness last winter and Anker promised to take good care of him.

It is very sad for all of us, particularly my husband who left him there, even though he advised him not to stay but the professor did not want to go back to the cold and dark of Norway. Birkeland prepared to start working with an old acquaintance of his and so my husband felt he was in good hands. What a shame it ended so sadly for Birkeland. Can you tell me how it happened? I will be very thankful. I'm glad your work is going well and let's hope that when the war ends we will see you again in Egypt next winter.

With much love,

Gerda

17

Brittle Remains

Tokyo

April 1917

I am happy that among Kristian's papers there is clear agreement from
Eyde that Kristian is the inventor of the nitrogen method. Everything
should be kept. One beautiful day it will be useful.

Letter from Richard Birkeland to Tønnes Birkeland,
November 1917

WHEN BIRKELAND arrived in Tokyo he went almost
immediately to the Faculty of Science at the Imperial
University. He was met by Professor Terada, who had
traveled to Norway to meet Birkeland ten years previously and later
wrote an account of Birkeland's visit to Japan:

I will try to relate the events in the form of an objective
memorandum while I still remember the facts. One morning, towards the end of the European War (World War I),
when I happened to visit the central office of the Faculty of
Science, I found an old European, rather short and bald, who
was talking with the secretary. The secretary showed me the
visitor's card and asked me how to deal with his wish to see
the library of the Physics Department. It was the famous
physicist, Professor Birkeland from the University of Christiania. I remembered his face from the past because I had

255

visited him once in his country and had seen his famous vacuum electric discharge experiment concerning aurora. Moreover, he had invited me to his home for tea. He did not remember me at once.

Birkeland wanted to see his own book, the *Norwegian Aurora Polaris Expedition 1902–1903*, to check some figures against work he had been conducting in Egypt with the Zodiacal Light, but the book was still unavailable in the library. He was very disappointed but Terada offered him use of the department's facilities and introduced him to the departmental chairman, Professor Nagaoka, and the eminent retired Professor Tanakadate. Terada noticed immediately that Birkeland had changed since they met in Christiania; his manner was listless and lethargic. Despite this, they talked for several hours about the connection between Terada's field of study, rapid magnetic variations, and Birkeland's investigations into the movement of charged particles in the upper atmosphere. Birkeland had received copies of Terada's published papers, and was flattered by his Japanese colleague with his familiarity with his work. Birkeland decided that he could carry out useful research in Japan and decided to stay for a while.

The Danish consul, Eriksen, reluctantly left Birkeland in the hands of the Norwegian consul, Anker, who invited the professor and a small party of Scandinavians to Hakone, a resort about a hundred kilometers southwest of Tokyo. Birkeland soon grew tired of having nothing to do and wrote to Terada asking him to recommend a quiet hotel in Tokyo. Terada booked him into the Hotel Seiyoken, a small establishment of a few rooms annexed to a teahouse in Ueno Park. Birkeland left Hakone with assurances to Consul Anker and his wife that he would take good care of himself, although he did not tell them where he was going to stay.

The Seiyoken was perfect for Birkeland's needs. The location was peaceful and the rooms a good size, with beautiful views over the hotel's azalea gardens to the cherry trees in the park beyond.

Birkeland made almost daily visits to the physics department, where he talked with Professor Terada and worked on his own complete cosmogony. Although he worked hard and remained lucid, it was clear to Terada that Birkeland was not well. As he later wrote:

> During our repeated discussions it became clearer and clearer to me that Birkeland was somehow melancholy and very nervous. He seemed feverish and as he talked he was continuously wiping away sweat from his brow. His sparse gray hairs were standing out on his head and it seemed as though they were steaming away from him. His face looked cherry-colored and his eyes were vivid.

While Birkeland was in Tokyo, Eyde was preparing to retire from Norsk Hydro. The company's board of directors had decided that a new ethos was needed. Eyde's style—his extravagance, large gestures, big risks, and feudalistic management style—was perceived as anachronistic during the war, when teamwork, efficiency, cutting costs, and consolidation in the face of industrial and military hostility were paramount. Despite the board and shareholders' frustration with Eyde's inventive accounting and self-aggrandizing schemes, they decided to honor him with a week-long retirement party in June. He was presented with so many gifts that there was no room for them in his large house and he had to store some at Norsk Hydro. One such present was a waist-high replica of a hydroelectric power plant cast in silver etched into which were long columns of grateful employees' names. Eyde was treated like a hero; his rewriting of history had proved successful and in all the celebrations Birkeland's name was barely mentioned.

Eyde officially retired on 15 June. That same day, on the other side of the world, Birkeland went to the telegraph office near the hotel and sent a message to his lawyer, Johan Bredal:

REMEMBER WRIEDT COMMITTEE.

When Bredal received the telegram later that day he did not understand what Birkeland meant by it and put it to one side, puzzled. Only the following day did its meaning become clear.

Sending the telegram was Birkeland's first excursion in nearly a fortnight. He had been closeted in the hotel, working on his treatise in the bright corner of his room near the doors into the garden. Every few hours he would send for a servant, asking him to buy more paper or bring him coffee. He did not eat, take naps, or stroll around the garden but wrote furiously and continuously until he collapsed into bed and called the servant to take a note to Professor Terada at the Institute of Science. In Terada's words:

One day he asked me to come to his hotel because he had something to tell me which would take some time. I went immediately. He was lying on his bed in his pajamas and he apologized for talking from the bed but he did not feel very well. He said that he was tired and would not like to use German or English, would I mind if he spoke French? Then he began to tell slowly the following story, that was completely unexpected.

Professor Birkeland invented some device for military purposes and had recommended its adoption to the French government. Since they declined his proposal Birkeland then went to the British government who performed tests on his invention but finally also rejected it. From that time on he felt that he was being followed by spies from Britain. He went to Helwan in Africa for the purpose of research and to escape the shadow of espionage. While he was observing the Zodiacal Light one night alone in the desert, someone tried to shoot at him out of the darkness.

After that he decided to make a sea journey to the Orient but he felt a spy was already on the ship and watching him day and night. Even after landing in Japan he felt shadowed, in Tokyo and Hakone as well. Only in the Seiyoken Hotel did he feel free but he said he could not be sure for how long he would be safe.

After finishing the story he closed his eyes and became silent, as if exhausted. I left his room without disturbing him.

Terada had no idea what to make of Birkeland's account. In these strange times of war in Europe he could well believe that such a brilliant man might be pursued for his inventions, but if someone wanted to kill Birkeland it would have been easy to do it in Egypt— why follow him to Japan? He felt alarmed for the professor's safety but wondered whether Birkeland's fears were illusory, the result of too much work or some sort of illness. He decided to call his medical friend Professor Miura in the morning and ask him to visit Birkeland. Miura went to see Birkeland and found that he was taking large doses of veronal. He took Birkeland to the hospital for blood and urine tests and to measure his blood pressure, then prescribed him potassium bromide in place of veronal. After a few days Birkeland contacted Terada again to say that he was not sleeping and Miura gave him more potassium salts and a weak compound of veronal salts as well, as Birkeland had insisted on it.

On the morning of 16 June, Professor Terada arrived early at the institute to be told that there had been a phone call from the Hotel Seiyoken to say that Professor Birkeland was gravely ill. He immediately called Professor Miura and together they went to the hotel. When they arrived, the servant boy was waiting for them, extremely agitated. Apparently he could get no response from the professor's room, however hard he knocked and so he had opened the door with a spare key and seen that the professor appeared to be lifeless. He had called the police immediately, as well as Terada at the institute. When the men entered the room, they saw Birkeland on the bed, behind a mosquito net, and on the table beside him a large, flat pistol and a glass at the bottom of which was a residue of white powder. The servant explained that Birkeland took the pistol with him whenever he left the hotel.

Shortly afterward, the police and a physician arrived. Their examination of the body revealed a deep depression in the skin at the side of Birkeland's head. They looked agitated until they realized that it was caused by his head touching the edge of the bed. The servant explained to the police that Birkeland had been angry with him when he had returned from the chemist with veronal salts rather than the stronger powder that he usually took. He sent the servant out to buy proper veronal, despite the young boy's protestations that it would be bad for his health. Birkeland had insisted that it was the only way he could sleep. When Miura checked, he found Birkeland cold, already blue, without pulse and unusually stiff. Assistants from the hospital were called to pump Birkeland's stomach, attempt artificial respiration, and inject camphor. But, as Miura noted in his account of the case, "it was all in vain and we were not able to wake the world-famous professor from his sleep."

Professor Nagaoka, from the institute, and the Norwegian consul, with his wife and sister, who had been with Birkeland in Hakone, arrived during the resuscitation attempts. They conferred and the consul decided that, until he heard from Birkeland's family in Norway, the corpse should be stored at the Department of Anatomy and injected with a fluid to aid preservation. As the physician was doing this, Birkeland appeared to sigh loudly and relax deeper into his sleep. The consul's sister let out a cry of shock but Professor Miura explained that "sighing" was a common postmortem phenomenon caused by air trapped in the chest escaping as the muscles relaxed.

While Birkeland's body was prepared for removal to the anatomy department, Professor Terada looked around the sparse hotel room. He noticed that Birkeland had been shopping during his stay in Hakone, as there was a large brass dragon in one corner of the room and a calendar, decorated with a black cockerel, hanging from a pillar near the bed, which had not been there when he had come to inspect the hotel for his distinguished guest. Birkeland's clothes hung neatly in the closet—the work of the servant rather than the professor—but his other belongings, hair and clothes brushes, collar box, cufflinks holder, a number of books, and some small instruments, were strewn across the dressing table and the floor, as if Birkeland had been searching for something or had been reviewing his life through these ordinary possessions. As Terada remembered:

On the table in the corner of the room was a stack of paper that looked like a draft for a treatise; so here he had been sitting every day writing this manuscript, I thought, taking up a sheet of the papers and glancing at it. When Professor Nagaoka noticed this he hurried over to me, tore it out of my hands and shouted to the servant to tie it up. Then he delivered the package to the consul and solemnly requested that the manuscript be properly sealed and sent home to Norway's university.

After the body had been removed and only Professor Terada remained, the servant took Birkeland's pistol into the garden where two other boys from the hotel joined him in a thorough examination of the weapon. After a few minutes they started firing the pistol into the azalea bushes at the edge of the garden, talking and laughing loudly. When all the bullets were spent and the bush was completely destroyed, they wandered off. The ground around the azalea bush was littered with shredded white blossoms.

Science College, Imperial University,
Tokyo, Japan
16 June 1917

To the Rector of the University of Christiania,
We feel it our painful duty to convey to you the mournful news that Professor Birkeland was found dead in his hotel on the morning of 15 June. He was suffering from insomnia and

seems to have taken an overdose of veronal. The physicians took every available means of recovery, but all in vain. We tried every means of making him tranquil; he was sometimes quite cheerful, but sometimes extremely depressed. This melancholy seems to have resulted in insomnia and the sorrowful end. It is an irreparable loss to science, and heartrending when we consider that he was solitary and far from home.

Yours very truly.   H. Nagaoka   T. Terada

Professor Birkeland's body was kept in the morgue of the anatomy department at Tokyo University until a telegram was received from his brother, Tønnes, with instructions that Birkeland be cremated and the ashes returned to Christiania once the war was over. A postmortem revealed that Birkeland had taken ten grams of veronal the night he died instead of the 0.5 grams recommended. The time of death was estimated at three in the morning. When Professor Miura researched the popular sleeping drug, he found a large number of letters to the *British Medical Journal* warning of the side effects; many doctors, indeed, had discontinued its use. Although a very slow poison, its excessive use by sufferers of insomnia had resulted in grave disorders of the nervous system, ataxia, hallucinations, tremor, and even death. In addition, a deterioration of the moral sense occurred, as in the case of morphine and cocaine dependency, which led to a reckless use of the drug, with dangerous or fatal overdosing often a consequence.

The Norwegian general consul, Mr. Anker, arranged for a Christian service to be held in a church in Ichibanchoo. The rainy season had ended and a strong, dry wind shook the leaves on the trees, revealing their delicate, white undersides as the cortège moved slowly along the path to the church doors. As there was no one present who knew Birkeland well, the consul gave the address. A Norwegian music teacher sung an aria, which shocked the Japanese mourners: such a noise would never be allowed to disturb the silence of a Japanese funeral. Professor Nagaoka made a short speech and closed with the statement:

> What Birkeland has achieved in the fifty years of his life is as brilliant as the dazzling waves of the aurora, which have exerted such a mighty attraction on him.

After the service the body was taken to the crematorium, from where the ashes were collected the following day by Professors Nagaoka, Terada, and Tanakadate. As Professor Terada recollected:

> The very brittle remains were placed in a snow-white urn. In the unusually large cranium there were still remains of unburnt brain, which looked like asphalt. Professor Nagaoka lifted it up with a bamboo stick and said, "In this there have been many great ideas" and then he carefully placed it in the urn.

A month later the consul sent Terada the bronze tiger that Birkeland had bought during his stay in Hakone, accompanied by a message explaining that it was a souvenir of Professor Birkeland. As Terada did not like the sculpture, he kept it in a closet for many years, where it jolted painful memories on the rare occasions he glimpsed it. The events weighed heavily upon him and he did not tell anybody what Birkeland had related to him until late in his life, in 1935, when he wrote an account of the scientist's sad last days, to be published posthumously. Every year, when late spring turned into summer and the azalea bushes were in full glory, he was reminded of Birkeland's death.

THE MORNING that Birkeland's body was discovered, telegrams were sent by the Norwegian consul to the Foreign Ministry in Christiania advising them of the sad event. Birkeland's lawyer,

Bredal, was the first to be informed and it was then that he at last realized the significance of Birkeland's mysterious telegram. He must have known that death was near—either he knew himself to be ill or he was convinced that spies were closing in on him—and was telling Bredal to see if a medium could contact him after death. That way, they could have conclusive proof as to whether there was any truth in the claims of spiritualists or not.

To Bredal fell the difficult task of relaying the tragic news to Tønnes and Richard Birkeland and Ida—all beneficiaries in the professor's will. Birkeland's affairs were in disorder; his will was in a bank box which had to be broken open because no one could find a key. There were no clear records of his assets or bank accounts, and it took Bredal several months to prepare the final settlement of the will. Ida Birkeland was given the interest on 60,000 crowns for as long as she lived, after which it was to be divided equally between Tønnes and his children. She also bought Birkeland's grand piano for 1,000 crowns. The rest of Birkeland's considerable fortune was divided equally among Tønnes and his ten offspring. Richard Birkeland had the pick of the professor's books; all his instruments were donated to the university. The contents of his beautiful house on Incognitogaten fetched the considerable sum of over 53,000 crowns at auction. His personal letters were given to Tønnes and Ida; his fez and slippers went to Norsk Hydro as mementoes. The house in Helwan was a difficult matter to settle from Norway, and Bredal wrote to the consul, Hooker, to establish the state of Birkeland's affairs in Egypt.

Norwegian Consulate, Cairo, Egypt
Ayerst Hentham Hooker, Acting General Consul
To: His Excellency the Secretary of State for Foreign Affairs, Christiania
14 August 1917
Professor Birkeland Deceased

Dear Sir,

I have the honor to report that on receipt of your telegram since confirmed announcing the death of Professor Birkeland at Tokyo, I at once proceeded to his house in the town of Helwan and in the presence of the consular janissary, placed consular seals on the doors and windows of the house and laboratory. I was unable to enter the house as the keys were left with the Danish consul's wife who has since handed them over to me.

I found a considerable number of firearms, four rifles and an automatic pistol with ammunition, these I have removed to the consulate in order to avoid possible conflict with the military authorities. I would suggest that the property be liquidated as early as possible as current expenses are considerable—taxes, watchman, water rate etc.

In the laboratory I found items of furniture belonging to a Greek lady who I last heard was in Athens seriously ill with consumption.

Best regards, A. H. Hooker

On 22 September 1919, Birkeland was buried in the Vestgravlund, Christiania, at the expense of the university but not of the state. No reason was given why such a prominent Norwegian citizen was not afforded the honor usually accorded to individuals who had made great contributions to the nation. Due to the circumstances of his death, the shadow of suicide hung over his name and unfairly obscured the glory that should have been his.

Birkeland was buried in the afternoon as the sun was dropping toward the horizon and the long shadows of the birch trees standing sentinel around the cemetery threw the mourners into and out of darkness with every step. Birkeland's brother was there with his cousin Richard, who had been the closest to Birkeland of all the family and was one of the angriest about his lonely death and the lack of recognition for his work. Kaya Geelmuyden and her brother and sister, the Mohn family—accompanying Ida—Brøgger and several other professors from the university gathered at the service and around the grave. Other mourners included engineers who had been inspired by the professor, his lawyer, and past colleagues whose lives had been deeply affected by knowing Birkeland, including Olaf Devik, Sem Sæland, Bjørn Helland-Hansen, Ole Andreas Krogness, and Karl Devik, who mourned deeply for his friend and resolved to return to Africa to settle Birkeland's estate in Egypt and recover any of his papers and personal effects that he could. Sam Eyde did not attend.

During the service a hymn was sung whose poignancy reduced many of the mourners to tears. It reminded them of Birkeland's extraordinary life, climbing Arctic peaks to gaze at the Northern Lights, bringing the universe into his laboratory and combing the deserts of Africa for ultimate proof of his prophetic theories.

Imagine when once that mist has disappeared
That is obscuring our life down here,
When the bright, eternal day has dawned
And brilliant rays of light surround all my small steps.

Imagine when every puzzle on Earth is solved,
Every "why" that I have pondered upon
But could not answer for all my trying, is mastered.
Imagine when I the ways of God shall clearly understand.

Imagine when every heartache is extinguished
Every wound is healed and every longing satisfied,
Every tear of pain is wiped away and each deep sigh is
Quenched in the embrace of love.

*The appearance of the aurora borealis in the North at Bossekop
(Finnmark)*

Epilogue

*I have dwelt a long time on his publications because they make clear that
the first correct theory for the aurora is Birkeland's. For such a problem,
the idea is not only the first thing, it is also the greatest thing—
the basic solution was Birkeland's and no one else's.
What he achieved in his fifty years will be remembered in our science for
a long time. His work* The Creation of the Worlds *ends with the
words of Henri Poincaré: "Our thinking is like lightning in the dark
night. It was dark before man started thinking and it will be
dark again if we stop." Birkeland's work was such lightning.*

SEM SÆLAND, memorial address, 22 September 1919

IRKELAND's treatise, which he had described to Helland
as important and which he worked on furiously in the
final months of his life, was given by Professor Nagaoka
to the Norwegian consul to post to the University of Christiania.
Perhaps the consul thought it safer to send it with the rest of Birkeland's belongings, which were entrusted to Captain Johan Bang-
Melchior of the ship *Peking*. A 360-foot Swedish steamship, the
Peking left Karatsu harbor on Kyushu Island at the southern tip of
Japan on 31 August 1919, bound for Hull in England. A wireless communication was received on 2 September from the vessel north of
Korea, where it was struggling in a violent storm that had pushed it
off course, but it was never heard from again. The *Peking* was

entered into Lloyd's List of Missing Ships in October with the captain, crew, and cargo deemed "Missing."

After Birkeland's death, Johan Bredal told Olaf Devik of the strange telegram he had received from Tokyo, and they decided to try to make contact with Birkeland's spirit. They wrote to Sir Oliver Lodge, an extremely eminent English physicist, author of nearly a hundred books and a pioneer of radiotelegraphy who was also known for his efforts to reconcile the ideas of science, religion, and the paranormal.

Christiania, Norway   23 May 1918

Dear Sir,

I should like to call your attention to an event, which might be of interest to you. It relates to Kristian Birkeland, whom you undoubtedly know very well from his nitrogen process. He some years ago attended séances in Christiania by the medium, Mrs. Wriedt, although at the same time he found no proof of the hypothetical connection with the next world. Last year, Professor Birkeland died in Japan and two days before his death, a friend of his in Christiania (also a member of the committee to assess Mrs. Wriedt) received this telegram from Professor Birkeland: "Remember Wriedt Committee." Undoubtedly, Birkeland meant that if there was any way for him to contact us, he would do his utmost.

Could you ask some of the best mediums to try to communicate with the professor, taking care to write down everything, even if not understood by them? Obviously, Prof. Birkeland might give special references, only known to us three. The communications should be sent separately to us (friends and former assistants), Professor Helland-Hansen, Karl Devik, and myself, who would then reply to you about the possible meaning of the communications without conferring with each other beforehand.

Epilogue

I think this would be a crucial test and I should be very glad to hear your response to my suggestions.

Yours very truly,

Olaf Devik

Birkeland's spirit, however, remained silent, and memory of him faded as his friends aged and died.

For fifty years after his lonely death his scientific reputation sank inexorably into oblivion along with the *Peking*. One man in particular, Sydney Chapman, continued the tradition of opposition by British scientists to Birkeland's work. Chapman had seen Birkeland checking some magnetic records in Greenwich en route to Egypt, but they had not spoken. He was a young, ambitious mathematician who became the leading scientist in the field of geomagnetism after the First World War, holding a dominant position in British science until his death in 1970. Chapman's career was the mirror opposite to Birkeland's. He was elected to the Fellowship of the Royal Society in 1919 at the early age of thirty-one, was invited to serve as president of five important scientific societies, and was awarded numerous prizes for his work.

Chapman considered Birkeland's intrepid expeditions into the Arctic unnecessary and anachronistic and the Norwegian professor's theories too "curious" for consideration. His antipathy was caused primarily by his disbelief in Birkeland's main hypothesis: that cathode rays from the sun were guided into the Earth's atmosphere along magnetic field lines, causing the Northern Lights and magnetic perturbations. Chapman himself had once written, in a paper in 1918, that rays of a single charge could stream from the sun, but when his theory was attacked he abandoned the idea and ridiculed Birkeland for suggesting it. Apart from being somewhat hypocritical, Chapman's criticisms revealed an ignorance of Birkeland's work. In 1916 Birkeland had published a paper outlining his theory concerning the rays emitted by the sun, in which he stated: "From a physical point of view it is most probable that these new solar rays are neither exclusively negative nor positive rays, but of both kinds." Chapman later advocated this correct theory, without reference to Birkeland.

He appeared to have a general disregard for Scandinavian science, making condescending comments about Birkeland's colleague Størmer, and the Nobel laureate Hannes Alfvén, whom he called "that Swedish engineer." Over five decades he effectively eradicated the memory of Birkeland's work and entirely dismissed his contribution to science, as can be seen from his opening address to the Birkeland Symposium in Sandefjord, Norway, in 1967:

> Though Birkeland was certainly intensely interested in the aurora, it must be confessed that his direct observational contributions to auroral knowledge were slight.
>
> The apparently unshakeable hold on Birkeland's mind of his basic but invalid conception of intense electron beams, mingled error inextricably with truth in the presentation of his ideas and experiments on auroras and magnetic storms. His breadth of mind and wide interests led him astray.

One young American scientist at the symposium, Alex Dessler, questioned Chapman about Birkeland. "I asked him whether Birkeland's work had any influence on him at all. He glared at me and said, 'How could it? It was all wrong.' "

In the last three years of Chapman's life, however, space satellites found incontrovertible evidence supporting Birkeland's ideas of a flow of electric particles from the sun. In 1962 instruments on board NASA's Mariner II spacecraft on its way to Venus recorded the presence of an electrified gas traveling through space at speeds ranging from 300 to 700 kilometers a second. A similar phenomenon had been observed the previous year by the Soviet Lunik 2 spacecraft on its way to the moon, but western scientists had dismissed the Soviet data as unreliable. After Mariner, other craft were launched into space and soon it was acknowledged that "empty space" was not empty at all but filled with a million-degree electrified gas, hotter, thinner, and faster than any wind on Earth, blowing at hundreds of kilometers per second through the solar system and now called the "solar wind." Composed of an equal number of negative particles, or electrons, and positive particles, mainly protons, this wind forms a neutrally charged "plasma." Birkeland had predicted a similar wind more than sixty years earlier (although the term "plasma" did not exist then and he called it "solar rays," "beams," or "pencils") when he wrote: "Small storms are almost continuously present . . . almost any time pencils of electric rays from the sun are striking the earth."

It was not until 1966, however, when a U.S. Navy navigation satellite observed magnetic disturbances on nearly every pass over the polar regions, that Birkeland's own star began to rise. Since 1967 scientists have been looking at the satellite data in relation to phenomena such as the Northern Lights, rediscovering Birkeland's extraordinarily prophetic theories and completely reassessing his work. Today, he is credited as the first scientist to propose an essentially correct explanation of the aurora borealis, supported by theoretical, observational, and experimental evidence. He was also the first to give a three-dimensional and global picture of the currents giving rise to polar elementary storms, now called "polar substorms." Birkeland suggested that these magnetic perturbations were caused by horizontal currents running along the auroral zone, maintained by a "constant supply of electricity from without" that flowed almost vertically down to auroral heights along the Earth's magnetic field lines. The vertical currents, first christened "Birkeland Currents" in 1967 by Alex Dessler, are now understood to cause substorms and auroras and to drive most of the current systems in the ionosphere—the region, about a hundred kilometers above the Earth's surface, where ionized particles can reflect radio waves.

Birkeland's understanding that the same charged particles that caused magnetic storms also caused the auroras is fully accepted today, although a more sophisticated model of how the particles reach the poles is now available. Satellites have shown that the magnetic field around the Earth is strongly deformed by its interaction with the solar wind, compressing the field on the day side to about ten Earth radii and stretching into a cometlike tail on the night side, typically ten times the moon's distance or more. The magnetic field lines are drawn so far out into space in the tail that they explosively collapse back toward the Earth, generally every few hours, accelerating the plasma particles back up to the poles and creating the dancing auroral displays.

The magnetic field is constantly reacting to the solar wind, which, like an ordinary wind, has gusts and gales created by strong eruptions from the sun, called "flares" (explosive events related to complex groups of sunspots) and "coronal mass ejections" (usually referred to as CMEs). During these eruptions large amounts of plasma escape the sun's magnetic field and are accelerated outward. If the plasma travels toward Earth, it can cause substantial disruption to telecommunications, electric grids and pipelines, magnetic disturbances, and bright auroras. The sun also has "coronal holes," areas where hot plasma streams out unhindered by the sun's magnetic field, that can survive several solar rotations, giving rise to patterns of magnetic activity on Earth that are repeated every twenty-seven days—the time it takes for a complete rotation of the sun. Birkeland noticed this periodicity during his first expedition to Haldde and correctly linked it to particularly active regions of the sun emitting corpuscular radiation associated with, but not issuing from, sunspots. Large solar eruptions occur more frequently during the most active period of the sun's eleven-year cycle, although Birkeland's "polar elementary storms" are much more frequent, with two or three occurring most days, even during the sun's quiet phase. As Birkeland surmised, all these explosive events on the sun, which have a dramatic effect upon the rest of the solar system, are electromagnetic in nature, controlled by Maxwell's equations and not Newton's gravity.

His great work, *The Norwegian Aurora Polaris Expedition, 1902–*

1903, contained other ideas that were not to be proved until fifty years after his death:

1. "The earth's magnetism will cause there to be a cavity around the earth in which the [solar] corpuscles are, so to speak, swept away"—an early indication of what is now called the "magnetosphere," the region surrounding a planet or star in which the magnetic field controls the behavior of charged particles.
2. "It seems to be a natural consequence of our point of view to assume that the whole of space is filled with electrons and flying ions of all kinds. We assume each stellar system in evolution throws off electric corpuscles into space. It is not unreasonable, therefore, to think that the greater part of the material masses in the universe is found not in the solar systems or nebulae, but in 'empty' space." Here, Birkeland predicts the "stellar wind," a concept that emerged in astronomy after the solar wind was established. He then points out the possible existence and importance of stellar matter around which, in the last few decades, a discussion has been steadily growing. Today, interstellar matter is regarded as a key component of the universe.
3. That comet tails and their direction (pointing away from the sun) may be a result of the interaction of material sputtered off the comet head, interacting with the solar corpuscular stream.

Birkeland's wider cosmogonic theory, in which he claimed that electromagnetic forces played a role as important as gravity in near and more distant regions of space, is certainly correct, although it took decades for his assertion to be generally accepted by astrophysicists. Since the satellite revolution, scientists can see even further into space, and the physics of plasmas and electromagnetic forces introduced by Birkeland has emerged from the shadows to dominate current views about the cosmic environment.

In addition to his extraordinarily advanced solar-terrestrial theories, his geomagnetic work, and his early application of Maxwell's equations on a global scale, Birkeland was also hugely inventive. He showed the finest craftsmanship in his development of the terrella chambers with their unique artificial re-creation of the aurora and other cosmic phenomena. Birkeland's development of photocell equipment came to revolutionize astronomy, although it was not used again for Zodiacal Light observations until the 1930s. His steady stream of patent applications is proof of his fertile imagination and the intense activity of his mind. Some patents were not very successful, although later versions of them have been, such as the idea to treat patients with radiation (the solar blanket), to advance the design of hearing aids, to produce margarine from hydrogenated vegetable fat, to make caviar from cod roe, and to use the force of cathode rays to propel rockets. No country's armed forces ever adopted his electromagnetic cannon but the technology has since been developed to make "railguns" (electromagnetic mass accelerators) for the American Strategic Defense Initiative, popularly known as Star Wars. Since the 1970s there have also been several proposals to use the same technology to launch scientific and military rockets and to design an electromagnetic carrier for mass transport between Earth and space stations.

Birkeland now has a crater on the moon named after him, which, together with Birkeland Currents and the wider acceptance of his work, should prevent his memory from fading, but rejection of his theories probably slowed the advance of geomagnetic and auroral physics for nearly half a century. The harsh treatment he received while he was alive also affected the people closest to him. Karl Devik, who was convinced that Birkeland's life had been significantly shortened by the Norsk Hydro affair, was sufficiently disillusioned by the actions of his countrymen to leave Norway and start a new life in Rhodesia. He traveled to Africa in 1920, stopping en route in Egypt to sort out Birkeland's estate there.

British Colony in Rhodesia   25 August 1920

Dear Father,

My private correspondence has been infrequent so far but many things have been very turbulent for me and I have postponed writing until I have got some order in my life.

It was wonderful going back to Egypt and our old friends there were very kind although the Norwegian consul in Cairo was far from a support to Birkeland and his behavior has been simply disgusting. It didn't really suit him that I came out here to settle Birkeland's affairs and a good deal of the mess is due to him.

The work concerning Birkeland's estate was very painful and the whole tragedy around his death was all the time clearly before me. I realized that the time after I went home in 1916 had been terrible for him. His enormously intense work for many years and the very bad treatment he was subject to from Eyde and certain scientists eventually wore down his nerves to the extent that he no longer had confidence in any human being. In his darkest moments he even thought I was playing tricks and being evil to him. It will be to my greatest satisfaction to tell publicly what Eyde has done to damage Birkeland in many ways and that this has shortened his life by years. The truth will come out in future and it may well be that Eyde will meet his nemesis . . .

With warmest regards,
Karl

Karl's prediction for Sam Eyde came true in some measure. After Eyde resigned from Norsk Hydro in 1917, he purchased a manor on the west side of the Christiania fjord and became a farmer. In 1918, however, he was elected to Parliament as a representative of the conservative party, Høire, with the support of the Farmers' Association. His career as an MP was even shorter than that as a farmer as he was sent as a trade envoy to Poland in 1919. In 1920 he was appointed Norwegian ambassador in Warsaw, a position that gave him the title "Minister," which he used on every possible occasion. Shortly afterward he was involved in a major financial scandal, and, although he was acquitted after a long public investigation, he resigned from his position as ambassador and went to live abroad. His reputation never fully recovered from the rumors that surrounded his resignation and he was written about unusually frankly in several publications after his retirement from public life. William Keilhau in *The Life and History of the Norwegian People,* published in 1938, wrote:

> Providence had hardly imbued Eyde with the ability for self-criticism and nothing indicates that he was able to adjust and discipline his actions. It made him ignore the limits and restrictions observed by most people. This absence of inhibitions was particularly visible when he saw a possibility for financial profit. Respect for others' interests did not concern him much.

Despite the shadows that clung to both Eyde and Birkeland, their achievements concerning Norsk Hydro could not be denied. Within Eyde's lifetime, the company had become the largest, and for many decades the only, multinational enterprise in Norway, employing 20,000 men and women, with capital equal to the Norwegian state budget. After the First World War, the company switched to a purely chemical method of fertilizer production, synthesizing ammonia by the "Haber-Bosch method," developed initially by BASF. It remains the leading multinational enterprise in

Norway, employing 38,000 people, still producing fertilizer but also having diversified into light metals, oil and energy provision, and petrochemicals, with an annual gross income of about 12 billion crowns.

After her divorce from Birkeland, Ida did not return to her family in Raade but moved to a smart new apartment on Elisen-bergveien, not far from the church where she was married. Financially well off from Birkeland's settlement, she spent most of her summers in the south of France, on the Côte d'Azur. She did not remarry, nor did she appear to maintain links with her family other than her sister Camilla. Ida died on 21 August 1926, at the age of sixty-three. The main beneficiary of her will had been her neighbor, but three days before Ida died she altered it and left everything to her sister Camilla on condition that, after Camilla's death, everything would go to Julia, the only one of the six daughters who had married and had children.

Amund Helland died in November 1918 from heart disease, saddened by the untimely death of his great friend, Birkeland. Henrik Mohn had died on 12 December 1916, but it seems unlikely that Birkeland would have heard this before his own death.

Birkeland's assistants went on to achieve great things, and one of his lasting contributions to science was considered to be the inspiring leadership he gave to the younger generation. Sem Sæland was elected rector of the Norwegian Technical High School in Trondheim in 1910, despite being the youngest professor there. He later became a professor at the University of Oslo, having been elected rector there too in 1927. He was reelected to this post for a record three terms and died in 1940. Lars Vegard, an assistant of Birkeland's, was elected to his professorship in 1917, and spent his life identifying and measuring the different spectral lines of the Northern Lights in order to determine which gases are excited in the course of an aurora. He made some pioneering discoveries and accurately compiled a list of about forty auroral colors and the gases with which they are related. Ole Andreas Krogness became the first director of the permanent observatory at Haldde in 1912 and lived on the mountain summit with his wife, Dagny. One of his two children, Synnøve, was born at Haldde. Olaf Devik joined him there in 1915 with his wife, who gave birth to two of their three children, Finn and Ingeborg, on the summit. In 1918 Krogness and Devik established a new geophysical institute in a more clement location, Tromsø, with Krogness as director and Devik as leader of the embryonic field of weather forecasting. Olaf Devik worked as a high-ranking civil servant in the Ministry of Education for many years before he retired; he lived to be over a hundred. The much-loved, jovial Krogness died in 1934, at the age of forty-seven. His friends and colleagues brought a stone from Haldde Mountain to place on his grave. Thoralf Skolem became a professor of mathematics at the university in 1938 and enjoyed an international reputation as a pioneer of modern mathematical logic. Carl Størmer, Birkeland's colleague in the mathematics department, developed important equations concerning the movement of charged particles in a dipole magnetic field (inspired by Birkeland and his terrella experiments) and accurately triangulated the height of auroras. Bjørn Helland-Hansen, having lost his fingertips to frostbite on Birkeland's expedition to Haldde, became an internationally respected oceanographer. Karl Devik never returned from Africa and little is known about his life in Rhodesia.

Birkeland devoted his life to an extraordinary journey, to unravel the complex and powerful relationship between the sun and the Earth. In doing so, he introduced modern physics to Norway and almost singlehandedly raised the funds necessary to build an up-to-date physics environment at Christiania University. It is a sad irony that he died while a working committee was considering his nomination for the Nobel Prize, in conjunction with Professor Størmer, for their work on the aurora borealis. The prize could not be awarded posthumously and thus Birkeland never received the recognition he deserved and so wished for. Although his life ended tragically, his resurrection has been steady and continues to this day. As Birkeland himself said, sitting round the fireplace in the administration building in Notodden, in 1910:

> A very few lonely pioneers make their way to high places never before visited. Others follow these new paths, and sometimes the pioneers build roads so wide that the masses may follow. These pioneers create the living conditions of mankind and the majority are living on their work.

Select Bibliography

I N A D D I T I O N to help I received from the people listed in the Acknowledgments and the information gathered from archives also mentioned there, the following books proved to be valuable for research. The titles of Norwegian books are listed in their original language followed by the English translation.

Akasofu, S.-I. *Sydney Chapman, Eighty from His Friends.* Privately published (available at the Royal Astronomical Society, London), 1968.

———. *Aurora Borealis: The Amazing Northern Lights.* Anchorage: Alaska Geographic, 1979.

Alfvén, Hannes. "The Plasma Universe." *Physics Today,* September 1986, pp. 22–27.

Alfvén, H., and A. Egeland. "Auroral Research in Scandinavia," *The Kristian Birkeland Lecture 1.* Oslo: Norwegian Academy of Science and Letters, 1987.

Al-Sayyid Marsot, Afaf Lutfi. *Egypt in the Reign of Muhammad Ali.* Cambridge, U.K.: Cambridge University Press, 1984.

———. *A Short History of Modern Egypt.* Cambridge, U.K.: Cambridge University Press, 1985.

Andersen, Ketil Gjølme, and Gunnar Yttri. *Et forsøk verdt* [Worth Trying]. Oslo: Universitetsforlaget, 1997.

Birkeland wrote around sixty scientific papers. Among the most important of his publications for this book are:

Birkeland, Kristian. *Expédition Norvégienne de 1899–1900.* Christiania: Norwegian Academy of Science, Jacob Dybwad, 1901.

———. *The Norwegian Aurora Polaris Expedition, 1902–1903,* vol. 1, parts 1 and 2. Christiania: H. Aschehoug, 1908, 1913.

———. "Sur la lumière zodiacale," *Académie des Sciences*, session of Monday, 15 February 1911, Paris.

———. "Sur la lumière zodiacale," *Comptes Rendus*, Paris, 20 July 1914.

———. "On a Possible Method of Photographically Registering the Intensity of the Ultraviolet Light from the Sun and Stars." *Cairo Scientific Journal*, vol. 8, 1914.

———. "On a Possible Crucial Test of the Theories of Auroral Curtains and Polar Magnetic Storms," *Videnskapsselskapets Skrifter*, I Mat.—Naturv. Klasse no. 61, Christiania, 1915.

———. "Are the Solar Corpuscular Rays That Penetrate into the Earth's Atmosphere Negative or Positive Rays?," *Videnskapsselskapets Skrifter*, I Mat.—Naturv. Klasse no. 1, Christiania, 1916.

———. "Simultaneous Observations of the Zodiacal Light from Stations of Nearly Equal Longitude in North and South Africa," *Cairo Scientific Journal*, vol. 9, March 1917.

Bødtker, Henning. *En advocat forteller* [A Lawyer Reports], Oslo: H. Aschehoug, 1970.

Brekke, A., and A. Egeland. *The Northern Light: From Mythology to Space Research.* Berlin: Springer-Verlag, 1983.

Brundtland, T. "The Laboratory Work of Professor Kristian Birkeland." Report to the Department of Physics, University of Tromsø, 1997.

———. "Instruments in the Arctic: The Norwegian Auroral Expedition to Novaya Zemlya in 1902–03," *Proceedings of the XVIII SIC Symposium Institute for the History of Science and Technology.* Moscow: Russian Astronomical Society, 2000.

Chapman, Sydney. "Frederick Carl Mülertz Störmer, 1874–1957," *Biographical Memoirs* 41, Royal Society of London, 1958.

———. "History of Aurora and Airglow," in *Aurora and Airglow,* ed. Billy M. McCormac. New York: Reinhold, 1967.

———. "Historical Introduction to Aurora and Magnetic Storms," in *The Birkeland Symposium on Aurora and Magnetic Storms,* ed. A. Egeland and J. Holtet. Paris: Centre national de la recherche scientifique, 1968, pp. 21–29.

Cowling, T. G., and V. C. A. Ferraro. "Obituary—Sydney Chapman," *Quarterly Journal of the Royal Astronomical Society,* vol. 13, 1972.

Danielson, R., et al., eds. *Norway: A History from the Vikings to Our Own Times,* trans. Michael Drake. Oslo: Scandinavian University Press, 1995.

Select Bibliography

De Mairan, Jean-Jacques d'Ortous. *Traité physique et historique de l'aurore boréale.* Paris: L'Imprimerie royale, 1733.

Dessler, A. J. "Solar Wind and Interplanetary Magnetic Field," *Reviews of Geophysics* 5: 1–7, 1967.

———. "Solar Wind Interactions," in *The Birkeland Symposium on Aurora and Magnetic Storms,* ed. A. Egeland and J. Holtet. Paris: Centre national de la recherche scientifique, 1968, pp. 13–19.

———. "Nobel Prizes: 1970—Swedish Iconoclast Recognised after Many Years of Rejection and Obscurity," *Science* 170: 604–606, 1970.

———. "The Evolution of Arguments Regarding the Existence of Field-aligned Currents," in *Magnetospheric Currents,* Thomas A. Potemra, American Geophysical Union Monograph 28, Washington, D.C., 1984.

———. Honors Ceremony for Hannes Alfvén for the American Geophysical Union, *EOS,* 70, 10, Washington, D.C., 1989.

Devik, Olaf. "Kristian Birkeland As I Knew Him," in *The Birkeland Symposium on Aurora and Magnetic Storms,* ed. A. Egeland and J. Holtet. Paris: Centre national de la recherche scientifique, 1968, pp. 13–19.

———. *Blant fiskere, forskere og andre folk* [Amongst Fishermen, Scientists, and Other Folk], Oslo: H. Aschehoug, 1971.

Devik, Olaf, and Ole Andreas Krogness. "Professor Kr. Birkeland," *Naturen,* 1917, pp. 193–204.

Eather, Robert H. *The Majestic Lights: The Aurora in Science, History, and the Arts.* Washington, D.C.: American Geophysical Union, 1980.

Egeland, Alv. "Kristian Birkeland: The Man and the Scientist," in *Magnetospheric Currents,* ed. Thomas A. Potemra. American Geophysical Union Monograph 28, Washington, D.C., 1984.

———. "Birkeland's Electromagnetic Gun: A Historical Review," *Plasma Science 2,* vol. 17, April 1989.

———. *Kristian Birkeland.* Oslo: Norges Banks seddeltrykkeri, 1994.

Egeland, Alv, and E. Leer. "Professor Birkeland: His Life and Work," IEEE *Transactions on Plasma Science,* vol. PS-14, no. 6, December 1989, pp. 666–67.

Eyde, Sam. *Mitt liv og mitt livsverk* [My Life and My Life's Work]. Oslo: Eget Forlag, 1956.

Friedman, Robert Marc. *Appropriating the Weather: Wilhelm Bjerkenes and the Construction of Modern Meteorology.* N.Y. and London: Ithaca Press, 1989.

———. "Civilization and National Honour: The Rise of Norwegian Geophysical and Cosmic Science," in *Making Sense of Space: The History of*

Select Bibliography

Norwegian Space Activities, ed. Jan Pettar Collet. Oslo: Scandinavian University Press, 1995.

Fuglum, Per. *Norge I Støpeskjeen, 1884–1919* [Norway Reshaped, 1884–1919], vol. 12 of *Norges Historie* [History of Norway], ed. Knut Mykland. Oslo: Cappelen, 1979.

Gilbert, William. *De Magnete*, London, 1600. English translation by P. Fleury Mottelay. New York: Dover Publications, 1983.

Hartmann, Edel. *Kjent folk gjennon årene* [Well-known People Through My Years]. Oslo: Olaf Norlis Forlag, 1936.

Haslip, Joan. *The Lonely Empress: A Biography of Elizabeth of Austria*. Cleveland, Ohio: The World Publishing Co., 1965.

Hassan, Hassan. *In the House of Muhammad Ali: A Family Album, 1805–1952*. Cairo: The American University in Cairo Press, 2000.

Hellemans, A., and B. Bunch. *The Timetables of Science*. New York: Simon and Schuster, 1988.

Hestmark, Geir. *Vitenskap og nasjon, Waldemar Christopher Brøgger, 1851–1905* [Science and Nation, Waldemar Christopher Brøgger, 1851–1905]. Oslo: H. Aschehoug, 1999.

Holmboe, Carl Fredrik. *Ingeniør ser seg tilbake* [An Engineer Looks Back]. Oslo: H. Aschehoug, 1948.

Holst, Helge, ed. *Opfindernes Liv* [Lives of the Inventors], part 2. Copenhagen and Christiania: Nordisk Forlag, 1915.

Huntford, Roland. *Nansen*. London: Duckworth, 1997.

Keilhau, Wilhelm. *Det Norske folks liv og historie 1875–1920* [The Life and History of the Norwegian People, 1875–1920], vol. 10. Oslo: H. Aschehoug, 1935.

———. *Det Norske folks liv og historie i vår egen tid* [The Life and History of the Norwegian People in Our Own Time]. Oslo: H. Aschehoug, 1938.

Kitroeff, Alexander. *The Greeks in Egypt, 1919–1937: Ethnicity and Class*. London: Ithaca Press, published for the Middle East Centre, St. Anthony's College, Oxford, 1989.

Lang, Kenneth R. *Sun, Earth and Sky*. Berlin and Heidelberg: Springer-Verlag, 1995.

Lauritzen, Åse Katherine. *"Vitenskapsmann som teknolog, Kristian Birkeland, 1901–1908"* ["A Scientist as Technologist, Kristian Birkeland, 1901–1908"]. Unpublished thesis in history, University of Oslo, autumn 2000.

Select Bibliography

Luetken, André, and Helge Holst, eds. *Opfindelsernes Bog* [Book of Inventions], vol. 2. Christiania and Copenhagen: Nordisk Forlag, 1913.

Mehren, Tonje Maria. *"Norsk Selskap for Psykisk Forskning"* [The Norwegian Society for Psychical Research]. Unpublished thesis, University of Oslo, spring 1999.

Mohn, Johan B. *Christian Joachim Mohn, hans forfædre, liv og etterkommere* [Christian Joachim Mohn, His Ancestors, Life, and Descendants]. Oslo: Mostue, 1928.

Nelson, Nina. *Helwan Shepheard Hotel—A History.* Cairo: Al-Ahram, 1992.

Nielssen, Alf Ragnar, and Arvid Petterson. *Nordlyspionerene* [The Pioneers of the Northern Lights]. Oslo: Grøndahl og Dreyer, 1993.

Norman, Howard. *Northern Tales: Traditional Stories of Eskimo and Indian Peoples.* New York: Pantheon, 1990.

Norsk biografisk leksikon [Norwegian Biographical Encyclopedia]. Oslo: H. Aschehoug, 1923–83.

Peratt, A. L. "The Legacy of Birkeland's Plasma Torch." *The 9th Birkeland Symposium.* Oslo: Norwegian Academy of Science and Letters, 1995.

Potemra, Thomas A., ed. *Magnetospheric Currents.* American Geophysical Union Monograph 28, Washington, D.C., 1984.

Rypdal, K., and T. Brundtland. "The Birkeland Terrella Experiments and their Importance for the Modern Synergy of Laboratory and Space Plasma Physics." *Journal de Physique* 4, supplement of the *Journal de Physique* 3, October 1997.

Savage, Candace. *Aurora: The Mysterious Northern Lights.* San Francisco: Sierra Club Books, 1995.

Schuster, Sir Arthur. *The Progress of Physics.* New York: Arno Press, 1911.

Sonbol, Amira, ed. and trans. *The Last Khedive of Egypt.* Reading, U.K.: Ithaca Press, 1998.

Soueif, Ahdaf. *The Map of Love.* London: Bloomsbury, 1999.

Stadler, Valerie. *Legends and Folktales of Lappland.* London: Mowbrays, 1972.

Störmer, Carl. *The Polar Aurora.* Oxford, U.K.: Clarendon Press, 1955.

Sæland, Sem. "Professor Kristian Birkeland," *Fysisk Tidsskrift* 16, 1917–18, pp. 34–53.

Terada, Torahiko. "Death of Professor B." *Literature,* Japan, July 1935. Trans. into Norwegian by Lars Ulsnes, 1978, and into English (main part) by Professor N. Fukushima, Tokyo, 1989, and (last part) by Truls Lynne

Select Bibliography

Hansen, Tromsø, 2000. All Norwegian and English translations are unpublished.

Tromholdt, Sophus. *Under the Rays of the Aurora Borealis: In the Land of the Lapps and the Kvæns.* London: Sampson Low, Marston, Searle and Rivington, 1885.

Turner, H. H. "From an Oxford Notebook" [about the Helwan observatory]. *The Observatory*, vol. 32, 1909.

Wikan, Stein. *Johan Koren.* Oslo: Christian Schibsted, 2000.

NEWSPAPERS AND REPORTS

Det Kongelige Fredriks Universitets aarsberetninger [Annual Reports of the Royal Norwegian Fredrik's University]. Christiania, 1885–1919.

Det norske Stortings forhandlinger [Proceedings of the Norwegian Parliament], Christiania, 1898–1920.

"Soflekker og nordlys, et budskap fra solen" [Sunspots and the Northern Light, a Message from the Sun] in *Verduns Gang*, Christiania, 16 September 1898.

"Professor Birkeland's elektromagnetiske kanon" [The Electromagnetic Cannon of Professor Birkeland] in *Aftenposten*, Christiania, 7 March 1905.

"Birkeland-Eyde, hvorledes den Birkeland-Eydske opfindelse er bleven til" [Birkeland-Eyde, How the Birkeland-Eyde Method Was Developed], open letter from Birkeland in *Aftenposten*, Christiania, 24 June 1915.

LETTERS

The letters quoted in this book come from the archives of the Norsk Hydro Industry Museum at Notodden, the Norwegian Technical Museum, Oslo, and the Manuscript Department of the National Library of Norway, Oslo.

PICTURE CREDITS

The photograph of Birkeland on deck is from the archives of the Norsk Hydro Industry Museum, Notodden.

Index

Index

Index

Index

Index

Index

Index

A NOTE ABOUT THE AUTHOR

LUCY JAGO is a former documentary producer for Channel 4 and
the BBC. She has been awarded two academic scholarships and a
Double First Class Honours Degree from King's College, University
of Cambridge, and a master's degree from the Courtauld Institute,
London. She lives in Dorset, England.

A NOTE ON THE TYPE

THIS BOOK was set in Monotype Dante, a typeface designed by Giovanni Mardersteig (1892–1977). Conceived as a private type for the Officina Bodoni in Verona, Italy, Dante was originally cut only for hand composition by Charles Malin, the famous Parisian punch cutter, between 1946 and 1952. Its first use was in an edition of Boccaccio's *Trattatello in laude di Dante* that appeared in 1954. The Monotype Corporation's version of Dante followed in 1957. Although modeled on the Aldine type used for Pietro Cardinal Bembo's treatise *De Aetna* in 1495, Dante is a thoroughly modern interpretation of the venerable face.

Composed by North Market Street Graphics,
Lancaster, Pennsylvania
Printed and bound by R. R. Donnelley & Sons,
Harrisonburg, Virginia
Designed by Virginia Tan